Elk Hunting
My First 50 Years

By Charlie Butz, Jr.

Dedication

This book is dedicated to the best friend a person could ever hope for. An honorable, dedicated hunter and a fantastic human being:

Bob McManus - "Tonka Wi Con" (friends forever).

Also, in loving memory of a dear friend and terrific hunting partner, Sam Mitzel.

Contents

Foreword

Through the years, Charlie has learned every inch of wilderness, downed trees, and the main water source where "Greybeard Camp" resides for ten days during the season. More importantly, several lifelong friends have been born after a stop to say hello near the American flag that stood tall at the entrance of camp.

Charlie's nickname "The Legend" is a true testimony to the respect other hunters in the area have for him, his creditability, passion, and love for the elk.

Every year, he keeps the same schedule to the hour. The hotels, gas stations, breakfast diners, making sure the tradition is kept as alive and successful as possible. While gearing up for the pack in, he loves spending time and catching up with old camp buddies.

The seven-mile hike into the wilderness always starts off the same, leaving candy or snacks for the horses and riders that pack in the tent and supplies. The pack out is also a routine as Charlie times himself while heading up what he calls "Heart Attack" Mountain. It's steep and has very little oxygen. But Charles, who might be half Billy goat, continues to shave seconds off his time.

Then there's the traditional stopping in to drop off fresh potatoes to his lifelong friend, JC Trujillo. As Charlie drives up the mountainside, the two yell to each other in Spanish something about friendship that defies language.

In 2015, a lifetime of knowledge and dedication put Charlie in the right place at the right time when one of the largest bulls harvested in the area stepped out of the dark timber behind his herd of 70 cows. With a steady hand and calm nerves, the hunt was over in the blink of an eye. His bull ended up scoring in the 360s and is now displayed beautifully at his home.

When I was asked to write Charlie's foreword, I immediately felt tears welling up in my eyes that he would give me the honor to share a glimpse into his journey.

I was invited and welcomed at Graybeard Camp in 2015 and had no idea how one hunt would change my life forever. During the hunt, I traded (never gifted) a coin for the most incredible deer-antlered knife with a sheath that read "Graybeard Camp 2015," which was handmade by Bob McManus. Since then, that knife has been with me on all my elk hunts.

Charlie is an inspiration to me in life and in hunting. He had shared countless stories with me and others about his life's journey over the years. Most of the stories were true. But, just as all hunters need a license to hunt, we also get poetic license to stretch a good story a little.

All jokes aside, I'm truly honored and grateful for your friendship and Charlie's continued faith in me. He's impacted my life and his story will be shared throughout my lifetime.

With love and respect,
Foster Bartholow

Introduction

In the dense mountain forests of North America, between towering pines and sweeping valleys, roams a creature of unparalleled majesty - the Wapiti (Elk). Wapiti is a word used by the Shawnee and Cree Indian tribes that means white rump.

Known for its imposing antlers and regal form, the Elk commands attention.

The Wapiti are adaptable creatures, able to thrive in various ecosystems as long as there is sufficient food, water, and cover. Perhaps its most striking feature is its impressive antlers. These antlers, primarily sported by males (bulls), can reach lengths of up to four feet and weigh as much as forty pounds. They are used primarily during the rutting season for display and combat, showcasing dominance and attracting mates.

Elk are among the largest species in the deer family. Bulls can weigh anywhere from 600 to 1,000 pounds, while cows (females) typically weigh between 400 and 600 pounds. Their coat coloration varies, ranging from reddish-brown to tan, with a lighter coloration on the rump and underbelly.

Elk are social animals, forming herds that can consist of dozens to hundreds of individuals. These herds are often segregated by sex outside of the breeding season, with bulls forming bachelor groups and cows leading smaller groups with their calves.

During the rutting season, which typically occurs in the fall, bulls engage in fierce battles for dominance and mating rights. Their bugling calls echo through the wilderness, signaling their presence and challenging rivals. The victor earns the privilege to mate with receptive females.

The antlers of Wapiti are not only awe-inspiring in size but also intricate in their formation. Counting the points on elk antlers is a practice deeply embedded in hunting culture and wildlife observation. Points, or tines, refer to the branches that protrude from the main beam of the antler. Several scoring systems exist to quantify the size and complexity of elk's antlers. These systems take into account the length, width, and number of points on the antlers to assign a numerical score. This score is used to rank and compare individual elk based on the size and quality of their antlers.

They are glorious creatures indeed, deserving of our respect and admiration.

This book is a collection of the experiences I have personally had over the past 50 years of hunting the mighty Wapiti in beautiful Colorado. Although I have hunted elk in two other states, these stories are strictly about my Colorado experiences.

Like my mother-in-law used to say, I may have started to "stretch the gum" a bit to make things interesting, but I can assure you – everything in this book actually happened — both good and bad.

I hope you can take something away from these stories to help you in your future elk ventures and inspire you to answer the call of the wild.

Be safe, enjoy the great outdoors, and please respect the majestic, magnificent Wapiti.

Good Hunting!

How Not to Prepare for an Elk Hunt

My elk hunting career started in 1973 as my family, some friends, and I prepared for a fishing trip to "Rainy Lake" in Ontario, Canada. A few days before, an acquaintance I had met a week or so earlier, Bob, had heard that I did quite a bit of hunting and asked me if I would like to go with him to Colorado on an archery Elk hunt that weekend. I was thrilled, excited, honored, and grateful. My wife, Rosie, shot me a look. She wasn't about to have her plans changed. I think her exact words were: "No way, we're going on a fishing trip to Canada!"

Needless to say, after I took my skirt off, I told Rosie I'd finish packing the supplies for our planned trip to "Rainy Lake." Bear with me – the elk hunting episodes are coming, but I would be remiss if I failed to give you a glimpse of our personalities and include you in the fun (hell), excitement (torture), and quality time (cussing/fighting) we all had on our Rainy Lake adventure.

A tent wasn't really an item in our must-have category at that time since most of our camping trips were *one-dayers* or an overnight stay at a nearby relative's house. But, this time, I came up with the brilliant idea of renting a tent at a new Rent-All place in town. I was the first customer to rent this particular tent.

But what could go wrong?

My friends showed up in the late afternoon, and I was all packed with food for a week: six coolers, one-and-a-half sleeping bags, an air mattress, kitchen chairs (no table), lanterns, a Coleman stove and tank with no white gas, three kids, the wife, and me. We all packed into a regular-sized 1970 Ford F150. The kids and wife were up front with me (no seatbelts – how did we survive?)

We left, excited for our drive to Canada and several days of fun when I remembered that I didn't have the rented tent. Thankfully, we weren't more than three miles down the road.

That little wrinkle might have been the clue that this was the beginning of the trip from hell. Chevy Chase's "Vacation" could have used what happened next to write his script.

We traveled as a convoy — three vehicles — in the darkness through the northern woods of Minnesota, dogging deer, moose, a million frogs, and trying to see through the heavy fog that eventually turned to heavy rain. All the while, my mind was constantly replaying Bob's words: "Would you like to go on an archery elk hunt in Colorado?"

I've always loved the mountains and, as I drifted away, imagining sneaking up on a big bull elk, Rosie screamed at me.

"Stay on the road!"

It was late at night, the kids were getting cranky and hungry, and the snacks that might have calmed them down a bit were packed back in the pickup bed.

It was a long drive, but we finally reached the border crossing at daybreak where I was asked the normal questions from the border guard.

"Where are you going?

"Elk hunting – no, fishing and camping."

"Where at?"

"Colorado – no, Rainy Lake, Ontario."

"How long?"

"Too long," I joked.

The border guard didn't crack so much as a smile.

"No, we're just going for the weekend." My ear rang from the impact of Rosie's left hand against the side of my skull for cracking jokes at a government checkpoint.

"Are you bringing any alcohol or cigarettes?"

Oh, God, I knew I shouldn't have brought that 12-pack of Pabst Blue Ribbon. "Yes, I have a 12-pack in the back."

"Can we check your vehicle?"

"If you've got time, good luck. I mean, yes, of course."

And finally, "Are those your children?"

"No, they're adopted." My ear rang again! "Yes, they are."

"Where were they born?"

"Oh, come on!," I said in frustration. "We're just going on a wonderful family fishing/camping trip."

"You may pass through."

I pulled over after being allowed into Canada and waited for the other two vehicles in our caravan. Vehicle #2 came right behind me, but #3 was being questioned. After thirty minutes, I walked back to see what the holdup was, being told not to accidentally cross back into the U.S. in the process.

My friend had brought his dog and, unless you belong to the Queen's Club, you can't bring a dog into Canada without having updated rabies' shot information. He didn't! We had to wait for a local veterinarian to show up to give the poor dog another rabies shot. Even though the dog had already received his shots, my friend couldn't prove it. So, the poor pup would have to have another painful jab.

After another long wait, we asked the agent again how long it might be and were told that, due to it being Saturday, they were having a hard time finding a veterinarian. A few hours later, the vet showed up and we were back on our way to Rainy Lake.

It was a new frontier for all of us, but I kept thinking I could have been in Colorado already on the archery elk hunt and there would have been no border patrol! I was sure I'd never be asked to go elk hunting again.

As we neared our camping spot, the sky cracked open releasing a torrential downpour and muddying our path. We took it slow, slipping and sliding through Canadian back roads until we finally saw Rainy Lake and pulled over to set up our weekend retreat at what we thought was the shoreline.

Forgetting the tent turned out to be a happy accident because I had no choice but to pack it last, making it first to unload. Truth be told, I am no expert at assembling a tent. In fact, I'm terrible at any assembly-related gear. Worse, since it wasn't my tent, I had to give up winging it and search for the instructions.

What?! No instructions?!

While I searched the bag for any help in assembling the tent, the kids got out to enjoy the rain, drawing shrieks from the adults and pleas to "Get the kids out of that mud!"

Turning back to the incorrigible tent, I realized I had to hurry. The sun had long since given up its warm golden glow, shielded behind thick, ominous clouds. But now, clouds or not, the sun was going down. I couldn't afford to lose daylight when I still had to get the tent up and cook a hot meal to feed my weary travelers.

What?! No one brought a hammer?

Les and Little V's tent went up quickly. Not a swear word or a stomp of the foot between them. And Marly? He fell asleep in the back of his vehicle after watching this three-ring circus.

As I pounded a stake with my bare fist, I wondered if it was raining in Colorado or if it was a brilliant starlight night — one as beautiful as John Denver always sang about.

After assembling the tent framework three times, I finally figured it out, resigning myself to the fact that the door opening doesn't necessarily *need* to be on the bottom. This was a great adventure – things shouldn't always have to go the way I expect them to.

With the tent finally up (or at least most of it up off the ground), it was time to think about the flooring. Why didn't this new tent have a floor in it? I wished I had brought some plastic sheeting.

Thoughts of sheeting quickly morphed into thoughts of shitting when a child's voice rang out, "Dad, I have to go poop!" Our campsite inn didn't offer such facilities. So, I would have to rally my troops.

"Okay, this is a team effort – whoever needs to pee or poop, come with me. I found a good bush, but now it's dark. So, we'll stick together."

"Dad, I'm scared," my daughter says.

"Don't be scared. Just pee."

"But what's that buzzing noise?"

"Dad, I need toilet paper," Oldest Son pipes up.

"Wait here, I'll be right back."

Daughter again, "Dad, seriously. Something is buzzing. Is it going to sting me?"

I hurried back with toilet paper. But due to the rain, it was soaked to the tube. "It's good, son, you can wipe and clean at the same time. Pretend it's a baby wipe. And give some to your sister, too."

Then I heard what my daughter must have. *What is that buzzing noise? Oh, my God, it's the ruler of the Canadian Woods, known to drive man and beast insane, the subject of horror movies – the Giant Mosquitos on Steroids! They can suck every ounce of blood out of you in seconds. A swarm of just a dozen can carry away a small child. Oh no, the kids!*

"Hurry, kids," I said trying not to show fear. Mosquitos can smell fear! "We have to get to the tent!"

"But, Dad, I didn't wipe yet!"

"That's okay, we have to go!"

"Is it a bear, Dad?"

"No, bears don't buzz. Besides, there's no bear here; we're too close to the water."

"Bears love water," I hear someone mumble.

Trying not to let the kids see my panic, I grabbed each one by the arm and ran screaming to Rosie to open the tent door.

She struggled to reach high enough to unzip our bizarro tent with the door at the top. *What a dumb design. Whose idea was this?!* Finally, we were safely in the dark tent interior with the mud floor. I braved the rain once more to search for the air mattress and lantern in the back of the truck. I grabbed what I could as I was under attack from a mosquito impersonating the Canadian national bird.

My mind drifted again to that "other" trip. I was sure there were no mosquitos in the Colorado Rockies. *Sure wish I was there.*

Back in the tent, I started barking out instructions: "Put the one-and-a-half sleeping bags on the air mattress, while I light the lantern. There's got to be another mantle somewhere."

I searched but… no matches and no lighter. "I'll just run over to Les's tent and get his lighter." But a quick peek in their direction and the darkness inside their tent put the brakes on that idea. *Great, they're sleeping already.* It was a long day that had become a long, dark night.

I raced to the truck where I was certain I had some matches and finally lit the lantern. I didn't know the glass lens was cracked.

The rain was really coming down now, but at least we had light and some heat and our *au naturale* floor was a slippery, slimy mess and somehow getting wetter by the minute.

Another trip to the truck yielded some food, but I needed more supplies. As I turned to go back, I noticed the nice skylights above us in several spots. *Wait? Skylight? No! It can't be. Holes in the tent?*

Rosie quickly made us sandwiches with wet bread so we could eat and jump in the sleeping bag and a half. With everyone still and quiet finally falling around us, I realized that my fear was correct; rain was coming through unsown areas of the tent. That meant... *Oh God, the mosquitos are coming in.*

Everyone jumped in my bag and covered up as I turned out the lantern and covered up with the half bag, and we all fell asleep on the oversized air mattress.

The next morning, I noticed it was still raining at Rainy Lake but, for some strange reason, the tent door was down where it was supposed to be and the tent was much smaller. The rain had beat so hard and so long against it, the small tacks the tent supplier furnished as stakes had pulled right out and tent was in partial collapse. This didn't make sense though, as there was no wind.

Then it became obvious as I noticed that my oldest son, daughter, and myself were outside the tent while Rosie and my youngest son were inside the tent. But we were all still on the air mattress. It wasn't just the six inches of water on the floor of the tent that washed us outside; I had assembled our Taj Mahal on the downside of a small hill.

Hey, it was dark out!

Trying to find some humor in the situation, I told the family it was a good thing we had the air mattress – it was our life preserver! I kept secret the fact that we were ten feet away from washing over a twelve-foot drop-off. No need to cause panic.

After a good hot breakfast (translation: cold, wet sandwich), I bid the family farewell to get ready for my fishing adventure. We only had a day and a half left of our dream (nightmare) vacation.

My friends and I threw my yate – a twelve-foot duck boat – into the mighty Rainy Lake. The lake was huge and intimidating, but I knew, with the help of one good paddle and one broken one, my 5-horse Johnson engine could zip us around wherever we needed to go to skillfully catch enough fish for supper.

Everyone was a little hungry since we skipped real food the night before. I didn't even get to eat my wet sandwich!

Little V and I weren't very big men; Les and Marly outweighed us by a quite a bit (no offense, guys!). As we shot away from shore, I mentioned it might be a good idea if nobody moved except to bail the water out from the boat floor.

I had been in several boats but never one where you could dangle your fingers in the water only three inches below the outer edge of my Titanic Cruiser.

We tried several areas and caught a few walleyes for supper, but no one realized we had driven and/or drifted several miles from camp. It didn't matter at the time because it wasn't supposed to storm for at least another half an hour.

I'm not much of a fisherman, but I had visions dancing in my head of casting for brookies in the clear cold waters of Colorado. Instead, there I was, watching my buddies bailing water more and more frequently.

As I watched the sky darken above us – it was only noon – I felt a strike that almost pulled the rod right out of my hands. I immediately adjusted, finding my footing and reeling it in.

The fight was on. This was Moby Dick. This was Jaws. This was the monster guys like me always hoped for. This is the truth — the real deal!

Yep! Uh-huh!

The monster fish was so massive, it pulled all four of us and my mighty boat around in circles. After what felt like an hour (two minutes), we finally got to see this humungous predator of the deep. It was at least a twenty-pound plus northern pike, or as the locals called it, a "Big Snake."

It started to rain harder and the wind picked up, but I was too excited to care. Except for my screams of excitement, it was very quiet for some reason. Then I realized why — the old reliable 5-horse Johnson had quit after being thrashed about by the titan on the end of my line.

The only thing still going in the boat was Les's lit cigarette. How it survived the rain, I will never know. The downpours were starting to block my vision.

We realized we were in serious trouble. The boat had no working engine and was filling up with water. Although it was a very realistic "live well" for our walleyes, the situation was growing more precarious — bordering on dangerous.

The giant fish surfaced for what must have been the eighth time, prompting me to scream for someone to grab the net.

Yeah, right!

This thing was fifteen times the size of our little net. Perhaps that's why they called it a minnow net? With the absence of proper brain functioning properly on my part to comprehend the seriousness of our predicament, Les came to the rescue. He knew the giant fish was half the size of my boat, and we needed to get the motor running. We would have to drag the thing to shore immediately.

No one wanted to risk losing a hand in this giant's mouth, so Les took his lit cigarette and pressed it against my super strong, greatly stretched line. It singed the line, and my dream fish was gone.

My first reaction was upset until I noticed that the waves were so high, we couldn't see the shore in any direction. I prayed I could close my eyes and, when I reopened them, I'd be standing on the top of a beautiful mountain in Colorado with Bob. I knew I wouldn't die from drowning because at any moment the other three were sure to start kicking me, punching me, and wrapping their hands around my neck.

With Les praying, Little V bailing water, Marly paddling with the good paddle, and me masterfully controlling the Johnson tiller with one hand and using the broken paddle as a rudder with the other, we managed to drift backwards at least another mile or so to the closest shoreline.

I docked us (crashed us) onto a deserted island. The storm, in full force now, made me long for that leaky tent back at the campsite. Better yet, I could have been skinning an elk by now in the mountains of Colorado.

We went out to explore the island only to find that it wasn't deserted. In fact, one lone tent served as a hidden getaway for two very scared newlyweds.

We assumed they feared the dangerous storm; after we talked to them, we realized they were scared to death of us! It took a bit a talking to convince them we were just good old North Dakota boys on a Canadian adventure. They were nice and welcoming.

When the weather let up a little, we apologized and challenged the mighty Rainy Lake once again on a quest to return to our camp. Halfway across the largest part of that body of water, we realized we couldn't continue; our two gallons of fuel were getting low. We had no choice but to backtrack to sail along the nearest shoreline and follow it back as far as we could. The closer we got to camp the better the weather got; so, I suggested we fish some more. The guys answered something about throwing me in and hoping I was a good swimmer.

After we made it to camp and before I could tell Rosie about our life-threatening ordeal, she let loose with a string of questions — rapid fire:

"Do you know what time it is? Where the hell have you been? Do you know the kids haven't had a hot meal yet? Do you have any idea how uncomfortable it is sitting in the pickup all day with hungry, wet, muddy kids? Did you see that the tent fell to the ground?"

I explained what happened while, simultaneously, quickly cleaning the three walleyes I had caught. Following that, I put the tent back up and tried to start a campfire.

Bellies full and everyone getting closer to dry, all seemed well again.

As we ate, we talked about how lucky (or unlucky) we were that day. We still had a half-day left to enjoy (or survive). The rain even slowed down to a steady enjoyable pace — if you're a farmer!

Just as darkness fell, we got ready to crawl into our wet tent and even wetter sleeping bags. I couldn't shake my joy at how lucky we'd been to survive the whole ordeal. That thought was interrupted by the sound of someone driving toward our camp at seemingly a hundred miles per hour and screeching to a halt. Two men jumped out of their truck and ran toward us in a panic. Trembling, they asked – no, begged – to stay with us because a huge black bear had destroyed their tent and camp; they figured they were next on the menu.

All of the kids screamed in harmony, "Dad! You said there were no bears here!"

Rosie couldn't speak due to shock – she really was never the outdoorsy type.

I thanked the two young guys for scaring the crap out of my kids and forever instilling the fear of bears in my family's mind. That said, I told them they were welcome to stay. We all had a restless night, sleeping in our vehicles. Two nervous adults and three scared kids crammed together in the front seat of a pickup.

Wow!

Needless to say, the next morning we decided to cut our adventure (nightmare) a little short. After wringing out our wet bags and tent and changing our shorts, we headed back toward good ole North Dakota, stopping only to indulge in the first hamburger joint we could find. We left with grateful hearts that no one was harmed and a healthy respect for the body of water that was aptly named Rainy Lake.

I still think I should have gone elk hunting!

Next Year ———————▶

The Beginning

Bob invited me to go hunting again the following year. Having learned my lesson, this time, I said, "Absolutely!" Even though I was extremely busy with work, I couldn't contain my anticipation and kept wishing September would come soon.

It was only January 1, 1974.

Although I had (kinda) hunted elk one time before in Montana, this was truly my first legitimate Elk Hunt.

Bob had moved to Minneapolis. So, I invited a new friend, TD, to accompany me on the journey. I proceeded to call Bob nearly every day for eleven months to see what I needed to bring for the 10-day archery hunt. I had my old 58-pound Browning recurve bow, plenty of old dull wooden arrows, one rusty knife, and a pile of hunting clothes.

The closer it got to September, the excitement grew until it became overwhelming. I had just bought a new 1974 F150, so we decided to use my vehicle for the trip.

Finally, the day of departure came. I picked up TD on the way to Minneapolis, and we talked about hunting all the way to Bob's with the radio blasting country tunes.

It was around 1,100 miles to Colorado from my place, so we had a slight detour (264 miles east, then 265 miles west) to and from Minneapolis.

We arrived at Bob's house and greeted his family. Bob's wife, "Dear Marie," had recently given birth to a boy – I called him "Speckmouse," a term of endearment.

We loaded up Bob's supplies. He had many items, including a down-filled sleeping bag, packed in this funny-looking metal framed contraption. I wasn't sure we'd have enough room for Bob's big pack because I had so many hunting clothes in the back of my truck.

I never had paid much attention when we loaded TD's things in the dark. Plus, Dear Marie purchased groceries and snacks that Bob thought we needed for the hunt. No one had asked me what I liked to eat, but food was the last thing on my mind.

The groceries were quite heavy with stacks of canned goods. We probably should have waited to pack the bread and eggs last — a fact we found out later. We each contributed $25 to the kitty and headed out.

I really didn't care to drive in the big city, so Bob took over the reins from Minneapolis and drove almost all the way to Nebraska. Just before dusk, I took over and drove and drove and drove. Dusk settled in the sky as I headed into Nebraska; but, being the wide state it was, it was nearly dawn when I drove out of Nebraska.

"Did you guys have a nice nap?!" I asked my companions as they stretched and yawned themselves awake. Bob too over and drove on from there to Cheyenne, Wyoming, where we stopped at a truck stop for fuel and lunch. This would be the first of many visits to the same truck stop over the years.

Bob stopped at a sporting goods store in Laramie, Wyoming, for last minute necessities. As we walked around, Bob said, "What kind of backpack do you have?"

"What? What is a backpack?" I answered.

There went another $60 – a lot of money back then.

"Do you have knife?"

"Yep!"

"A hatchet?"

"Nope." Another $20 gone.

After the spending spree, off we went to Walden, Colorado. There we purchased our over the counter $25.00 Elk Hunting Licenses. Wow! $25.00 represented almost 4 hours of work for me at the time!

Bob had another question. "Got a warm cap and coat?"

"Oh yeah," I proudly answered.

Next stop – the mighty, majestic Rocky Mountains. Even though I had seen the mountains in Montana, going through Colorado was breathtaking for a flatlander kid from North Dakota.

The End of the Road

As we drove up dangerous and rough mountain roads, I noticed outfitter ranches every once in a while. "Pack In on Horseback" the signs read. Such luxuries were for the rich and famous. Who could afford to pay $25.00 per horse and $50.00 for a guide fee ($150 and $300 in today's dollars)? Besides, we didn't need a guide. Bob had hunted here for years already.

Eventually, we turned off the main rough road onto a very nearly impassible narrow trail full of ruts and boulders for a couple of miles. Since we were hunting a wilderness area, we had to stop at the entrance of the National Forest – not that we could have driven any further anyhow. It was far too steep and rough.

Since we were all flatlanders, presently at 9,000 feet above sea level (8,500 feet higher than my house), Bob said we should stay for a day or so to get acclimated to the elevation.

Midmorning the next day, after unpacking a bit, I felt awe and excited welling up inside me. I grabbed some jerky and headed up the trail with the guys. Our campsite was about six miles from the truck. Bob explained that there was a 'Y' on the trail about one mile up and warned us not to go farther than that. As I headed out, the trail angled down and down and then steadily climbed back up again.

Piece of cake! I reached the 'Y' in no time. In fact, I ran most of the way on that warm, dry day, sprinting over deer and elk tracks on the trail which sparked a joyous feeling I can't put into words.

I headed back, even though I wanted to keep on exploring. I reached the base of the final mountain, eyeing the spot where my truck was parked at the top. I was in great shape, so I imagined I'd zip right up the mountain.

Yeah right.

I climbed and climbed. *It certainly wasn't this steep when I went down it.* We later named this "Heart Attack Mountain" for obvious reasons. I don't know why, but the altitude changes never affected me except for one time later.

We dug out our sleeping bags, ate some cold food, and slept under the stars.

"Do you have a good warm bag," Bob asked?

24

"Oh, yeah. Got it at K-Mart." Another lesson learned. There's no way I could sleep anyhow with all the anxiety and excitement that was bursting inside me.

Pack-In Time

We got up at daybreak – a little stiff and sore but ready to go. The first thing we started packing in our backpacks were the canned groceries (Rookie). Now I know why I needed a backpack. The packs were filling up fast and getting very heavy; we still had half of the truck's load to go. Bob suggested we make a couple of trips.

No problem.

We helped each other put the 50- to 60-pound packs on each other's backs and started to head out… rather, head up!

"Wait a minute," Bob said, as he reached into his pocket, handing both of us a piece of Anise candy and a chunk of Levi Garrett chewing tobacco. This was new territory for me.

"Just keep the candy on one side of your mouth and the tobacco on the other," Bob instructed. "Make sure you only swallow the candy juice, not the Levi Garrett."

I learned that this strange combination was a tradition among hunters and one I was proud to learn and someday master.

The most important thing I didn't pack was toilet paper, which would later become a necessity for me. Many a tree was sacrificed for the sake of my brown eye (my rear end). I never had diarrhea in my life before. But, after this trip, I referred to this miserable attribute as the big "D."

My 50-pound pack got heavier and heavier as we climbed in elevation, but the scenery, so beautiful and overwhelming, distracted me until we reached our campsite six miles later at an elevation of 10,000 feet.

We had packed a small pup tent and some clear poly. We put the groceries in the pup tent and made a large tent with lodge poles and the poly. We cut firewood, dug out the small Coleman stove, and made something to eat. That's when I realized just how worn-out I was from the hike. We laid out our sleeping bags and just slept on the ground anywhere.

Thankfully we arrived a few days before the season opened giving us extra time to go back down to the truck for more supplies. Damn, that Heart Attack Mountain seemed to grow each time. Finally, after a few more twelve-mile roundtrips, we finished setting up camp and got our archery gear ready for the hunt. Each morning and night, we could hear the bulls challenging each other with their constant bugling that echoed over the mountains in every direction — a sound that, once you hear it, you can never forget.

We had a beautiful campsite right beside a crystal-clear stream full of trout (Brookies). The water was cold and delicious. We weren't aware of Giardia Lamblia parasite in such waterways at that time, intoxicated by the scenic forest-filled mountains surrounding us in our plush valley meadow.

I was kind of shy back then, so I would go inside the tent to change my clothes. It didn't help that it was a clear plastic tent.

Smart move, Chaz!

After four or five days, it got musty in the tent requiring all occupants to take a sponge bath now and then. Of course, I would retreat to the clear plastic tent for my cleaning. Not only was I shy about the bathing, but I also had to have my own private shitter. This consisted of just the right log at just the right height in a hidden area of the forest – but not too far from the tent.

The First Hunt

Up at 4:00 am, dressed and ready to go, I downed a cup of hot chocolate and a couple of cookies. And, of course, I shoved the Anise and Levi chew into their respective cheeks.

The thrill of sitting in a tree stand was always exciting to me. I had been hunting since I was fourteen years old, so I planned to show my new hunting partner how good I was. Then I learned the awful truth… no tree stands when hunting elk! I had a lot to learn.

Bob explained our itinerary. Unless we were on the trail of an elk, we would come back around 10 a.m. or so for breakfast. Then he pointed in the direction he thought each of us should go, find a trail, stalk, stop, and listen.

At that hour of the morning, it was mighty damn dark in those woods. My imagination took me to some wild places and conjured up dangerous critters behind every tree. Right at daybreak, I found a well-used trail on top of "The Draw." I stalked. I stopped. I listened. And it worked. I could hear the elk moving in the timber; occasionally, I saw a cow.

Damn, they're huge. Let the games begin.

I got so close, I thought I could smell them. But they were constantly moving. Although I didn't see any bulls that morning, they were bugling everywhere around me. It was legal to shoot an elk of any sex during archery season, but I wanted a bull – any bull – for my first elk. My heart was about to jump clear through my skin and out of my chest. I had a whole herd around me — about 35 yards away — but no clear shot.

The wind shifted causing the elk nearest me to freeze. After a moment of eerie silence, all hell broke loose. The lead cow bellowed out a bark louder than any Doberman I had ever heard. I had no idea they could do that, and it scared the crap out of me. Bob had warned that if I spooked them, I should back off and work my way out of there. Unless the wind was right, I wouldn't want to drive them to the next county.

I slowly worked my way back to camp, or so I thought. Compass...in the truck (Rookie). There were three high points to watch for to keep my bearings straight. Once I saw one of them, I turned around and went the right way.

As soon as I saw our camp way down below, I decided to take a shortcut... bad idea! I ended up walking through a knee-deep marshland on the side of a mountain. *How is that even possible?* Not to mention, every other step was over downed timber. I still had so much to learn.

Back at camp, Bob cooked breakfast over the Coleman stove. He's a damn good cook. I couldn't even boil water back then.

I took off my outer layer of soaked pants and the second layer of wet pants beneath them, hanging them out to dry. As I took my top two coats off, Bob asked, "Didn't you get a little warm?"

"Oh yes, but you said to pack plenty of warm clothes."

The other guys took off only one jacket — some kind of down-filled thing.

We ate breakfast and talked about the morning hunt, detailing what we screwed up and what we should've done. But we were all excited that there weren't other hunters around – even if it was a bit strange. We spent the rest of the afternoon cutting firewood and telling lies… I mean, stories.

Evening Hunt

Bob didn't like going after the elk during the afternoons; it took me a few years to really understand why. Once they got your scent, they were gone and could have moved up to 15 miles away if they were aggressively pursued. If we stayed all day, the elk would certainly catch our scents.

For the evening hunt, we used a different strategy. We resolved to find a meadow near the heavy timber where the elk had been feeding and make a ground blind, so to speak. Again, we split up to better our chances. We were all seeing elk, just not close enough to get a shot off.

Sometimes hunters sit there in the quiet where everything is still except for an occasional bugle or the chatter of chipmunks giving your position away. But the quietest of all is gang of elk — a dozen members strong — standing right behind you never making a sound.

The next sound the hunter hears would sound like a herd of elephants crashing through the downed timber as they burst into the meadow.

Archery hunting is likely to coincide with rutting season — you just never know. Obviously, the bulls are more active when they are mating, but the cows are extra cautious and watchful.

The sun set over the beautiful mountains, causing the temperature to drop so low, sending a chill through my three layers of sweatshirts and two coats. By the time you're

29

halfway back to the camp (in the deep darkness), you're already shedding clothes. Everyone else had two layers, I had five!

I had never been so close to the stars and galaxies. It was like I could reach up, grab a shooting star, and fly off into space.

Amazing!

The first one back to the camp would start the fire and pump, pump, pump the white Coleman gas lantern, then light it (at his own risk). The lantern would burst into a fireball. We were careful to loosen the cover on the can of gas! None of us smoked, so we didn't have any dry matches or a lighter, it was very hard to start the lantern with a chew of Levi Garrett!

After chowing down some beans, bacon, and fried "badadas," we hit the sack in our cold sleeping bags after sharing a little shot of peppermint schnapps, of course.

"How's your bag?" Bob asked.

Squeezing my teeth together to stop them from chattering, I told him I would get two K-Mart bags next time.

Lesson learned.

Daily Routines

As each morning arrived, I learned to accept the pain in my back from a protruding tree root or a pointed rock poking through your sleeping bag. The bugling bulls and the tremendous anticipation of another day's hunt outweighed a little back pain.

All three of us had our chances to get an elk, but something would always prevent us from scoring the kill. A branch would block our shot, or the elk would hang behind a big tree, or the wind would change and give a one-hour stalk away. Regardless, it was still exciting and the thrill of a lifetime.

As each day passed, we shared more stories and became more comfortable with and confident in each other. Little did I know that Bob and I would become lifetime hunting buddies and the best of friends over the next 49 years.

One day, we cut down an old dead tree for firewood. We left about a four-foot stump. As TD and I cut up the log, Bob grabbed his homemade hatchet and threw it at that stump. THUD! It landed right in the middle. I had never seen anything like that before. *Let the lessons begin!*

Bob gave us a few pointers. Eventually, even I could stick the hatchet in the stump — though it was the lower left corner and took thirty tries to accomplish. Then TD tried the axe. After fixing the broken handle twice, we decided we should probably save the axe for chopping the large amount of wood we needed. Still, throwing the hatchet became our afternoon hobby.

The air cooled often, especially at night and in the early mornings. One morning, we grabbed our bows, jerky, anise candy, and a chew of ole Levi Garrett and headed up the trail towards a lake we heard of about two miles away. We walked quietly most of the time, enjoying the sights and sounds of chipmunks, squirrels, Canadian jays, blue grouse, and, of course, elk.

Beautiful!

As we walked around the corner and stepped out of the dark timber, the sight of that beautiful mountain lake took my breath away.

Around noon, with the sun high in the sky, we walked to the shore and noticed large trout in the shallow lake. We didn't have any fishing equipment, so I told the guys to watch me.

"I am going to catch one with my bare hands." After all, I was as fast as the Karate Kid and could snatch a house fly right out of the air with my bare hands! Besides, fresh fish for supper sounded really good.

I noticed a log the fish were travelling under, so I laid on it ready to spring into action. I tried thirty or forty times, only managing to brush across the slippery skin of a trout once. My failure meant fresh beans and "badadas" for supper again.

Even though there aren't many deer in the high country, one of us would purchase a deer license. This time, it was Bob who got the license.

The sun was now directly overhead, and it was very hot out. Before heading back to camp to get ready for the evening hunt, TD and I laid down and took in the beauty of the lake and mountain ridge. Our bows rested on the ground near us. Bob walked in front of us, stopped, and whispered to us to stay still and quiet.

Another prank from the prankster himself?

He slowly bent down, grabbed his bow, slipped out an arrow and explained, "There's a muley buck right behind you guys."

Yeah right!

I moved to get up when Bob drew back his bow full length. Since I didn't feel like an arrow in my cranium, I laid still as the arrow flew over us and SMACK! We turned and saw a muley buck with an arrow in its lungs. I couldn't

32

believe it. As he stood up, we ran down the trail towards camp. By the time we caught up to him, he had died on the trail. All that was left to do was gut him, skin him, and carry him two miles back to camp.

Bob and I processed him while TD searched for a 50-pound pole to tie him on. (Well… maybe not 50 pounds but almost as big as the deer.) We tied him on and carried the pole on our shoulders just like the frontier men did ages ago.

Rookies!

TD and I carried it all the way to camp — dang near running half the time… nonstop. At camp, we cooled it down in the creek. It's then that I noticed I was soaked, so I took off my outer wool shirt and sweatshirt, leaving my soaked, so-called, long johns on.

"I told you I had lots of hunting clothes," I chuckled.

Rookie.

Bob just shook his head.

I dressed lighter before we carried it along the six-mile trek to the truck up "Heart Attack Mountain" where all the aspen trees had changed to their fall colors. Absolutely magnificent.

We headed back up to camp and prepared to leave for home, packing up all our gear and gathering the empty food cans, bones I just had to take with me, and all my hunting clothes. I swear my pack was as heavy going down as coming up.

Rookie!

When I got back to work, I had to take a bit of ribbing from my colleagues because I spent so much money ($200.00), traveled all that way, and didn't even get an elk. That really bothered me at that time; but as years went by, I learned the difference between being a hunter for yourself or a game killer for others. I didn't want to make a kill just for the sake of not being called a loser or accused of wasting time.

Besides, next year, I'd be more prepared.

Next Year

The Beginning "Charlie Butz" 1974

Chapter 3   **Weather Change**

The following year brought the three of us together again. Same prep, excitement, and anticipation of what was to come as we had a year earlier. This time, Bob met us in North Dakota and we headed south to Omaha. As before, my turn to drive was the stretch through that damn lengthy Nebraska again.

I wish I knew how these experiences would impact my life. It took nearly twenty years before I realized I should write them down.

All these stories are true… for the most part. True, I may have stretched the gum a little here and there. But I'm confident that the important parts are accurate. In recalling the first twenty to twenty-five years, I relied on old pictures, stories from my hunting partners, and my memory (sometimes a problem)!

Favorite landmarks along the way help to revive some of the memories. On this road trip, we made the same stop at the Cheyenne Truck Stop and picked up our licenses in Walden – still $25.00. Only this time, the weather was not pleasant. Rain and sleet in the high country cast a shadow over the mountains. Still, it was beautiful.

Did I pack a rain suit? That's right. We brought the next best thing: garbage bags.

I thought the trail road was bad last year, but it looked even worse with all the rain. A few vehicles had challenged the road ahead of us, so I locked in the 4-wheel-drive and the carnival ride began — slipping along, avoiding huge washouts, and rumbling over rocks everywhere.

As we drove into the wooded area, we slid completely off the narrow trail. I came to a stop, the guys got out, and they said I'd have to back up or risk hitting the trees. After thinking about it for three seconds, I responded.

"Get out of the way. This is the only way in."

After all, my pickup was a year old by this time, and I knew what it could do. I floored it and realized I should have heeded my friends' warnings. I was never that good at pinball, but man, could I bounce my truck off those trees.

We got through with minimal damage to the truck — just a couple thousand dollars — and reached our parking area just before dark. We were thankful to have leftovers from our last restaurant stop and didn't need to cook anything. We decided to sleep in the truck (as if we had a choice – it was raining) and pack up in the morning.

Our packs were even heavier this year. We brought a teepee-style tent, giving up the clear plastic of the prior year. Same canned goods, but we added cup-of-soups, which were lighter and delicious. Thank God we had plastic garbage bags to put over our packs or they would have been soaked through and through.

As was his custom, Bob handed us the anise candy and a chew of Ole Levi before we headed out. A chew at 6:00 a.m. threatened to disagree with my stomach. But I soldiered on.

Going down Heart Attack was always the easy part; but with the rain, it was more precarious than the climb up. We might as well have had skis on; it was terrible, and there were areas that went straight down about 200 feet. To say the trail was challenging was an understatement. Furthermore, we had to cross three streams that we walked across the year before. This year, they were only passable by using logs or rocks. Before long, we were soaked and covered in grayish mud.

There were more signs of elk on the trail this year. That, along with the changing colors, filled us with joy enough to clog along farther. This time, I remembered the toilet paper and only had to use it twice on the way up. I neatly tucked it in my back pocket, later learning that was a mistake. By the time I reached for it again, it was soaked. Having no choice, I realized I had invented a bidet before I ever knew what a bidet was.

Patent pending?

My wife would always say as I hurried out of the house, "Have Fun!" Yeah, it was fun. I bet she had a chuckle thinking about our "fun-filled" Rainy Lake excursion two years earlier.

We continued along feeling our boots get heavier and heavier as the muck covered them. I fell four or five times, learning the sad truth of getting up from a deep rut with a 60-pound pack on your back. But my wife would be happy to know that this was what I called "having fun!"

We ran into a hunter or two on occasion. It seemed strange to me to know there were other people who wanted to have all this fun in the mud just to pursue the mighty elk with a bow and a little sharp stick.

Setting Up Camp

With our dark blue teepee tent, I rejoiced at the thought of privacy where I could change clothes in peace. We managed to set up camp in between the downpours, then set off on the near-impossible task of finding dry firewood. We wondered how the elk would react with this wet weather. As we would find out later, they were active and everywhere again, unbothered by the rain.

We dried out our packs and clothes as best we could before storing them in the tent. Remember to bring thin pads to lay on the ground under our sleeping bags turned out to be a great advantage.

Getting smarter!

Bob set up the cook stove and a makeshift kitchen as I hurried out across the trail to scope out my private toilet in the woods. I even found some dry toilet paper. Good thing, since I had the same bowel movement problem as last year: the Big "D" even though I hadn't even eaten anything or drank from the stream! came better prepared this time with a large package of Imodium-D.

Besides collecting firewood and old bones, my assignment was to assist Bob when he was cooking. As I mentioned, I couldn't boil water. But how tough could this assistant's job be? Turns out it was quite easy since Bob just wanted me to taste everything as I walked by and peeked over his shoulder. I started walking by him a lot after that.

The canned goods were heavy, but a large can of whole chicken we brought made the best soup I ever had, bones and all.

Scouting Time

All three of us had a general idea of where we wanted to hunt from scouts last year, but one never knows about the elk's movement. We came up with names for the areas this time so we would know the locations each other was talking about. Bob had what would later be called "Old Dad's," TD had "TD's Mountain," and I had, well, everywhere else. Seriously, I walked miles during those early archery seasons.

I loved stalking in the heavy timber; it turned out to be quieter and even more exciting in the wet weather. We hunted in the timber for morning hunts mostly and concentrated more in the open meadows in the evenings. Bob had found an area filled with elk, so he would hunt that in the evenings.

After two days of scouting, we discussed our findings and decided to hunt the same areas as last year. With very few other hunters around, we expected a great hunt. Either way, I was on Cloud 9 again and all the work was made worthwhile because, after all, I was having fun!

The season opened the next day. That evening, we double checked our gear. In my case, I laid out all my "heavy" hunting clothes and filled every pocket with candy and jerky. I had invested in a new camo sweatshirt. Before jumping in my bag, I headed back across the trail to do my thing, lighting my makeshift bathroom with flashlights, matches, and flares.

The Hunt

4:00 a.m. - Not much sleep due to excitement and the bulls and coyotes that screamed all night long. Breakfast consisted of hot chocolate and a cookie and then some candy and a chew and we headed out in the dark.

Bob wasn't a big fan of flashlights and told us to use them only if necessary. Walking in the dark required knowing when to lift a leg and how high. We carefully crossed over all the dead fall with no light. As I worked my way to the top, I could hear the cows and calves chirping as if they were speaking to each other. Occasionally, a squeaky bugle could be heard, which Bob told me was a young bull. My mind was a sponge, and I gratefully took in all Bob had to say, absorbing the sights and sounds that surrounded me each time out.

As daybreak slowly approached, I stopped to rest from the climb and realized I could smell the elk quite strongly, indicating that I was in the middle of a herd again. The wind was right, so I rushed on quietly to get ahead of them. I reached a large log and got ready. Since I didn't have a compound bow yet, I couldn't pre-draw. I could see the animals' legs about 45 yards away, but they were moving toward me.

Until you've been there in these situations, there's no way to describe the excitement and feeling of your heart beating out of your chest.

Suddenly everything stopped just as it had the year before. Just then, I caught something out of the corner of my eye. I slowly turned my head to find myself staring eye-to-eye with a yearling cow less than ten yards away. I think we both thought, "How in the hell did we get this close to each other without knowing it?"

Word of advice, albeit from a Rookie: You'll never win in a stare down with an elk. Motionless, I stood there for thirty minutes (okay, ten seconds) trying not to fall off the 4-foot-high log when the inevitable happened. She let out that horrible, deep "Mad Dog" bark. Then she stomped her foot (like I've seen deer do), barked one more time, and then the crashing began. It sounded like I was in a fireworks display. I could hear them breaking branches all the way down the side of the mountain.

Damn! Defeated, I worked my way back down for real breakfast. At least I didn't go through the swamp this time. Learning.

Bob was alone back at camp, so we talked about our adventure while making breakfast and waiting for TD to return. Bob explained how he had a bull going in "Old Dad's," but didn't see him. He knew how to use a bugle call; I didn't.

Just as I was telling him about my harrowing episode, our conversation was interrupted by the sound of TD hollering as he ran down TD's Mountain. He had struck a bull ten yards from him, but it was behind some bush. He saw the hit and found blood, so he came for help.

We were all excited, but Bob said, "We'll have breakfast first and then go find him."

It had finally quit raining, so Bob was confident we should be able to find the blood trail. TD had tied a piece of orange tape where it was standing when the shot hit, so Bob found the blood right away. I was too embarrassed to tell them I was partially colorblind, so I wasn't much help unless the blood was wet.

The last of the blood trail ran way down the other side of the mountain, nearly a mile and a half from camp. We looked for hours. After splitting up, we all met again in a beautiful valley meadow that we appropriately named "Lost

Meadow." There were no signs of an injured elk anywhere, and worried we may not find him… or maybe it was a non-vital hit.

Exhausted and hungry, we worked our way back to camp. We stayed close to camp that night with upset stomachs, but we still had hope.

The next morning, Bob asked me to go with him to "Old Dad's." I was thrilled for the opportunity to hang with the pro. TD headed back up to keep looking for his bull, and we told him we'd be up after our morning hunt. This time, we'd take food, candy, and Levi Garrett with us.

Bugling Them In

As Bob and I entered "Old Dad's," the king himself started to bugle. Younger bulls spoke out their juvenile challenging calls followed by the sound of a mature elk. They were lucky the big boy didn't come to find them.

We stopped several times as the bugles got closer — perhaps approaching through narrow openings within the dark pines. Bob sent me ahead of him about 50 yards or so while he stayed back and challenged this magnificent creature with his homemade elk call.

The answer back from this big fellow went right through me. I don't know how my heart withstood all the excitement. I understood in that moment why TD was yelling all the way down. The bull finally stuck his head and neck out from behind an evergreen. He looked huge to me – I was too excited to count the points on his horns.

He was quite far away (75 yards or so), but I was ready if he kept coming. He stepped back into the dark timber, not aware of us at all. Moments later, he disappeared but kept bugling for quite some time.

The wind picked up, so we quietly backed out of there. Even though I was calm about the whole thing, I didn't shut up talking to Bob all the way back to the camp.

We grabbed some snacks and headed back up to help TD. We ran into him over the top of TD's Mountain and spent several more hours searching to no avail. Reality had set in; we had lost an elk after injuring him. Sickening, but sadly, it happens.

Saying Goodbye

Even though the weather more challenging than it was the year before, those ten days went by awfully fast. TD didn't feel much like hunting the last four days. Bob had a couple of chances, such as his bow string getting caught up in a branch while a bull stood twenty yards from him. As for me, I'm proud to say I shot a blue grouse at twenty yards, and we had him for supper.

Packing up was harder this year. We were all quiet… even me. The thought of waiting another year to return was depressing and losing the elk made it worse.

We got everything down and packed, picked up all our trash, and put it in our packs. Just as we were ready to go, I grabbed my toilet paper and threw on my heavy pack. "No, wait," I said.

I took off my pack, ran across the trail to my secret toilet, and let the "D" fly again. I came back, washed up, grabbed my toilet paper, and put on my heavy pack again. I took a piece of candy just as Bob gave us a chew of Ole Levi, and we were off.

I can't sing, but I "sang" Merle Haggard songs all the way down. I only had to stop once to clean the ole brown eye.

Our trip home was uneventful, but little did I know this would change in years to come.

Next Year ⟶

Charlie - 1975

A Year to Remember

Another year of adventure awaited. Bob met TD and I early, so we went to a Steam Thresher's Reunion. We took the wives out for breakfast before packing up TD's new Blazer and headed out leaving the ladies behind.

We had gotten to know each other a little better and TD mentioned how ten days felt like a long time to be away from his beloved wife. (Horniest guy I've ever met.) After all, we all missed our families, but we had waited a year for this. Next thing you know, they'll be sending love letters back and forth!

The road trip down was uneventful in the new Chevy Blazer. We made the same stops on the way down as we had in the past. The locals at the rest stops started to recognize us.

Leaves had already started to change color in the Aspens. Mother Nature put on a fantastic kaleidoscope show of beauty. Every year when we went over the summit of Rabbit Ears Pass, the scenery was jaw dropping. It never got old.

The weather was decent so far this time. Even the last two miles on the mountain trail were doable. The ruts seemed to be even deeper though, perhaps sinking with time and wear. TD didn't want to take his new Blazer up the last stretch, but we shamed him into it. After all, it was a four-wheel-drive. I think he remembered what happened to my new truck and felt it wasn't right to risk his new vehicle just as I had.

Arriving at the forest edge earlier this year, we packed some stuff in. Next morning, Bob set up camp while TD and I headed down for the last of the supplies. Our breakfast was a Pop Tart, a piece of anise candy, and a chew of Levi Garrett for the trip down. By now, I had learned which juices to spit and which to swallow.

I remember to take plenty of toilet paper with me, thank God. There was just something about Colorado that brought the big "D." When my brown eye had to go, it said when, where, and how – no debating and nearly no delay allowed.

We returned to camp in the late afternoon and helped Bob finish up unpacking. We had the same blue teepee tent again. It was small, but I loved the privacy. You never know when a chipmunk or elk might stop by and peek in when you're changing clothes.

We were getting smarter with our dining habits and brought paper plates, bowls, and plastic utensils this time. Of course, "Dear Marie" provided all the groceries again. There were even a couple dozen eggs in unbreakable containers. Unbreakable, my ass. We only broke three or four.

We brought a few bags of freeze-dried food. It was not very tasty back then. When you're hungry, though, anything is better than anise candy and a chew of Levi Garrett!

The Night Before

We knew which way we were heading for the morning hunt, but the weather was very warm. Due to this, the elk were likely to be higher even though we were based at 10,000 feet. There were elk signs everywhere, so we unpacked and got things ready for morning: wax the bowstrings, sharpen the arrows (we didn't have the razor tips yet), and get the hunting clothes out. As we were unpacking, TD got all excited, jumping around like a teenager on his first date.

"What the heck is going on?" Bob asked.

"Look-it here!" TD proudly showed us pictures fresh out of a Playboy magazine. His wife had to remind him all the benefits of skipping the hunt and staying home with here.

I told him that was ridiculous and that we were there to hunt elk.

As I reached deeper into my clothes bag, I felt a square piece of paper. *Huh, puzzling.* I turned my back to the guys as I slowly pulled it out. It was an envelope with red hearts all over it. *This can't be.* I opened it with caution and removed the contents as I turned my back to the guys. I certainly didn't want them to see it.

Just as I quietly opened the single piece of paper, Bob popped over my shoulder and said, "What's that?"

Oh boy! I had no choice but to confess that it was a kissy-face, miss-you, love note from "Rosie," my wife. At least it wasn't Playboy Girls.

Opening Day

Opening morning was spent climbing, searching, listening, and smelling elk. Although it was a straight up, tough climb, I concentrated more on one of the highest peaks in the area which eventually was named "Chuckie's Mountain." Go figure, it was the most miserable to get to. Steep ravines, swamp areas, and large deadfall were everywhere; but there were elk!

TD headed to TD's Mountain, but this time Bob tried "Boob's Meadow" for the morning hunt. TD and I didn't see much, but Bob reported that elk were in and out of his meadow for quite some time that morning. He followed some trails and set up a plan for a ground blind for the evening hunts. He arrived back at camp very optimistic.

Bob was late getting back because he didn't want to scare the elk out of the meadow – a lesson we all had to learn.

Since neither TD nor I could boil water, we hung on Bob like two little puppies as he made breakfast. Eggs, bacon, and taters. *Mmm.* It was worth carrying all that extra weight up on our backs.

After that gourmet meal, we rested and gave our morning report. Other than a lot of signs, the only report I had was a damn squirrel cussing me out for ten minutes. At least TD had seen several cows.

TD had hunted with Bob a year before me, so he had rank on me. That evening he got to go with Bob to Boob's Meadow. I decided to check an area we would eventually name "Hog Pen."

Good choice!

I made a makeshift blind and settled in. The weather was warm so far, so I was careful not to overdress. But the weather was misleading; when the sun went down behind the mountains, an evil chill crept in. No problem shooting a bow while shivering, right?

Just before the magic hour, elk stealthily appeared in the meadow from several directions. The wind was right for me but, up that high, it would shift constantly. There were several spikes, a few satellite bulls, and many cows and calves — all chirping constantly.

I didn't have a Range Finder so, prior to making my blind, I stepped off certain areas up to forty yards. An elk is so large, sometimes that distance can be deceiving.

As luck would have it, a calf walked right by me at ten yards. What a thrill! I didn't move, but he quickly turned his head and looked at me. *Here we go again*. He peacefully turned back and kept eating, having no idea a hunter was right beside him.

I was tempted to take a shot at a spike, but he was too far from my marked spot. They were all still there at dark. Remembering what Bob had just told us, I snuck back down in the timber to the trail and smiled all the way back to camp. What a thrill – every outing an exciting adventure.

As I arrived back at camp in the deep dark, the area stood empty and still. I started a huge fire, grabbed my hatchet, and sat back in the shadow of an evergreen. I didn't like the dark and didn't love being alone!! Suddenly there was a noise by the tent… then another one.

I stood up and shouted, "Okay, you sons-of-bitches, come on in!" I held my hatchet cocked in the throwing position. Sure enough, those two clowns emerged, thinking it was easy to pull pranks on me and get me all worked up.

Their evening story was similar to mine except they had many more elk come out of the dark timber to feed in the luscious meadow. Unless they needed help with a kill, it would be a few more years before I would be asked to hunt in Boob's Meadow.

49

The Kill

The next morning, our routine continued with snacks, anise candy, and Levi Garrett. I headed to Chuckie's Mountain and those two went back to Boob's.

I spent a few hours sitting, stalking, and trying to learn all I could on the movement of the smaller herds. It was such a beautiful morning that I ended up walking farther than I thought, so I was much later getting back to camp. Strange – the guys weren't back when I returned. We had no way of communicating, not even two-ways. So, I opened my own can of fruit cocktail and ate a Mars bar. Just before noon, they came.

"What's that all on your pants," I asked?

"Blood."

"No way. You got one? Did you find it? Where is it? How big is it? Who got it?"

To say I was excited again would be an understatement!

"Let's go get it!" I continued.

"Settle down – we'll have breakfast and grab our packs, some mesh bags, a meat saw, and a hatchet and head back up," Bob said.

Bob had killed a spike bull and they gutted it out before coming in. I couldn't wait to see it up close – not realizing how heavy it was going to be to carry back to camp.

Never being in Boob's Meadow before, I couldn't wait to see it and entered it with the commensurate respect and awe. The trail into the meadow was windy and long with lots of downed timber. Popping around the last corner and seeing the meadow for the first time was like looking at a "Monique" painting to me.

I was probably as excited as Bob and never stopped asking questions all the way. As we approached the downed animal, I couldn't believe how enormous it was. Yes, I was close to them in the woods, but I couldn't touch them in that setting. We all took out our polaroids and grocery store Kodaks to cherish the memories.

The Work Begins
We skinned the critter and proceeded to saw it right down the middle, head to tail, like butchering a beef. We cut it into 4 quarters, ribs and all, and put it in the mesh bags.

It was mandatory for each of us to have a bundle of parachute cord for tie-down. We secured three-quarters of it on our packs and helped each other put those heavy packs on our backs. Bob grabbed the antlers and we headed down. He said he'd come back up and get the other quarter later that afternoon.

Back at camp, we cleaned the meat the best we could, deboned the ribs, and removed them. Bob went to get the remaining meat while TD and I hung the quarters on a makeshift game pole.

When Bob got back, we finished the process. Since it was so warm during the day, flies grew to be a problem. Even though we were going to take the meat down the next day, we had to put pine boughs under the mesh and sprinkle pepper over the quarters to help keep the insects away.

We were all plenty tired that afternoon, but I still went out for the evening hunt. Now I had more reason and hope than ever — not that I needed any more.

Bright and early the next morning (before the heat), we loaded the three packs again and divided up the smaller fourth piece to get it all down in one load. The packs were very heavy with unboned meat. I couldn't tolerate the slow walking pace my companions chose, so I went ahead and walked very fast. I would stop more than the others for a few seconds, but I ended up way ahead. The trail was mostly downhill until we got to Heart Attack where I waited for the guys to catch up.

The trip up Heart Attack with a quarter plus elk in tow was a challenging, unforgettable feat. Too bad horses were so expensive to pack out. *$25.00 – are you kidding me?*

Rookies!

Thank God I was young and in good shape but, at 5'8" and 175 pounds, I was basically carrying myself!

What a sight to see the top of the mountain. That beautiful Blazer was right there, cheering us on and offering to take the load off our hands. Turns out there were a couple guys camped there that Bob knew. They couldn't believe we carried an entire elk that far.

They helped us lift the two-ton packs off our backs and put them in the large coolers. As Bob was talking to them, I overheard them call us something like *insane* or *stupid* – something like that.

One of the men said, "My God, you can rent a horse for $25.00."

Please don't remind me.

As I walked by them, they said, "That was quite a feat."

I responded, "You'll never see me do something this stupid again!"

Bath Time

We trudged our way back up in the heat, grabbed something to eat, and laid down for a while. TD was even too tired to stare at the Playboy pinup girl he hung above his bedroll. Upon awakening, someone commented that it was getting pretty rank in the tent with the stench attached to each of us.

Bob said, "That's it, no sponge bath will do, guys. We're going in." There was a deep fishing hole (3 feet or so) around the corner from our camp.

I didn't want any part of jumping in that hole, but that damn TD agreed. I boisterously repeated my disapproval of such a childish endeavor.

If you know the song, "Please, Mr. Custer," you can imagine me bellowing out the tune in resistance as Bob grabbed the soap and some towels, TD grabbed my arm, and we headed for the unimaginable 39° fish swimming (bathing) hole.

"Please, Mr. TD, I don't want to gooo! There's cold water waitin' out there, fixing to curl my hair."

I pulled away like a scared dog heading for his first bath to no avail. Three grown men, of whom I was the only one who wasn't naked, walked across a field beside a public national trail.

Are you kidding me?

Those two jumped right in and said, "Come on in, the water's fine."

Are they nuts? It's 39 degrees! I have to admit, I smelled pretty bad, so in I went, shorts and all. I figured they needed a cleaning too.

I jumped in and the shock made me shoot up in the air twice as fast, screaming like a schoolgirl. That water was so cold, it shriveled the Dew Berries up so tight, I talked like a girl for two days. I had a lot more respect for those little trout swimming in that ice cold stream. I admit, though, that I felt so good though when I got out.

Back at the tent, Bob said, "Now we're going to change shorts."

What?

"Chaz, you change with TD and I'll change mine." *Pranksters.*

Not Again

TD and I continued hunting the same areas we had stalked before. TD went to Boob's. It was two days after Bob shot his elk. I walked even further, going clear across the top. By about noon, I headed back to camp to keep Bob company. When I arrived, TD was not there. That was strange. He usually beat me back.

Bob and I started a late breakfast, when suddenly, just as before, TD running up to us like a mad man, grabbed me up off my stump, dancing and whipping me around like a rag doll, shouting, "I got one, I got one!"

When he finally let me go, we congratulated him and tried to calm him down, forcing him to eat something. We grabbed our packs and necessities and headed back up to Boob's. He told us on the way up, it was only a large cow.

Bob instructed him to never use the word "only." An elk was an elk.

By the time we got to the cow, it was getting late and would be dark soon. TD had already gutted the animal, so we decided to wait until morning to quarter it up. We worried about coyotes though. They were always looking for something to scavenge.

TD came up with the "brilliant" idea of hanging it in the trees. *A gutted whole elk cow?* We were dumb enough to tie it to a pole like we did the deer in the past and hang it high. How in the world the three of us lifted that elk up in the trees is beyond me; somehow, we did it. We took some pictures and headed back down.

Here We Go Again

The next morning, we returned to see that our idea for keeping the meat safe actually worked. Camp robbers (Canadian jays) had helped themselves to some of the fresh meat, but no coyotes. We finished skinning and quartering the cow. She was huge with lots of meat. Strangely, I had never tasted elk yet and was looking forward to it.

It took most of the day to get everything down to camp. Since we only had a day or two left on our hunt, the decision was made to take a quarter down to the Blazer that day and the other three quarters the next day. TD was floating so high, he said he'd take a front shoulder down and come back up. He packed up the cleanest shoulder and headed down. Bob and I cleaned up the rest of the meat and started to clean the camp.

As the only one who hadn't scored a kill, I went out hunting that evening, focused more on reminiscing and enjoying the sights and sounds than anything else. I got back to camp right at dark and TD arrived an hour or so later. He was very tired and I thought I noticed a new limp.

We planned to take the two hind quarters (heavy, with bone-in) and the remaining front shoulder down and come back up so we could pack out the next day. Obviously, there was no more time for hunting. I would end the season without getting an elk again.

The next morning at daybreak. TD could hardly move. He said something was wrong with his hip. *Great!* He was in a lot of pain. Bob asked him if he could at least carry down his pack with his things. He said he'd try, but he didn't think he could make it back up.

"We'll figure it out," Bob said.

What do you mean, figure it out? We had 3 quarters of an elk, the tent, and supplies to go down yet and only me and Bob to carry it.

Holy shit!

Bob and I tied the front shoulder onto a pole and put the heavy hinds in our packs. We thought it would be best to hang the shoulder straight down from the leg bone to make the weight equal for both of us. TD was well ahead of us by the time we got going.

"My God, this is heavy," I commented.

Thankfully it was mostly downhill until… *Oh shit, Heart Attack.*

We heard that some weather was moving in, but the trail was still good and dry. As we headed down, we noticed we were out of step a bit as the hanging shoulder started to swing sideways, making it twice as miserable. We had to make quite a few stops and rest up.

"Well, here we go," I said, as we headed up Heart Attack, challenging each other. I was holding the front of the pole when I looked up and saw the top where the Blazer was.

"Another 100 feet, Bob. We did it!" I couldn't carry this thing any further. We limped up over the last knoll and Bob's friend walked over to us in disbelief.

"You guys are crazy," he stated. "You said you'd never do that again just two days ago. You could've got a horse for $25.00."

"Don't remind me," I said.

We didn't want to put the heavy packs down until we got to the new Blazer just behind this fellow's camp. As we walked around his camp, we were shocked. No damn Blazer. *What the hell?*

Bob's friend said, "Your partner heard there might be snow moving in, so he drove his new Blazer down to the main road."

Another mile away! It's a 4-wheel-drive, for crying out loud!

We got the meat down to the Blazer and didn't say much for fear of revealing how furious we were. There was no way TD could go back up, so Bob and I took off for camp. We slept well that night. The next morning, we packed up the remaining items, cleaned up camp, said goodbye for the year, and headed back down again.

We were happy and thrilled about our success, but the trip home was a little quieter if you know what I mean. By the way, it did snow – a whopping two inches.

Next Year ⟶

Bob - 1976

A Different Area

Chapter 5

For the first and only time, we had to hunt a different area just south of our main area because of a high fire danger listing. Bob and his new friend, "Porcupine," were going to meet TD and me at the trailhead. The season was already open. I drove my 4-wheel-drive truck – weather change or not!

Since we weren't in a wilderness area this time, we could bring in small mechanical things, such as carts. TD made a one-wheel contraption with two handles on each end. We had no idea if it would work. All we knew was the wheel was round, so we were willing to give it a shot. Now that we had this carry-all unicart thing, we could bring more stuff.

Bob had meetings at work, so Porcupine met up with us first. He was a wonderful gentleman. I was still in my twenties and he had to be in his 50s at least. That was elderly to me back then.

We packed the groceries, stove, fuel, and tent on TD's wonder-cycle. "I think we can put more on," TD said, as poor Porcupine stood there with a puzzled look on his face. We only had to pack in a couple of miles this time and it wasn't as steep.

Piece of cake.

We put on our packs which were much lighter now since we put so much on the cart. TD took the front end and I took the back. *His hip must be fine this year.*

We took off like we were on the interstate. On the first little curve, everything on top flew off.

"There's a speed limit on our curves," I stated. We probably should have tied things down. I can still hear Porcupine laughing.

After regrouping and tying things down, we tried again. The thing was heavy and, when we reached our first incline, there was a lot of grunting and moaning. As stubborn as we both were, we trudged on, reaching our new campsite by mid-morning.

We set up a makeshift camp and decided to go scouting. Porcupine was a great asset to our little team — a true outdoorsman. Bob was to arrive there the next morning, and I knew he'd be impressed with the camp set up nice and neat.

Bows in hand, off we went in different directions. There were elk and deer signs everywhere. We saw a few small groups here and there, but this was a huge area. Refusing to head back to camp with all this fresh sign, I ended up deeper and farther away than the others. As always, I had to stop and find a decent place to get rid of the big "D" before I could post somewhere. (Yes, I buried it.)

I nestled in a small group of trees just to observe things for morning. None of us intended on actually hunting that evening.

Leaves were starting to change again and the steep cliffs surrounding the area were magnificent to see. I sat with my bow hanging on a branch when, out of nowhere, three of four cows and calves walked ten yards past me. It's a good thing I had done my business earlier or I might have filled my pants. The slight breeze was perfect to conceal my scene. They were so close, I could see the veins in their eyes. I wanted to pull back and try to get my first elk, but I really wanted a bull and let them walk away. *The guys aren't going to believe this.*

It was starting to get late. Never being in this area before, I decided to try and find my way back; I didn't like the dark! I had to go through a small ravine with younger pines and a crystal-clear stream running through it in order to get back to the main trail. As I started down the ravine, a young muley buck (3x3) jumped in front of me. We surprised each other.

I decided that, if he stopped and gave me a good shot, I would take it. Sure enough, twenty yards away, he stopped broadside, looking back at me. I didn't have sights on my 58-pound Bear bow, but I knew the distance and where to hold it. I quickly drew back and let one fly.

SMACK! I got him right behind the shoulder, a double lunger. He jumped over to the other side of the ravine. *No way, I can't lose this one.* I waited ten minutes or so, but the sun was disappearing over the horizon. I hated the dark; besides, there were bears in this area. Thankfully, I had a small flashlight in my fanny pack and followed what I thought was blood. Since it was on both sides of the track, it had to be.

Less than 50 yards away, there he laid – expired. I didn't see my arrow at all. I turned him on his back to start gutting him out when a sharp object poked me in the leg. It was the business end of my arrow. I bled a little bit but was too excited to worry about that.

I got back to camp late. The smell of fresh Mountain Man coffee Porcupine had brewed was a refreshing scent. I grabbed a bite to eat, poured a hot cup of that coffee, and proceeded to tell my story. We couldn't believe how this day had ended.

The next morning, I told the guys the general area where the deer was. While they went out hunting, I headed up to it to start skinning and quartering him. Mid-morning, they found me and helped me carry him back to camp. They had heard and seen elk everywhere. I had heard lots of bugling also.

It was starting to get very warm, so we did our best to keep the meat in the shade. Bob arrived that afternoon and couldn't believe I got my first Colorado kill. He was happy for me until I told him I had a cow ten yards away also.

Porcupine wasn't going to be able to stay with us for very long. It was getting warm out. He said he would leave in the morning and volunteered to take the meat to the nearest locker plant. The remaining days were spent stalking elk a few miles from camp.

At the end of the first day, we headed back to camp in the dark. We hunted in the same general area but had split up. The constant screaming of the bulls echoed through the canyons.

I was first to get back to the camp again, so I prepared my best defenses against the deadly critters and, God forbid, strangers. I built a huge campfire, grabbed my hatchet, and hid in the dark. Worked every time. The only sounds in this pitch-black darkness were the crackling fire and bulls off in the distance, until suddenly branches broke behind me.

Oh, shit! A bear?! A mountain lion?! With hatchet in hand again, I shouted, "Okay, you sonsabitches!"

Two pranksters popped into the light, laughing their asses off.

My poor heart.

Earlier that day, I had found a very nice log for my private toilet. While we were sitting around the fire talking about all the bulls, I figured I may as well let the "ole brown eye" finish what had already started when the two idiots scared the shit out of me… literally.

Shortly after I got back and sat by the fire again, TD said, "I smell shit."

What? I always cleaned up and besides, I had my bidet sheets to make sure. I had to admit, though, the pungent odor getting stronger, prompting Bob to start an inspection.

"Here it is," he said. "It's on his damn shoe."

I was embarrassed. I didn't dare tell them about my shorts which I burned when they weren't looking.

After a lot of laughter, we made a plan for the last two days. We packed in the necessities – a small plastic tarp, some food, anise, Levi Garrett, and our bows – and stayed up on top the next day and night.

"Fine with me," I said when I was told the plan. "But by dark, I'm sticking to you guys like glue."

The next day, bulls bugled from every direction. Bob and TD went one way and I went the other. We all had chances but never a clean shot.

I got closer to the guys towards dark. It had clouded over and started to rain. *Great, no tent.* But we had remembered to bring a small plastic tarp. We discussed flipping a coin for who gets the tarp. After all, it was only big enough for one person. Instead, we made a lean-to and tucked our damp, cold sleeping bags under it. Plenty of room if you're a sardine. We were able to start a small fire somehow, just under the edge of the tarp. We should have brought more food. I was starving. Being the smallest, I slept in the middle. Good position to stay warm.

The next morning, stiff and sore from the cold wet ground, we slowly hunted our way back to base camp. Even though we split up at one point, we met again at the base of a large ridge about a mile away. Midday, wet and hungrier than a bear, we stepped it up a notch, found the main trail, and headed down.

A hunter sat under a pine tree with a small stove going. The aroma of something gourmet filled the air and our nostrils forced us over to this gentleman. After introducing ourselves, we couldn't help but notice four pieces of brown, delicious-looking blue grouse simmering away. We put on our sad and homeless-looking faces, all the while explaining to him how we stayed up on top all day and night with very little food.

He said, "You should have killed a "fool's hen" (blue grouse). They are very good eating. Good luck hunting!"

Damn.

Back at camp, we packed everything for the two-mile hike down.

We had started a tradition of giving each other a small gift in camp each year. Bob asked me if I'd like one of his homemade fantastic knives.

Mama didn't raise no fool. "You betcha!"

Just before we got to the trucks, the wheel came loose on the two-ton, one-wheel cart, so that thing was retired for good.

Next Year ⟶

TD & Charlie – 1977

Charlie – 1977

Chapter 6

Back to the First Camp

Over the course of the next year, Bob bought a collector car from TD. So, when it was time for our yearly hunting trip, we hooked up a car trailer behind my heavy-duty, half-ton pickup and headed for Arvada, Colorado. I thought people were staring at me and my beautiful truck as they went by, but in truth they were gawking at Bob's awesome '53 Cadillac.

Twelve hours later, we arrived at Bob's. *Holy shit has "Speckmouse" grown.*

"What are you now, five?" I remarked. "And you're only 5 feet tall?"

This fantastic kid and I hit it off from the day he was born. He hung on me like glue, taking my hand and leading me around the neighborhood, showing me to all his other 5-year-old friends like I was something special.

He would say, "This is 'The Chaz' and he's a mountain man." Those little shits would stare up at me and just say, "Wow." His little buddies stood all of three to four feet tall. I felt like Jeremiah Johnson standing amongst them — all except 5-foot-tall, 5-year-old Speckmouse.

Bob and Porcupine surprised us by purchasing two horses, Jake and Spice, and by getting a horse trailer. Now we could really have fun! They pastured these two throughout the Arvada area for a few years.

We had to get panniers now and ropes to tie them onto the horses. Porcupine taught me several knots to tie the packs. The main one I remember to this day was the Squaw Hitch Knot. It didn't matter how tightly you secured the knot, though, if you didn't have the saddle on tight. The result? A rodeo with your items all over the mountainside. (Ask me how I know.)

Since we were hunting in a wilderness area, we had to take in certified feed. This meant extra trips up and down; but having the horses was much easier on our backs. We also had to water and care for them every day.

We loaded things up while "Dear Marie" gathered the final bundle of groceries as she always did. I wouldn't realize just how much work that was until a few years down the road.

Porcupine brought his things over that evening. The four of us headed out early in the morning. I can't explain why the anticipation and excitement was happening to me again, just like the first year.

The Road Trip

We took a new path this year. I rode with Bob, a mountain-driving Mario Andretti, in his new 4-door pickup. This man knew how to take a curve. Or, at least, I hoped he did as I squeezed my eyes shut so as not to see him speed around the bends. Going up the mountains at 70 to 75 miles per hour was bad enough. Going down a 7-degree road and seeing signs "Runaway Truck Area Ahead" was… well, let's just say the ole brown eye was puckering up.

Bob impressed the hell out of me. Like I said, Bob Andretti. Going up and over Eisenhower Tunnel (14,000 feet) was unbelievable, all the while pulling a horse trailer with Quarter horses in it!

Traveling this new route to our destination meant stopping in Kremmling, Colorado for burgers, onion rings, and malts. Kremmling was a beautiful little town where the elk migrated for their winter-feeding ground. We also went by a small town that read "Toponas," which Bob said meant "sleeping lion." From that day forward, I would inform anyone riding with me what it meant and then question them the following year to be sure they remembered. This was the beginning of a wealth of roadside information I would share with others to enrich their craniums.

We arrived at the trailhead and, as always, the last mile was worse than the year before with huge washouts now. Slowly, we crawled in 4-wheel-drive through a maze of boulders, trees, and deeper ruts.

We packed the panniers on the beautiful horses and tied them securely. Instant pros. We probably should have bought canvases to cover the packs with. *Oh well, it won't rain and I'm sure these two mountain horses will stay on the trail and not brush against any trees.* Wrong on all accounts. They bounced into every tree they could and, yes, it rained. After a couple of rodeos and repacking, we reached our campsite.

We were still camping by our favorite spot at the stream. While unpacking, we got another surprise. Porcupine brought a real canvas tent. This was like a motel to us. We were actually able to bring up real pots and pans, some silverware, and our own cups. How quickly one learns to appreciate things that are commonplace at home. This was a treat in God's wilderness. With all these extra utensils, I helped Bob even more with the cooking by tasting everything more often. Porcupine also did some cooking. I had my own two chefs.

We cut and split some wood for the evening. I helped with this chore. It was the least I could do… literally. After laying our hunting gear out for the morning hunt, we sat around the fire taking in the sounds of the clear flowing stream and an occasional bugle.

I ran to fetch the gifts I had brought for the guys. I was so proud of the keychain (cheap), pen (free), and a small fridge magnet with my company logo on it. Big spender!

I said, "Okay, men, let's exchange our hunting gifts."

They went to get theirs. After a while, we were back around the fire again, sitting on our makeshift log branches. I couldn't wait to give them my fabulous gifts. (Well, I did have to pay for my company logo, after all.)

I proudly went first, walking around to each of them with a big smile on my face.

Complete silence.

I sat down, puzzled, waiting for some kind of acknowledgement. Five minutes later (okay, 5 seconds), they all said, "Thanks, Big Spender." I realized they were probably thinking, "This is a hunting trip in the middle of nowhere – what are we supposed to do with a keychain, a pen, and a damn magnet up here. We didn't have a fridge."

Then it was Porcupine's turn. He gave us each a pair of camo hunting gloves and a packet of jerky.

Oh my, what have I done?

Then Bob handed out anise candy, of course, and a nice hunting cap for each of us. My head started to droop in shame. Only TD to go and I'd be out of this embarrassing situation. He gave us each a bag of small candy bars and a lighter. When he got to me, he handed me a gift-wrapped box.

Wow! I felt special again! I ripped it open to see a one-inch putty knife with a small rope loop for my belt. As my smile started to slip away, TD ordered me to turn it over. There it was in bold letters it read: "Shit Shoe."

Damn asshole!

He said, "Keep it on your belt, we know you're going to need it."

Just before we headed to the tent, Bob revealed another gift— my first beautiful homemade knife. I was back to feeling proud again.

Now that we actually had a real tent, we also upgraded our bedding. It had been awfully chilly at night the year before, so a friend of mine lent me his miliary mummy bag. I gave my K-Mart bag to the kids for summer camping. Maybe they could use it to stay warm in July. We even brought up foam pads so we wouldn't be on the ground.

Porcupine would have his evening cups of cold coffee. The others would be in the sack. It never failed that I was always last, even to this day, to settle into bed. I was more comfortable around the guys, so I talked a lot more. But I never learned to shut up until I was told. Since I was the last one down, I always had the job of turning off the gas lantern. It would produce a puff and pop when it finally quit burning. The drift of white gas would fill the tent as the guys started screaming at me as if I did it on purpose.

The Hunt

TD and Bob headed to Boob's Meadow, I went up Chuckie's Mountain, and Porcupine went to Porcupine's Meadow. Porcupine had a raspy, quiet voice. When we'd all get back to camp, his stories were detailed and riveting. The poor guy would get so excited when telling his experiences after each hunt, he would cough and choke while gasping for air. He would tell us how he either screwed up or just plain missed the elk. This would also start a tradition we carried on for years: when one of these two things happened, the man it happened to would bend over to receive a kick in the ass by the others.

Bob and TD saw lots of elk all around them. As for me, let's just say I got my ass kicked a few times that year.

The next morning, Bob said to me, "You may as well come up with us." I couldn't believe it. Finally, I would get to hunt Boob's Meadow. They sent me off in another direction which eventually would be called "Tom's (Speckmouse) Meadow," which ran parallel to Boob's.

After sitting around this meadow, I noticed a draw that angled around and up. I started to explore more and more after the morning hunts. Eventually, I found the right spot – the almighty X for waterfowl hunters. I made my blind and headed down for breakfast.

That afternoon, we headed back up a little earlier because the weather was changing — as always in these mountains. I settled in, full of expectations of finally maybe getting a chance at a bull. It was very quiet and when I tore open my Kit Kat bar. It was so loud, it sounded like I was using a microphone. I let it melt in my mouth so as to not make any more noise. As time went by, I had another Kit

Kat. Just like that, without a sound, I could see and hear elk all around me.

There were a lot more trees around me in this draw, so, my shooting lanes were limited. I stood up slowly and made sure no hanging branches would be in my way when I drew my bow back. Everything was fine.

Even though I was excited, I had been hunting long enough to know to take a deep breath and relax. There was no room for shaking or buck (elk) fever. All I could see and hear were cows and calves. Suddenly, a mature dry cow stepped out from behind a large evergreen and stopped at thirty yards.

Perfect.

I made the decision that enough was enough. It wasn't the bull I was after, but it was a large elk. I had finally had my taste of elk meat — delicious. As I drew my recurve back, she moved forward a little bit. I couldn't hold that 58-pound pressure for long, so I aimed right behind her front shoulder and released the arrow. The sudden sound could be heard all the way back to camp. One jump and she was in the timber as all the other elk were crashing all around me.

I waited until it quieted down before going to get Bob and TD to help me find her. First, though, I wanted to see if the arrow had gone through this mighty critter. I had a hard time following a blood trail. But I eventually came upon her to see that the arrow only went through about 4". The only reason I could be so precise on this information is because I had just killed a 4-inch sapling tree. She had stopped at a perfect place (for her) and, apparently, as I drew back, she moved, causing me to hit the tree. I could imagine how the boys would've laughed had I gotten them before I looked for my arrow.

It was getting dark, so I reached for my last Kit Kat and headed down to meet up with the guys only to find that the Kit Kat was gone, apparently dropped in the excitement. I caught up with the guys on the main trail a mile from camp.

Bob told me to take the lead in the dark timber. He didn't like us using flashlights on the trails, so I had to adjust my eyes and lead the way. The darkness didn't bother me when I had two bodyguards behind me.

Halfway down, I stopped to tell them something. I turned around, and they were gone. As panic set in, I stated the same phrase I had used a few times before when being alone in the dark. "Okay, you sonsabitches!"

I walked back to see what was going on and they jumped out of the timber, enjoying a big laugh. I had to excuse myself to go check out the ole brown eye again!

Nothing was as satisfying as getting back to camp, starting the campfire, and swapping stories (mostly true) about the day's escapades.

The next morning brought cold, wet, miserable weather. Porcupine got up and poured his cold coffee. I got up and made a "hot" chocolate for me and the other two yahoos who were still in their bags.

Bob started another tradition. As I opened the tent flap and he saw the rain and sleet pouring down, he made up an excuse to justify staying in bed.

"TD," Bob stated, "since you're not feeling well, I'll stay in here with you this morning."

Porcupine headed out first thing. As I moved toward the tent exit, Bob asked me where I was heading. I jokingly said, "I have to find my Kit Kat, so I'm heading up there." That draw was called Kit Kat from that day on.

Not much happened that morning, except I realized my clothes were not sufficient for this type of weather. I found my Kit Kat though.

Hardship and Joy

One very cool evening, the boys hit a cow. Just before dark, I met up with them again. It had been about an hour since they stuck it, so I went with them to look for her. This time we used our small flashlights, and I would help find the blood if it was wet. We trailed her over two mountains as the blood trail slowed to fewer and fewer drops. Finally, in an area I wasn't familiar with, our flashlights went dead.

Bob decided he would spend the night in this no-man's land and try and find her the next morning. "If you want to head back to camp, it's over that way."

Are you shitting me? Middle of the night, pitch black out? No way. I'm staying the night here.

We certainly weren't dressed for the very cold night, but we had some matches. We sat facing the fire until our face paint started melting, then we turned our backs to it. It was a freeze-thaw situation all night long with barely any sleep. I could hear the wife saying, "Have fun!"

As we sat quietly by the small fire, a few roars suddenly broke in the distance. As I jumped up in self-defense, we realized it was our stomachs roaring. Reaching in my pockets where I knew I had lots of candy and jerky, I intended to hand out snacks. *Oh no, empty, empty.* None of us had anything. As I pulled up my hood on my sweatshirt, I felt something in my shirt pocket.

I turned away from the others to check it out — a small box of raisins. I quietly ate them one at a time. The plan was working perfectly until I got caught chewing. It's

75

amazing how friendships can be hampered over a single raisin. I apologized by sharing the last six with them.

The next morning, we didn't realize we were about 100 yards from where the cow had laid down for a while. There was a small amount of blood there and just like that, nothing. We looked for hours to no avail.

Elk are amazingly tough animals; she probably survived the ordeal. Regrettably, we headed back to camp where Bob made a dozen or more pancakes for each of us.

Porcupine returned later to report that he had killed an elk. We all helped pack it back to camp. Sadly, we had to tear down camp again and get ready to head back down to reality. The horses certainly made packing out much easier.

Thus ended another year of hearing nothing but negative comments about the waste of money from the people back home because I didn't kill an elk. If they only knew the "fun" I was having. Just ask my wife.

Next Year ————▶

Chapter 6

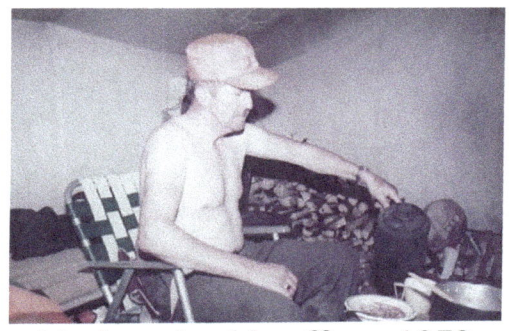

Noris and cold coffee – 1978

A real tent – 1978

Horses – 1978

Chapter 7

New Blood

TD never went hunting with us again, so I met up with my deer hunting buddy, Marly, from Bismarck, North Dakota. Of course, I had to get permission from Bob to bring the new guy first.

Bob had just purchased a new Ford truck with North Dakota plates (important to remember). We loaded my gear into his truck, stopped by a local station, and purchased some delicious broasted chickie. This was so good, I saved some for later.

Marly didn't care for loud music, so I cranked up his cassette player and Me and Merle Haggard sang to him most of the way. It was hard to hear him hollering at me because we were singing so loud. I can't sing, but, man, I love music. He did get excited when I told him about the beautiful wilderness and elk everywhere.

"How many times did you get close?" he asked. (Asshole)

"That's got nothing to do with it," I grudgingly stated. "Besides, how many mountain saplings have you killed, huh?"

The second stop for gas (and there were many with this gas guzzler), he suggested throwing the garbage out. I shook the chickie box and heard a rattle. Two crispy legs were left. It would've been devastating to throw that delicious chickie away. What could I do? I love chickie. I wrapped them up in the liner paper and stuck them in my pocket.

I didn't tell Marly, but Bob asked me what kind of guy he was. I said, "He's more like a brother to me. We laugh, we argue, we agree, we disagree, we drink together, and most importantly, we defend each other most of the time."

"What do you think he'll do if we pull a little prank on him?" Bob asked.

I said, "He's got a temper and he's tough, so not sure."

I would not be a part of this conspiracy, whatever it may be.

We arrived at Bob's early in the morning, but that didn't matter to Little (big) Speckmouse, who'd been waiting for us. He came running to my side of the pickup. I opened the door as chickie bones and aluminum cans fell out onto the driveway, something he would never forget. I never could understand how a kid could get so excited over a guy like me, but then again, I was his "Mountain Man," his show-and-tell subject at school.

Bob suggested we rest before getting the horses, but we were too anxious for that. As "Dear Marie" went to get groceries, we headed for the pasture to pick up the horses. We planned to head to the mountains in the early afternoon.

Spice, Noris's horse, would let anybody walk right up and put the lead rope on with no problem. Jake, Bob's horse, on the other hand, would always show us how fast he could run the other way. After three hours of tag, we managed to corner him. Once we haltered him, he was as gentle as any animal could be. Bob would get very pissed at him over the years about the initial ruckus to get him haltered.

Bob showed Marly his mountain truck's racing abilities.

"That seat belt ain't going to do much good," I told Marly, as he turned white as a ghost.

Since I was experienced at this carnival ride, I just sat back and talked all the way as always. These three didn't talk much ever, but maybe they didn't have a chance.

Going over the last pass a few miles from our destination was just as breathtaking for me as the first time I was there. Marly seemed in awe or maybe Andretti shock — I'm not sure.

As we approached our usual packing area, we noticed more hunters than before. Most were friendly, shared the states they came from, and bombarded us with questions once they learned we'd been here before.

We packed the panniers on the horses, and I had Noris show Marly the Squaw Hitch Knot I had taught him. Okay, I'm stretching the gum a little. Anyhow, we were getting much better at tying things down. We were down to only an occasional rodeo now and then. On the way up, I told Marly all the names we had given to certain areas. He learned all about Heart Attack quickly. I showed him another trick I learned — to get behind Jake and grab his tail.

"Are you crazy?" he said.

"No seriously, he'll pull you along. It really helps," I assured him.

"Oh, look at that. It really does help," he stated, as he grabbed on.

I said, "Just be careful if he has to shit," I quickly warned him.

Too late, lesson learned.

Same Campsite

Camp set up went smoothly with Marly proving to be quite helpful. We had brought up an army folding shovel which gave Marly an idea.

Marly said, "Give me that Mexican backhoe and I'll dig out this fire pit."

Bob and I just looked at each other in shock.

Bob hadn't noticed at first, but I took his advice and purchased a new PSE compound bow after last season. It had sight pins and everything. I became quite accurate with it, but I still had my Bear Take Down for a spare.

With the tent up and wood cut, we kicked back and had some lunch. Of course, I pulled out my two chickie legs! Midday found us milling around camp. Suddenly, three Mexican men on horseback came galloping over a little knoll between us and the trail. They were hollering in Spanish and looked angry. I had never met these three guys before, but I knew something was coming.

Noris and I walked across the stream and stood on the other side. Bob stood by the fire with a hatchet in his hand as Marly stood by his side. (Remember, Marly and I defended each other most of the time.) The men kept screaming.

Marly asked them what they wanted.

They shouted, "Pistola, pistola!"

Bob spoke back to them in broken Spanish. When they answered, Bob explained that they were looking for a North Dakotan who had molested their goat.

"What do they want with us?" Marly asked.

"I don't know," Bob said, "but I'm not from North Dakota, and you better take this hatchet."

Marly was so worked up, he didn't hear Bob ask the leader if he spoke English.

The meanest looking dude said, "No." Just then his horse reared a little and he said, "Whoa, Whiskey, you sonofabitch" in plain English.

Marly didn't even notice <u>that</u>. He was in full defensive mode now. That's when I decided I had better intervene, not knowing what Marly would do.

The three men got off their horses and Bob walked over to them. Noris and I walked beside Marly as Bob said, "Hi, Don, Paul, and Dave."

"Hi, Bob," the men answered. laughing.

As Noris and I shook their hands, Marly stood there bewildered. "You asshole, you know these guys?"

Marly didn't forgive me for a long time, but he would get even with his pranks on me. But we weren't done giving Marly a hard time.

As we all sat around, Bob asked Marly, "What did you call that shovel?"

Marly responded, "A goddamn Mexican backhoe."

We all got a good laugh, eventually even Marly. Turns out Bob knew these brothers from work. The two younger brothers said they had done all they could do to keep from laughing when their mean-looking brother was yelling at us.

They confessed that he had been yelling, "How far is the lake? I have a pistol and I'm going to shoot all of the fish!"

Hunting elk wasn't the only thing we did to have fun.

Bob thanked the brothers for the fun and for bringing up the menudo their mother had made.

Noris and I said, "Nice to meet you," while Marly just glared at them as they rode off.

"What's menudo?" Marly asked. "It was good.

"Cow's stomach stew," Bob replied.

Marly ran off with his hand over his mouth.

We spent more time fishing this year than we normally did. I had my favorite "honey hole." We cooked the little trout we caught in foil with onion and lemon over the open fire.

Delicious!

Bob and I showed Marly how we threw hatchets and axes and, of course, I showed off by shooting my new PSE bow. After several killing shots at a lit candle at thirty yards, the top limb of my new bow snapped loose. (You can't make this shit up.) The good news was that I had brought my take-down bow as a backup. The bad news was that it was down in the truck. A quick twelve miles later, I was ready to hunt. Bob said he had a connection with a PSE guy in Utah and we'll call him when we get out.

Exploring New Areas

I showed Marly some areas to hunt, but he mostly concentrated on the Draw area. He saw and heard plenty of elk through the hunt, but just didn't have any good opportunities. Noris hunted Porcupine's Meadow and brought back lots of stories. Bob killed another spike bull towards the end of our hunt in Bob's Meadow.

As for me, with more hunters around, I ventured out further and named many more areas. I had many close encounters. After killing a sapling tree trying to get a cow the year before, I made up my mind that my first elk (if ever) would be a bull. Many a cow and calf would sneak up on me as I was eating my Kit Kats in years to come.

Time to Move

A few days before we were done hunting, Marly and I took Bob's elk and some garbage down to the truck and rode back. That certainly seemed weird, but a lot easier. As in prior years, the color of the leaves on the aspen trees changing and the solitude of riding quietly up the trail left me speechless. It had to have been to make me quit talking. It was so beautiful, words were not sufficient to express it.

When we returned to camp, a forest ranger stopped by and said that next year, we needed to move our campsite 100 feet from the stream.

Looking around, Bob said, "Let's check over there."

"Oh no, that's my shitter!" I shouted.

Smell aside, it was a perfect campsite. It was set back in the woods from the main trail out of the wind. We made a plan on how we would set up for next year.

We packed up camp again and led the horses down. Marly and I reminisced about the hunt all the way until we got to Heart Attack where there is never any unnecessary talking. People on Heart Attack had one job: taking in all the oxygen they could going up this monster.

Finally on top, Marly said, "Now I know why you call it Heart Attack."

Bob and Noris had all the equipment to cut and wrap the elk. Before we got started, Bob called the PSE company in Utah. I could hear him complaining about me. "Yes, it broke on the upper limb. Yep, right off. It's new, less than a year old. What? Well, if you knew Jake..."

Bob told me the rep had said that one in a million broke prompting him to say, "If you knew this guy!" The company cheerfully offered to send a brand new one.

We took the horses back to the pasture and started to cut and wrap steaks, roasts, and burgers. After we split up the meat, we said our goodbyes. It was sad to leave little (big) Tom for another year. I gave him a big hug as he picked me up off the ground.

One good thing happened as a result of climbing mountains: Marly quit smoking after years of inhaling that crap. *You're welcome.* Marly wouldn't be able to hunt elk with us again until we started hunting the rifle seasons.

I always had a beard since getting out of high school, so I told Marly if I ever got a bull with my bow, I'd have Bob shave it off with the knife he made me.

"Yeah, right," Marly replied. Another year of memories. The trip home was uneventful again.

Next Year

Noris & Marly – 1979

Chapter 8 Is This the Year?

After taking crap from everyone at home for not ever getting an elk – could this be the year? After all, I had a new compound bow, and I also shot competitively on an archery team all summer. Not bragging, but I could put five in the ring at twenty yards. Of course, the target wasn't five feet tall and bugling at me either.

Bob called me midsummer and said he and Noris took the horses up to camp for a summer fishing trip. Noris had just bought a new heavy duty Ford pickup and wanted to try it out. I hoped he didn't let Bob drive it, but then again, it would've been broken-in properly for racing. (I mean, hunting.) The three of us had become great friends, but Bob and Noris were extremely close.

On a serious note, on the way back down from the fishing trip, Noris said he felt very faint and weak. He often got altitude sickness, but they were on their horses and were at a lower altitude.

Bob got off Jake and helped Noris to the ground, knowing immediately that Noris was having a heart attack, and knowing he needed to stay calm. It was another mile or two to reach the truck. Trying to encourage (or piss off) Noris, Bob leaned over him and asked, "Noris, if you don't make it, can I have your truck?"

Noris got color back in his face and, with that all too familiar raspy voice, said, "Shiiittt, help me back on my horse."

Bob took him to the hospital in the nearest town. After a complete check over, they told him he was very lucky, and he could go. Noris was much older than me, but he was in excellent shape, which I think helped him.

Later that summer, Noris called me and said he was still going to hunt elk, but he wanted to sell Spice. I told him I was interested and, after all, wouldn't that be fun? I lived on a 7-acre hobby farmstead and already had several different animals. Why not a horse, too? Once my daughter found out about a horse, there was no turning back. I bought Spice.

I also had a fairly new truck and asked Bob if I could borrow the trailer next fall to bring Spice to North Dakota. *Okay wife, now we're really going to have some fun.*

Labor Day – time to head out. "Have fun," the wife said again.

I drove alone this year. What could go wrong? Besides, now Merle and me could sing as loud as we want. I stopped in Bismarck, said hi and bye to Marly, picked up my broasted chickie, and headed south.

Midnight, Eddie Rabbit sang, "Driving my life away... with windshield wipers keeping time." *Wait a minute, it's pouring rain and one wiper blade is off.* It scratched the hell out of my window. It seemed dim out, so I pulled over and discovered that one headlight was out. Finally, I got into Colorado just before daybreak and heard a sudden rumble. Flat tire. *Jesus, what next?!* Good thing I had plenty of help nearby.

I got to Arvada and saw Tom (who was even taller) sprinting toward me. He opened my door and out fell the chickie bones and cans. He loved it when that happened.

Dear Marie had already picked up the groceries, so off we went to get the horses. Knowing how Jake was, we took as many people as we could to catch him. Of course, Spice would walk right up to us as the shit show began. Another two hours and we were ready to head out.

I settled up with Noris before we left, but I forgot about a saddle, blanket, reins, etc. He willingly sold me those also, making me a proud horse owner.

Off we went. *Drive carefully, Bob, I don't want my horse bouncing around back there*, I thought, as he took a 30-mph curve at 50. Damn, he was good.

After our annual pit stop at Kremling, we reached our old familiar parking area again. This time, I was unloading my own horse. I was anxious to pack my own horse, with Noris' help, of course. The weather was nice this time, so we didn't have to pack any extra feed.

Another journey up the trail, taking in all the beautiful sights Mother Nature had to offer, inspired appreciation in me more and more each year. The cold two-day-old chickie tasted good too.

Setting Up Our New Campsite
Arriving at our new campsite, my construction experience kicked in. After several discussions with Bob and Noris, we set up Bob's new tent in just the right spot.

"We'll have a makeshift kitchen here, store our supplies over there, and the meat pole can hang in those trees," I said.

Perfect. But wait, this used to be my toilet – now what? Off I went. "Found it!" I shouted from back in the timber. The perfect logs. It put a smile on the ole brown eye. Even though our tent was back in the timber, we could see if anyone came by on the trail. Not only was this a perfect campsite, it ended up being mine for the next forty-plus years. We named it Graybeard Camp after Bob's nickname. Officially, the crossing at the stream was called "Dead Horse." I never did know why.

It seemed as though we kept bringing more food, tools, and supplies each year now. I thought I even saw a big can of pineapple. *Hmm?* One warm afternoon, Noris made us pineapple upside down cake. Yum!

Our backpacks were still heavy, but the horses certainly made a difference. We had a day or two before hunting, so we caught fish for supper and sharpened up on our hatchet throwing skills. Though the weather was beautiful, we knew it could change in a moment.

Again, there seemed to be more and more hunters (people) each year. We often thought what it must be like during rifle season.

It's Time

The three of us went our separate ways the first few days, more or less to see where and how many elk were around. If the wind was wrong, Bob wouldn't go up to Boob's Meadow. He always told me a bad wind direction would just drive them farther away. Noris worked Porcupine and I climbed up to the most miserable place on Chuckie's Mountain.

Midway through the hunt, Noris had missed a couple of times. *Okay, bend over – ass-kicking time.* We were all seeing elk, but Bob was seeing more in the meadow than Noris and I were.

Then, just like that, Bob said, "Chaz, you wanna come up with me?"

Even though I had been up by Boob's Meadow, I never got a chance to hunt in it. I followed Bob up the trail like a happy little puppy.

He already had a makeshift blind behind a deadfall ten yards from a well-used trail. He had me sit right beside him in complete silence. There was a smaller dead tree lying a few feet in front of us. As the sun was starting to set behind the mountains, a little white weasel popped up on a dead log.

With complete silence and the accuracy of a laser, Bob blasted that little fellow with a full spit of Levi Garrett. Bullseye! He ran off, now a little more brown than white. I had to hold both hands over my mouth to try and keep from busting into laughter.

A little later, Bob instructed me to stand up and get ready; they were coming. I could hear a mouse fart 100 yards away, but I didn't hear anything that would indicate incoming elk. Bob had heard one branch break — that was it. I stood up and suddenly, there they were, coming right down the trail in front of us. I drew my new 60-pound compound back as the first one stopped behind a tree.

I whispered to Bob, "It's a cow."

As I let the bow string back down to the 60-pound pressure point, the elk stepped out just ten yards away. It was a large spike bull. He snapped his head and stared right at me. My arms were ready to fall off from shaking. He looked away finally and I had all I could do to pull my bow back to the relief point. I took a deep breath, put my closest pin sight on his heart, and released the arrow.

I saw the hit and turned to Bob. He never got up — just splattered another chew on the weasel log and said, "Nice shot, Chaz."

As we watched him slowly trot into the meadow, down he went, only 68 steps away. I did it. Overwhelmed with joy and having my mentor right there with me was one of the greatest moments of my life. As we were processing this magnificent animal, we noticed the arrow went right through and I had missed the heart by one inch.

A Deal is a Deal

Since it was getting dark, we decided to skin him out to cool and just cover him with his hide for the night. Noris helped us pack him down the next morning.

I was on Cloud 9. I finally did it. I just couldn't believe it… and a perfect shot and kill.

The guys hunted some the last few days without any results, but they were just as happy for me as I was proud. We had a little toast of moonshine that afternoon and then Bob said, "Remember what you told Marly?"

In all the excitement, all I said was "I wish he would have been here to share this with me."

Bob asked for the knife he had made for me.

"Oh shit, my beard…yeah, but…"

"No yeah buts," Bob said, as he sharpened it to perfection. "Sit down, Chaz. You better have another pull of that moonshine. Dry or wet?"

I didn't know. I'd never shaved it off. Even though he was excellent at sharpening knives, the dry shave was quite an experience. I didn't care; I couldn't wait to tell Marly. But I wasn't going to let Marly know about my bull until I got closer to North Dakota.

It was also a tradition to eat the nuts for your first bull. Noris soaked them overnight and did an excellent job cooking them up nice and crispy the next day. Very good.

We got back to Bob's place to cut and wrap the meat.

I said my goodbyes and prepared to leave when Bob's eyes got wide.

"Wait a minute, you have horses to take home," Bob said.

Hell, I would've driven off without them. We had to change some wiring in my truck; then we loaded up. It was always so hard to say goodbye, especially to Tom. We were getting closer each year.

The Trip from Hell

We loaded plenty of hay and feed in the trailer for the long trip home. I intended to let the horses out when I stopped for gas and let them walk around and eat some grass.

It was about an hour before dark, as I pulled into Luck, Wyoming, still full of joy and pride. I decided to call Marly. I kind of double parked on a side road in the small town. Surely, I wouldn't get in trouble for being there only a few minutes. I went inside a local tavern, ordered a drink, and asked if I could make a phone call (no cell phones yet).

No problem.

I told Marly I would be in Bismarck around 9:30 or so that evening and I had something to show him. We were to meet at our old stomping grounds in Bismarck. As I went back to my drink that I hadn't even touched yet, a Deputy Sheriff walked in and asked whose trailer was out front.

Nervously, I said, "It's mine. Sorry for double parking. I'll leave right now."

"That's not the problem," he said. "How many horses did you have in the trailer?"

Strange question.

"Why do you ask?"

"One door is wide open and there's no horse on that side," he stated.

Oh my God, please let it be Spice. I hurried out and felt my world turn upside down. It was Jake – gone. The levers on the doors weren't padlocked, but they couldn't just open by themselves. The Deputy said some kids more than likely came by and let him out. I explained to the Deputy that this horse was very hard to catch. He said he'd keep an eye out for it and wished me luck.

I drove all around town, the edge of town, and a few miles out in the country over and over again. No sign of him anywhere. I was worried sick that I had lost Bob's horse. I met the deputy at 3 a.m. at a truck stop.

"Still looking for him?" he asked.

"Yeah, no sign of him."

He said, "I have some things to do and then I'll start looking too."

Around noon, the deputy found me and let me know he had spotted Jake. As I followed him, I wondered what I was going to do to catch the horse. There Jake was, 100 yards away, standing in a field. The deputy reached for his gun and said, "Do you want me to wing him a little bit?"

"Can you shoot right here on the edge of town?" I asked.

"Absolutely," he said.

I was thinking to myself, if this was my horse, he'd be coyote food.

There were heavy woods behind Jake and a trailer court behind me. I was going to saddle up Spice, but I thought that would make things worse. I walked out and circled around him. He ran towards my truck and into the trailer park. I had to think fast. I drove around the park and blocked the rear exit with my truck and trailer. I ran back around to where he went in and there he was, looking at me like he was ready for a jousting match.

I was so tired and pissed, I said, "Bring it on, you son of a bitch."

People watched us from their windows as the episode unfolded. Thankfully, a husband and wife came out to help me. We slowly approached him. His only way out was to jump the fences or leap over my truck. The last 50 feet, he charged my truck and reared up at it. I just couldn't believe what I was seeing.

Then, just like that, he stood still and let me grab him. Totally exhausted, I put him in the trailer and thanked that wonderful couple for helping me.

Later, I told Bob about the ordeal. He listened quietly until I was done and then said, "You should've shot him."

I met Marly at the same place and time, just twenty-four hours later. I walked into the tavern with my cowboy hat in front of my face, just peeking over the top of it.

He yelled, "You didn't!" When I pulled the hat away to reveal my missing beard, he ran at me and danced me around like his prom date.

When I arrived home, the kids were all excited, especially my daughter. "You bought me a horse, Dad!" she exclaimed.

The wife said, "You finally got an elk. Did you have fun?"

"Oh yeah, I had lots of fun!?"

Next Year ⟶

Charlie's first bull – 1980

Bob shaved me with my knife – 1980

Chapter 9

Horses — A New Experience

The kids loved the horses, especially my daughter. She continued to insist that I bought Spice for her. The horses weren't that big of a problem except for one winter night when my folks were visiting us.

Somehow, the horses managed to push the water heater out of the water tank and up against the wood barn siding. As we were eating supper, my dad said, "I think your barn is on fire."

I looked out and, *holy shit*. We ran outside and, sure enough, fire was shooting right up the side. I grabbed an axe and told my dad and son to start throwing water on it. I chopped wood off the side and ran up in the loft to open that up. I carried buckets of water up and dumped them down the siding from the inside. It was cold and snowy, but somehow, we managed to put it out.

Horses are so much fun.

Hay was expensive too. No winter pastures this far north.

The following summer was exciting for my daughter at least. Me, on the other hand... I put up a barbed wire fence to keep that monster, Jake, in. Apparently, he felt my ranching skills were amateurish as he completely destroyed it, cutting his front shoulder to the bone at least 16 inches long. I had a vet come out to see what could be done. He gave him a shot, put some salve on it, and left me some medication to give him later.

"You're not going to sew it shut?" I asked.

"No, it will heal. Just keep him calm," the vet replied.

Calm – are you kidding me? Don't you realize… this is Jake.

Heading South

Fall came quickly. I checked the lights on the trailer and had my truck serviced. Ready to go. This time I was more prepared – saddles, reins, panniers, and, *oh yeah*, the horses. After I loaded them into the trailer, I padlocked the levers down this time. Lesson learned.

My daughter yelled out, "Take care of my horse and bring him back!"

I said goodbye, dear to my wife as she shouted, "Have fun!" If she only knew.

The trip to Bismarck was no problem. I grabbed some broasted chickie and headed out. From there on, the fun began. I forgot that the gas mileage went way down while pulling the horses and ran out in the middle of nowhere. At least I was smart enough to have a full two gallon can with me. *Two gallons – what was I thinking? That won't get me twenty miles.* I held my breath and drove a lot slower.

There was one building alongside the road up ahead that I had driven by many times but never stopped. There had never been a need. Sure enough, they had one gas pump. It was 50 cents higher than the other stations, but I didn't have much choice. I filled up and moved on.

When I pulled into Belle Fourche, SD around 6 o'clock or so, I heard a rattle in the back. I parked in front of a welding shop and went to survey the "situation." A weld had broken on the hitch. Boy, what luck; I was right in front of a welding shop.

I went to the front door. Closed. I checked all around town and finally got a name and number of the station owner. I am forever grateful to the man, even though I was three hours behind and $100 lighter.

What the hell, I was having fun!

Other than stopping for gas and getting a little bit of sleep now and then, the rest of the trip went surprisingly well.

I met up with Bob, his neighbor J.D., and Noris at the trailhead. We had one more guy again, so we had to make an extra trip packing in. Bob noticed right away that Jake had healed nicely.

Our new camp felt like home already. The camp robbers and pine martens greeted us right away as several chipmunks cheered in joy when they saw the feed bags we brought for the horses. The little shits were in them all the time.

The season was a little later this year and it felt cooler, especially at night. I even brought up a down-filled vest; I couldn't afford the jacket yet. The cooler evenings also brought the most dreaded, most filthy, most noisy, and most deadly (well, maybe not deadly) critter God had put on Earth – the almighty mouse. (I don't mean our beloved Speckmouse.) These little bastards were constantly trying to overtake our home. Eventually I set out on a mission to trap the little suckers.

Season Opener

There were more hunters than elk this year; at least, that's the way it seemed. We had talked again about maybe trying rifle season. This would be J.D.'s only time up there, so he had no vote. As always, Bob made him sign his life away that he would never disclose to anyone our location. Sitting around camp, Noris, Bob, and I decided that we'd try rifle hunting the next year.

In the meantime, off we went with our bows and arrows. Naturally, I had to climb up Chuckie's Mountain on opening morning just to check my physical attributes and stupidity. It seemed to get steeper and tougher each year, but I did it. There were elk up there, as was usually the case, but it was so hard to get within range. Still, I enjoyed the peaceful walk on top.

I trudged my way through even more downed timber as I worked my way back to camp. A certain type of beetle had infected this forest area years before and the destructive effect showed more and more each year.

As we sat around eating breakfast, we shared our findings. The results weren't what we were used to — very little bugling and not much sign, not even in Boob's Meadow. This continued day after day. There were several bow hunters farther up the trail from us, but that shouldn't have made all these elk disappear. There simply weren't as many elk around, and I walked more miles this year than ever before searching for them.

For several days, it rained so hard I only went out in the mornings. Elk wouldn't want to go to the meadows in the evenings when it was pouring like this. I got soaked each time I went out, but it was peaceful walking in the dark timber with an occasional tree squirrel scaring the hell out of me and giving my position away.

As the weather cleared, Bob said he wasn't feeling good and told me I could go up to his meadow if I wanted. *Are you kidding me?* Even though he hadn't been seeing much, that place was heaven to me and not just because I killed my first bull there either. It was and is to this day, elk or no elk, a very special place. We only had a few days left, so I went — full of expectations.

As I sat in the same spot where I killed my bull before, I could see elk coming out into the meadow from every direction like I had several times before. The only thing is this time it was just wishful thinking — my imagination working overtime. There were no elk around.

Then, an echoing bugle rushed across me like a jet. It came from up on top. Bob didn't want us trampling around in the timber unless the wind was right and we were sure we could get to it. The wind was right, and I was certainly able to get there quickly.

A Day I'll Never Forget

I hustled my way up, constantly watching for cows that would give me away. I ran as fast as I could towards the bull only when he was bugling. I had about 50 yards to pull myself up, root by root, to reach the very top. I noticed the bugle was getting closer. As I started to sneak amongst the smaller scrub pines, I saw him 100 yards away. He was coming towards me, ripping the hell out of the little pines. He was pissed. The antlers looked quite heavy. I had to think fast.

There was a small open area to my left almost twenty yards in diameter. *Perfect.* I got to the edge of this opening and knelt. Why I knelt, I'll never know. I didn't practice shooting from my knee that often. All I could see was his gigantic antlers as the ground trembled and he groaned twenty yards away. I quickly looked the situation over and noted a large log to my left, right on the trail he was coming down. It was nine steps from me. I then made a terrible mistake.

For those of you hunters out there that made this same decision, I hope you learned. For those of you who are about to start hunting, please heed this advice. Never ever decide what an animal is obviously going to do.

I drew my bow back. I was calm and confident. *As soon as he gets to that log and lifts his leg, I'll put an arrow right through his heart.* It was almost identical to last year. As he stepped out from behind the last little pine, I glanced at his very thick antlers, but quickly concentrated on his chest as he approached that log.

I couldn't shoot when he stepped out even though it was only ten yards away because there was ground brush blocking his chest area. I had a 3-foot window when he stepped over the log to make my move. He grunted and shook his head from side to side. This was something only seen in the movies. *One more step and he's mine. Perfect planning, Chaz!*

As he stepped from behind the brush, he turned right at me. *Now what?* Nine yards away and no time to think, I still didn't panic. If he turned a little bit left or right, the shot was there. Even though it was not advised, in hindsight, I should have shot him right in the frontal area. *Too risky.*

He was still at nine yards and had no idea I was there. Finally, he turned just slightly to his left. I put the pin right behind his shoulder and let fly. I heard the hit but didn't see my arrow. He groaned and let out a half-bugle, then walked right towards me. Why didn't I have another arrow in my hand? I would give anything if someone could've witnessed this. This humungous animal that I watched beat the piss out of those little pines stopped right in front of me. I looked down at his front right hoof inches from my knee. Talk about a mind rush.

Now what do I do? I had an angry, 900-pound bull elk ready to fight. I was 175 pounds and had no antlers. As I write this, I'm reliving the fear and excitement as though it happened yesterday.

I didn't feel like getting my ass kicked that early in the morning, let alone by a bull elk. I was still amazingly calm for being in a situation like this.

I didn't think I had any choice other than to look up at him. I slowly rolled my eyes up. He tipped his antlers towards my head. Believe me, I could see the glare in his eyes. My first panic attack started as I stood up. I don't know who was more surprised – me or the elk. His eyes got huge as he jumped away from me and threw dirt on me. He was at least a heavy 5x5, but that didn't matter now. I had to get another arrow in him.

I notched an arrow as quickly as I could. My only thought was to try and hit the femoral artery, so we'd be able to follow a good blood trail. But it was too late; he was in the timber. It would've been too risky of a shot anyhow.

A Little Peace of Mind

I marked the spot and went down to get the guys. We had something to eat and then put our packs on. I told Bob I felt terrible that it was up on top. He hadn't been up there in years.

"Not much blood," Bob said as we reached the spot.

That seemed strange. We found some drops where he ran when he saw me stand up.

Bob couldn't believe it. "Good job, Chaz," he said.

We looked until almost dark, but the trail went from little blood to no blood. The two of us searched the next day, circling at least a mile from the spot to no avail. I was just sick to my stomach. A hero one year and an embarrassing zero the next. Bob kept encouraging me that it happens to the best and, besides, not many people would spend two days on a dry blood trail.

He and I went back to the spot where I shot at him. He asked me if I saw the arrow in the bull when he stopped by me. I had not and there was very little blood on his shoulder. Bob figured I probably hit a bone in his leg somewhere, and my arrow didn't penetrate. So, we looked around for my arrow, but never found it. With Bob's encouragement and me wanting to believe the bull probably lived to beat the piss out of other trees and hunters, we finally gave up.

We readied ourselves to pack down. We only had one more day of hunting. But I was still sick to my stomach and ready to quit.

Bob kept saying, "How many rifle shooters do you think shot at an elk and if it didn't just fall over like a deer, they figured they missed. They probably didn't even look for blood, let alone look for two days."

I finally understood and tried to let it go. Other than me writing about this, few people ever knew it happened to me.

To lift everyone's spirits, Bob made chicken and dumplings that afternoon. I did a lot more than sample taste this time. I ate like a pig, cleaning the bones off like a camp robber would. *Where did I put my two broasted chickie legs from Dakota nine days ago? Found them! Still in my pocket – they'll be a good snack on the way down.*

We didn't get any elk this time, but what a chapter in my life. All that remained was the fun of taking the horses all the way back to North Dakota. To make matters worse, some idiot shot an arrow right through one of the tires on the horse trailer. Sure, why not?!

I couldn't wait to see what was ahead.

Next Year ⟶

Chapter 10

Summertime Blues

We had no major episodes with the horses during the past winter. With summer approaching, I reinforced the barbed wire fencing. My daughter spent many days riding Spice around. I even saddled up Jake so her friends could ride with her. Once you saddled Jake, you could put a baby on him – he was so gentle.

One mid-summer day, everything was about to change. A friend of mine had come to the farm to visit for the weekend. We had lunch in our kitchen and, as I looked out the window, I noticed a section of the wood corral that I thought looked strange. As I walked over to it, I noticed the top 1x10 was pushed out. The horses weren't in the pasture, but surely, they must be in the barn. No, they were gone. I grabbed my buddy, and the search began.

I had my wife call all the neighbors to let us know if they saw them. We searched all day, giving up at dark with no sign of them anywhere. We traveled well over twenty miles in every direction. Back at the farm, I went to the barn just to double check. I took a flashlight and looked all around the pasture – nothing. It was pouring rain as we went inside to have a late supper.

My wife mentioned something about getting rid of the damn horses. As we ate, I tried to figure out what else we could do. Did someone steal them?

Suddenly, there was a knock at the door. The young man standing there asked, "Do you happen to have two horses?"

"Yes, I do, but how would you know that?"

"Well," he said, "There are two horses standing on the highway right in front of your house."

Thank God. Our farmstead was right along a busy blacktop highway so we had to get them to safety quickly. As my buddy and I walked out of the house, we could see Spice in the ditch on my side of the road and wild Jake standing on the shoulder. What happened next happened so fast, it felt like the blink of an eye.

I saw a vehicle's headlights coming from the east and, by the sound of its engine, it was coming fast. I didn't want to spook Jake, so I called for Spice, and he came to me like a dog.

"Come on, Jake," I pleaded. No, he decided he'd wait and check out this vehicle that was speeding towards him. The young man, our good Samaritan, unfortunately had his headlights shining directly into the oncoming vehicle. Right at the worst moment, Jake turned sideways and smacked that '69 Pontiac on the rooftop. He reared up, and I was certain he'd be dead. Not Jake. He ran to the barn as the car slid sideways down the highway and then finally came to a stop halfway down the ditch. The vehicle backed up all the way to my driveway and turned in.

I had my friend run over to make sure Jake stayed in the barn. A young man got out of the Pontiac.

I yelled, "Are you okay? Is anyone else with you?"

"I hit a cow," he said.

It was quite obvious this guy was intoxicated. "What town am I in?" What a three-ring circus. Then he started screaming, "Look at my car!" He repeated the phrase again and again, jumping up and down in a frenzy.

I asked him again if he was alright and told him I'd take care of his car. The whole front of the roof of the Pontiac was pushed down towards the dash with maybe a 10-inch opening in the shattered windshield.

The owner kept screaming.

"Listen!" I shouted to get his attention. "I have a $2000 horse that is probably dying in the barn. I need to go check on him"

The young man who told us about the horses left, half in shock, I'm sure. I ran towards the barn just as it started raining harder. I put a lead rope on both horses.

As I looked at Jake's injuries, my friend said, "Hey, that guy is leaving."

I couldn't believe it. Maybe the $2000 cost of the horse scared him away. How he drove off with the condition of that smashed windshield was beyond me.

My wife called the vet around 9 p.m. She found him at a dance at the Eagles club in town. He left immediately to come see Jake.

All I noticed on Jake was his lips bleeding and it appeared he had a large lump inside his mouth where he had hit the vehicle. Most people would say the vehicle hit the horse, but it you knew Jake, I swear he purposely hit that vehicle. As we waited for the vet, I couldn't help but hope that intoxicated man got to whatever town he was headed for.

Finally, the vet showed up and we showed him where the horses were. He opened his door and reached for some rubber boots. As he turned to put them on, he fell right into the mud. It was pretty obvious he wasn't just dancing at the Eagles Club, he was also pretty full, if you know what I mean. If that wasn't bad enough, when we walked up to the horses, he asked me which one hit the car. *Are you kidding me?* You can't make this shit up!

He noticed Jake's lip was bleeding and checked over his front legs. He said, "I'll give him some antibiotics and check with you in a few days."

I showed him my concern with the large lump in his mouth, to which he chuckled and said, "That's a normal gland. I think he'll be fine."

Jake seemed to listen a little bit better after that ordeal.

The Long Trip Down

I traveled alone again to the hunt. I would've made a terrible trucker because I just didn't care for the long hauls, especially alone. Besides singing with Merle, I did a lot of thinking.

I stopped in Bismarck for the same ritual: "Hi," "Bye," and broasted chickie, then a stop at my folks' house for a minute. My mom always had cookies and banana bread for the guys, and my dad just loved to see any elk I may have shot and hear the stories.

My daughter was going to be very upset if I had to leave the horses back in Colorado. I had mentioned it to Bob and my wife was certainly for it.

114

Besides eating broasted chickie and singing away, the thought of my first rifle hunt in Colorado kept me going. I drove to Bob's this time and met up with the guys. Tom was in school, but when he got home, he checked out all the cans and chickie bones beside my truck. By now he was a foot taller than me and was excited to show me the poster picture of me in his room. What a kid.

We hooked the trailer to Bob's truck and off to the races, literally. After our traditional stops, we arrived at our turnoff. There were tents, campers, and horse trailers everywhere. What a letdown. We expected rifle season to be busier but not like this.

"We're up six miles from here," Bob said, encouragingly. "We know the area, and a lot of these hunters are probably only here for the opening weekend." That lifted my spirits

The forest service finally shut down that last mile of trail to vehicles for obvious reasons. Over the years, there were motorhomes up there that got snowed in and had to be left until spring. Even though it meant an extra mile to walk, we were glad.

The weather was beautiful for this late rifle season, two weeks after archery season closed.

As we were packing the horses, Bob said "You can't even tell where Jake got hit."

I laughed. "You should have seen the Pontiac."

Just a few rodeos happened on the way up – not a big deal. Someone forgot to check the cinch on Jake's saddle. Halfway up, the entire pack rolled over to his belly. Normally, that crazy horse would've scattered our things everywhere at a full gallop. But I'll be damned if he didn't just stand there. I immediately thought, maybe the Pontiac helped Jake's disposition.

We only met a few other hunters on the way up. At camp, we set up Bob's 12x12 tent. What a perfect campsite. We even brought up a small barrel wood-burning stove. Now this was living in the high country. A foam pad, a warm tent, and plenty of food. What more could you ask for?

The season wouldn't open for a couple of days, so we had time to cut wood and get our rifles ready. I laid out my newest knife — one my buddy, Bob, had made. I couldn't imagine anything better than to use this on my first rifle kill.

We didn't need to pre-scout. We were each going to the same place we went during archery. As we were setting up the tent, I came up with the bright idea of putting dirt all around the base of the tent to keep the killer mice out. It worked great. They got in through the flap opening and couldn't get out. *Great idea, Chaz.*

Opening morning, like an idiot, I headed up Chuckie's miserable mountain. There was a small tent set up at the base of my mountain right along the trail. They weren't supposed to do that, but it was none of my business. The people inside were sound asleep as I went by. It was still early and very dark, but I wanted to get up as high as I could before first light.

A faint bugle rang out in the distance every now and then — nothing like archery season. After remembering which logs to step over that I had tripped on for years, I made it to the main trail on top. As the sun came up, I noticed it was as quiet as archery season was in this dead timber. The damn squirrels would still signal that they were around.

I walked slowly, stopping often just like I did during archery. Then, I saw them — a bunch of elk's legs going up over a small ridge.

Since I was so far away (75 yards), I decided to sneak up on the herd to get a closer shot. I foolishly forgot that a rifle would shoot farther than a bow. My archery instincts were still strong, apparently.

The breeze was right, and I sat down within 50 yards of them. I don't know how many had gone by, but they kept coming. Even though the rules at that point in the season allowed hunters to shoot any bull, I was sure hoping for something more than a spike.

Cow after cow with their calves kept going by me. I was ready for the bull to make an appearance. Then, a slight bugle below the ridge sounded like it was coming my way. I remained still, calm, and ready.

Suddenly, the line of cows that was in front of me stopped. It didn't make any sense – the breeze was right, and I hadn't moved. The reason they call the front cow the lead cow is because they're the smartest. Sure enough, out of the corner of my eye, I saw her standing behind me. She had that look as if to say, "What the hell do you think you're doing?" Next came the earth-shaking bark and they were gone. It's then that I asked myself why I tried to sneak closer than 75 yards. Idiot! Rookie!

I had no choice now but to keep walking the trail. I checked over my scope on my trusty 25-06 – the only rifle I owned. After walking a distance and hearing rifle shots all around, I decided to sit on a log, have a Kit Kat, and take it all in. Just as I was going to take a bite, twenty yards to my left an elk head popped up from behind the evergreens. I dropped the Kit Kat and slowly reached for my rifle. As he stepped out, I looked at his antlers. A spike? No, a fork horn? No, there are more points. When I counted the fourth point, I turned and fired at the front shoulder.

He turned and ran over the ridge like he had been hit by a BB gun. How was I to know my gun was too small?

I knew I couldn't follow any blood, so I ran over to the ridge to see which way he went. Just before I got to the edge, I heard a crash. *Please Lord, I'll never bring this small caliber again if I can just find him.* At least I was smart enough to have my variable scope on 3-power instead of 9!

I searched for him, certain that I couldn't have missed at that close range. I didn't see any movement anywhere, so I walked in the direction I had heard the crash. I saw the antlers resting against a tree. What a relief. I was straight above camp now (albeit in a hell hole of downed timber), so I decided to dress him out and go get the guys to help quarter him. It was midday and in the 70s. *This is just like archery season.*

I turned the huge animal on his back and started to process him. As I finished up, I counted the points. Four on each side – what a beautiful animal. I was so excited, I didn't notice I had cut my finger on my left hand down to the bone. I wrapped it with my white hanky and headed down.

Two young guys standing by the tent that was near the trail asked if it was me who shot.

Excitedly, I said "Yes, it was me. I got a nice 4x4."

One of them looked down at my hand and said "Oh, my God, what happened?"

Blood dripped out of my now soaked hanky. "That's nothing," I said, and hurried towards camp.

Bob was the only one in camp when I returned. A fellow Bob knew from before, Bill, stopped by just as I was telling Bob about my 4x4. After eating a bite, we headed back up.

Bill said, "If you don't mind, I'd like to go with you and give you guys a hand."

Absolutely! With my injured finger, we needed another good pair of hands. We grabbed some mesh game bags and a saw and headed up. Bob said he'd stitch up my cut when we were done.

When we got to the bull, Bill turned the head a bit and said to Bob, "I could see Chaz was awfully excited, but apparently he can't count." The whale bone was sticking in the dirt. It was a nice 5x5.

Wow!

I can't explain the emotion going through me at that time. We were losing daylight, so we hung the quarters in the trees overnight with plans to bring the horses up as far as we could the next morning.

It snowed all night long. We received some snow over the years during archery, but not like this. I went ahead of Bob and Noris. Noris was sick; we told him to stay in camp, but he wouldn't listen. They tied the horses just below the top because it was just too steep of a climb and lots of downed timber.

I walked around looking for the quarters for fifteen minutes while waiting for them. When they got up there, I said, "I can't find anything."

Everything looked the same with all the snow, so it was embarrassing to lose the meat. I'd hunted this mountaintop for several years. Now, I couldn't find a dead hanging elk?

Noris was getting worse, so I said, "Let's head down and I'll come up in the morning and keep looking."

Noris stayed back the next morning. Bob said he'd come with me, but I suggested he go hunt somewhere until I found where I hung it. It was still snowing. This could be bad. I had to find it.

After looking again, we found the quarters hanging right in front of our noses all along. Unbelievable. I marked the trail this time and went to get Bob. We worked our way up again and packed him down. I was relieved and very happy. But then our concern shifted to Noris.

He insisted in his raspy voice, "I'll be fine."

"Let's operate on your hand," Bob said.

I damn near passed out as he cut off the loose skin.

With surgery over, we got to talking. Since I now had the largest bull, I decided we should have a belt buckle for the one with the largest kill in camp from here on out. Yep!

The first rifle season lasted only five days, and we only had a couple left. The weather stayed cold and snowy for the remaining days. One afternoon, Bob and I took my elk and some supplies down to the truck. Halfway down, we passed a camp with a gray-bearded fellow. We'll call him "Rich." He waved and asked if we'd like a cup of coffee. We thanked him, but we were in a hurry to get down and back as soon as we could.

We led the horses down and then rode them back up. As we headed back up, Rich asked us again about stopping for a cup of coffee. To this day, Bob and I both wish we would've stopped. But it was already dark and the only thing colder than walking was riding a horse. We were freezing.

120

Noris had a nice warm supper for us back at camp, even though he still wasn't feeling well. We made our plans for the next morning.

Noris toughed it out and went hunting a couple more times, and I went with Bob up to his meadow. We arrived there just before shooting time. There were a few elk in the meadow, so we had to crawl to the nearest downed trees. Two spikes stepped out about 300 yards away. The second one was bigger and had an extra point.

"Take the back one, he's bigger," I suggested.

"Maybe there's a bigger one coming out," Bob said.

I didn't want him shooting a bigger bull than me, so I said, "If you don't shoot that one, I'll stand up and holler." I was kind of joking, but he shot him with his 7mm. Bob was using Herter's shells at that time. I didn't even know they made shells.

When he shot, I said, "You hit him!"

Bob hit him again and again. Finally, the elk went down. The bullets didn't mushroom very well, but they were all kill shots. *Probably should get different bullets.*

We went to dress him out and I told Bob, "Nice bull."

"Thanks," he said, "but he's not as big as yours."

"Aw, shucks," I stated, with a smirk on my face.

Joy and jubilation filled our camp again. Bob and I made the long snowy pack down to the truck again. This time it wasn't so late. Rich invited us to coffee again as we walked by, but we had to keep going. On the way back up, Rich met us at the trail. We finally got to meet him properly and sit with him for coffee. He ended up being a lifetime friend from that day on.

Noris started to pack up leftover supplies to take down. We did what we could that evening to make it easier for the next morning. This was always the worst of the whole trip every year. Bob would always get cranky, and I just always had that sick feeling in my stomach from having to go back to reality and having to wait another year to do it again.

It was much warmer down below. We got everything loaded up and headed out. Several miles down the road, we pulled over at a small ranch outfitter. As Bob got out, a cowboy – we'll call him JC – came walking over. The two of them stood behind the horse trailer talking. We didn't know this guy. I was puzzled about their conversation.

As I watched in the mirror, Bob opened the trailer door and led Jake out. *Are you kidding me? Hallelujah, I think he sold Jake.* All Pontiacs were now safe – at least in North Dakota.

When I got out of the truck, trying not to show my exuberant emotions, I walked back to see what was going on just as Bob led Spice out, my horse. What?? JC shook my hand and thanked me.

"For what?" I asked.

Bob replied, "You're always bitching about the horses, so I sold Jake to this man for $600 and gave him Spice for free."

JC held out a bottle of whiskey and said, "Let's have a pull. Best damn horse deal I ever made."

No shit! I stood in disbelief.

As we drove off pulling Bob's empty trailer, we could hear JC holler as he was laughing, "How much you want for the trailer?"

"Not today," Bob whispered to himself as we kept on trucking.

My daughter is going to disown me! What in the world am I going to do? I ended up taking the trailer with me and told Bob we'd figure something out for next time.

"See you next year, Tom."

I stopped by and showed my folks the elk. My dad was very happy and as proud as I was.

"Biggest animal I've ever seen," he said.

"Thanks, Dad," I replied. "This is just an average one, but he's a trophy to me."

Next Year

Charlie - 1983

Chapter 11

A Year to Forget

I was right about my daughter. She was upset and remains so to this day. After all the crying and why, why, whys, I promised her I'd get another one for her birthday. On the other hand, the wife was happy those two troublemakers were gone. As promised, I found a smaller quarter horse for her. He was much younger than Spice and a little spunkier. She named him Rusty. Life was good again.

In June, we went on an annual fishing, boating, and camping trip with our friends from high school. At the risk of carrying on about the entire episode, I got a tube that is pulled behind a boat. Unfortunately, I hit a parked boat coming back to shore. The surgeons figured I hit it at a minimum of 50 mph. I was lucky to be alive since I ended up with head lacerations, a shoulder broken in twenty-two places, a broken wrist, a torn spleen, and a shattered hip.

I spent two weeks in the ICU and a month in the hospital, then I was off to the farm. I had to use a crutch and a cane for many months to come, so my daughter had to tend to her horse mostly on her own.

Bob, Dear Marie, and Tom even came up to North Dakota to visit me. I was a mess. I told Bob I would try to be healed by October.

"We'll worry about that later," he said.

Around September, I pushed myself to the limit. I still needed a cane, but at least I could walk. I asked my shoulder surgeon if he thought I could shoot a gun without damaging the steel plate he had installed over the broken bones. He asked me what caliber I was shooting. I told him it would probably be a 7mm.

"No problem," he stated. "You aren't going to break that plate. What are you shooting at?"

I told him about my annual elk hunt and how we typically walked up six miles. He checked with my hip doctor and gave me the all-clear, though he did question my sanity. After a laugh, he said it would actually be good exercise for all my damaged muscles, but it would likely be a lot tougher than I expected.

I kept in contact with Bob and told him I'd probably be a couple days late, but I would be there for opener. After a few more surgeries and removing staples all over me, I did more and more walking to try and get back in shape. The pain was still there, but I was getting around better, considering all the busted-up areas in my body.

As October approached, I told Bob, "I'll definitely be there. I'll go right to the parking area."

Since we no longer had horses, he said he made an arrangement with a friend to help pack our things in.

Noris and Bob went up early and set camp up the week before season opened. Bob told me they borrowed a horse for the hunt, and he'd bring it down to me when I got there. I told him not to worry about that since there was no way I could get on a horse. I'd take my time and walk up. I'd crawl if I had to.

The Drive Down, The Walk Up

The weather was a lot worse traveling down, especially through Wyoming and Colorado. With all my aches and pains, I had to stop and move around more often than I did before. I stocked up on extra broasted chickie for this trip and hunt. The drive down was almost as tough as the upcoming hunt would be.

I finally arrived where the guys had parked and grabbed my rifle, toilet paper, and snacks and raced off. Truth? I walked like a newborn deer. A three-year-old child would have passed me. Plus, I couldn't carry a backpack. I had to wear my extra coat because it was snowing and colder than usual. I couldn't figure out why the other hunters in the area were pointing at me and shaking their heads as I walked by. Didn't they realize I was from North Dakota? Some of us didn't make a full sandwich all of the time, if you know what I mean. Besides, now I knew I was possessed with the Elk Hunting Fever. My wife called it something else, but that's between her and me.

As I walked up, I attempted to hold the rifle with my left hand (broken wrist) and my cane in my right hand (broken shoulder) to take as much pressure off my left hip (busted) as possible. It was mid-morning, and I thought I had plenty of time to reach camp before dark – after all, it normally was only a two- to three-hour walk.

After several hours of smoking along, I saw an object on the trail ahead of me. As I got closer, I realized it was Rich. *My God, it's starting to get dark and I'm just now at Rich's?* He reached in his back pocket while shaking his head and pulled out a pint of brandy.

"I can't believe what I'm seeing. Are you crazy, Charlie?"

I wasn't sure which question to answer. "Yes, it's me and, yes, there's a good chance." I wasn't sure what I was going to do. It was getting dark and I certainly knew I couldn't outrun Bigfoot if I confronted him on the trail.

Then Rich had an idea, "Why don't you spend the night here in my tent?"

I couldn't spit out "OK" fast enough. My sleeping bag was up in camp, but he had extra horse blankets. He always set his tent up on a slanted area. I just had to figure out if I wanted my feet up or my head. The ground was pretty hard and cold without a foam pad, but I was in a heated tent, so I couldn't' complain.

All these years, I had fought off and blocked out those killer mice, Rich fed them like pets. They were everywhere.

"They're just trying to get warm," he explained.

Hell, for all I know, that could've been what he fed me for supper. At least it was hot.

I took extra pain medication that night. Not for the pain solely, but I thought it would help put me out long enough so I wouldn't feel all the mice running over me.

The next morning, Rich offered to make me a travois to haul me up to camp.

"No, I'll just truck on up there," I said. I had a cup of hot coffee with him and headed out glad that I had stopped for that first cup of coffee the year before and made such a great friend.

The Attempted Hunt

I don't know if the guys were happy to see me or were in shock. I think I was in a little worse condition than they had expected.

All Bob said was, "You're a dumb ass."

I always appreciated his blunt honesty.

They sure catered to me at first, serving me hot coffee and getting my bedroll ready.

"We cut some wood, but we thought we'd wait for you to help split and stack it," they said.

"No problem," I stated. I couldn't split it, but my cane and I made several trips back and forth, stacking wood inside the tent. There was too much snow and too cold this early, so we needed all the dry wood we could find, which was difficult with a foot of snow on the ground and more coming down.

Opening morning, Noris headed to Porcupine's and Bob had me go with him. There was no way I'd make it up Chuckie's Mountain in my condition.

Thankfully, Bob was never a fast walker. Still though, it was hard to keep up in deep snow. Moonlight reflected off the snow, which helped us see. Bob stepped over a two-foot-high log in front of me. I tried and fell flat on my face.

Bob turned around and asked, "Are you hurt?"

"No," I said.

"Well, then, get up and let's go." He seemed unusually grumpy and more serious than the Bob I had known over the years. I later found out why.

I tried to walk in his footsteps in the snow just to keep up. He had little sympathy for me. I hunted Boob's Meadow with him for a few days before I realized it was getting tougher than I thought. Besides, I was holding Bob up. So, the only thing to do was to let him go on without me.

I continued to go out each day, but I hunted closer to camp. Unfortunately, the only signs of elk any of us were seeing were occasional tracks heading down to lower elevation. The snow kept coming and I'm sure this was a factor for the elk going down.

We enjoyed each evening in our warm tent with the wood stove crackling away. This particular stove had a small lid to put the wood in. If the damper wasn't just right, smoke filled the tent instantly. As we ran outside in our shorts to escape, the guys cursed me for my blunder of smoking out the tent and said that they would fill the stove from now on. This was a lesson I learned the hard way, but I demanded that I be the only one to open that lid for years to come — determined to get it right.

There were several people who would try this on their own later with the same results, resulting in a smoke-filled tent and me bitching at them to leave it alone, just as I had been told years before. Thanks to my teaching abilities, I was able to train a few of the yahoos down the road on how to work this wood stove.

The season was all but over. We were running out of dry wood, and everything was either damp or wet. The snow kept coming and was waist high now.

We packed up most of everything and made the decision that when someone led the way, we would try to get in their tracks as soon as we could. We quickly cleaned up camp the best we could and started to follow in the tracks left by a pack of horses that came through earlier.

The stream we had to cross was mostly frozen over and was challenging to navigate on foot – especially with a cane. The snow was up to the curved handle of my stick.

Noris took the lead, and Bob and I tried to keep up in the rear. Walking on level ground was hard enough, but with waist-high snow, it was extremely difficult with the cane.

Bob reached a narrow, steep area of the snow-covered trail and then suddenly… down he slid. He was in snow up to his neck. I hurried as fast as I could.

Should I help? Hell no. As I hurried by as fast as I could, I looked back and asked, "Are you hurt?"

I don't think I got an answer, but I certainly got a look. As I took off in front of him lying there, I said, "Well then, get up. Let's go."

Payback is a bitch.

This wasn't something I normally would have done, especially to Bob, but I thought it was hilarious at this time. I could have sworn I heard a faint "Dumb Ass" again. I forgot Bob was in a very grumpy mood.

The walk down was tough and very quiet after my stunt. Heart Attack was almost impassable. Willpower and stupidity were great assets at this time.

We finally reached our vehicles and changed into dry clothes. We headed for the nearest town to have something to eat and settle up on the kitty. Bob still wasn't in his normal mood when we said our goodbyes. They went towards Denver and I headed north.

Did I hear "Dumb Ass" again?

The trip home uneventful, except for the rear end going out in my 4x4 truck. I pulled into a station, unhooked the rear driveshaft, and drove home with the front axle only.

Piece of cake.

A few days after I was home, Bob called me. I finally got to find out what was bothering him. *I'm such an idiot.* He and Noris had been worried sick that something would happen to me up on the mountain and they would not be able to help me.

Bob was the most honest caring person I had ever met. I told him I was so involved in what I could do, I never thought about what I couldn't do. This was very selfish of me. I told him so and apologized. This just deepened our lifetime friendship even more.

Just before we hung up, I swear I heard "Dumb Ass" one more time.

Next Year ⟶

Charlie - 1989

Chapter 12

Trip for Two

I drove my little-ass CJ5 Jeep down to Colorado on year twelve. When I stopped by my folks', my Dad asked, "How are you going to bring back an elk with this little thing?"

"I'll have to kill one first, Dad, but I'll figure it out."

It was just going to be Bob and me, so I drove straight through to Arvada, Colorado. Same old routine when I pulled in the driveway. Tom came running looking for chickie bones and cans laying on the floor of my Jeep. (He still laughs about that to this day.)

Bob made arrangements to use a big Quarter Horse named Jughead. He was one of the largest horses I'd ever been around, but he was very well-behaved. As far as I knew, he hadn't beaten up any Pontiacs or any other vehicles for that matter. You could even walk right up to him and catch him. *Gosh, I miss Jake. NOT!*

As we headed for our destination, Bob said, "The weather is calling for some snow again."

It wasn't bad so far. There were several inches of snow on the ground where we parked our vehicle. Rich was already there and packed in ahead of us. He had an older truck with a camper in the box. To our surprise, there still weren't many other hunters around yet.

We didn't need that many supplies with just the two of us and only one horse, so we packed Jughead and our backpacks and headed off. Other than an obvious limp and restricted use of my right arm, I was in much better shape this time. I had told Bob I wouldn't come if I couldn't carry my own weight or be able to help him if something happened.

The trail was slippery, and we had to be extra careful going down Heart Attack. As we worked our way towards Rich's, sure enough, Bob twisted his ankle. He had trouble with his ankle before, so this wasn't good.

"Don't worry, Bob, I'll be the doctor this year and take care of you," I said. That's what friends are for. I didn't even hear any "Dumb Ass" remarks.

We stopped by Rich's and had some hot coffee. He wasn't quite set up yet, but then again, Rich never was in a hurry with anything. He's what I would call "really laid back." He wished us good luck and said he might come up to our camp later on in the week.

Time caught us off guard, and it was getting late in the afternoon. It started snowing a little harder now. We arrived at camp with about an hour of daylight left. After feeding Jughead some grain, we attempted to set up the tent in the snow, clearing away an area with our feet and putting it up as fast as we could. We were only able to get the side poles on — not the center poles. At least we had a four-foot-high enclosure. I certainly wouldn't call it a tent, but we'd be out of the elements.

There were only two days until the opener, so we knew we had lots to do the next day. We just laid our bags on whatever we could to keep them off the cold ground. The only light we dug out were our flashlights. We had to belly crawl into our makeshift tent as the zipper would only go up about three to four feet from the ground. We were tired and worn out, so we hit the sack early.

As we woke in the morning, the tent roof was almost touching our bags. We crawled out from our warm bags and tried to dress as best we could. Bob struggled as he opened the zipper of the tent from a kneeling position. All we could see was snow. Apparently, it had snowed all night long and collapsed the roof. There was close to three feet on the ground and still accumulating. After the ordeal we had gone through last year, we didn't say a word to each other, yet we both knew what we were going to do.

We packed our bags, folded the wet tent, and loaded up Jughead to head back down. Sure, there might have been a bull or two still hanging out in this high country, but the odds were against us, especially with only two of us.

We arrived back at Rich's camp very depressed. Waiting all year and then getting punched by Mother Nature changes everything. There wasn't much snow down where Rich was, so he said he was staying put. His wife was coming up and we certainly didn't want to interfere, so we told him we were going to hunt down by the truck, even though that was new territory for us.

"Rather than you guys putting up a wet tent, just stay in my camper," he offered.

We couldn't believe it and quickly responding like they say in North Dakota: "You betcha we will."

He told us where the keys were hidden and to make ourselves at home. The beginning of another lifetime friendship.

There were still only a few inches of snow by the truck, and we were able to take care of Jughead much more easily. We threw our bags in the camper, made a hot meal, and got things ready for the morning opener. Life was good again.

Let the Hunt Begin

Over the years, Bob and I had walked by some openings that looked promising, but we never investigated them any further. The day before the opener, we walked back up the trail a mile or so and took a closer look, so we at least had a plan for the next morning. There were good signs all over. Obviously, some elk had come down. We picked our spots out and headed back to the camper.

A few more vehicles pulled in overnight. We couldn't understand how they could just get up and start hunting after arriving so late. Did they even know the area? As always, we were up early too. I got ready to fill the wood stove – no wait, we were in a camper with propane heat. What a treat this was. It was small, but warm and had all the comforts of sleeping in a closet.

I had caught so much grief for using a 25-06 that first year of rifle season, I went out and bought a 338 Magnum. Yes, I checked with my doctor about the impact on my shoulder from this cannon. I told Bob, "No elk is going to run away now. This Howitzer will tip them right over."

We walked up the trail together until we reached the area we were going to hunt. I went ahead and couldn't see Bob anymore. He veered off to the right, and I went left. I hadn't even reached my destination when right up above me on the ridge, there was a small group of Aspen trees 75 yards away. We didn't have many Aspens up on top, so I wasn't used to looking through them. Still, something looked out of place in that clump of trees.

I slowly pulled up my Elk-Tipper-Over cannon to look. *Holy shit!* It was at least a 4x4 bull looking right at me. Then again, I've been known to count incorrectly. I knelt down on one knee, took a breath, held the crosshairs right behind the front shoulder, and slowly squeezed the trigger. I could visualize him plopping over sideways from the impact of my 338 Mag. I looked up with half a smile on my face. Five minutes into shooting time on opening day, and I killed a bull elk.

Wow!

Strangely though, I could still see the figure of an elk standing there. I pulled my gun back up to look and sure enough, it hadn't moved. I got a good hold and fired again.

Nothing.

You've got to be kidding me! I had the gun properly zeroed in. *Did the scope get bumped?* I fired one more time. Again, absolutely no movement. *Is this a decoy of some sort?*

There had been no tree bark flying, so I couldn't have hit a tree, especially three times. Even if I did, my cannon would have chopped them over like a dull chainsaw. A similar *sitcheation* like this happened to me before while hunting deer on a reservation up north.

My native friend had explained, "That was a ghost deer," as it just disappeared.

Was this a ghost elk?

Finally, the bull took one step forward out of the trees. It was real. *What the hell?* I panicked. I had one shell left in my gun. I tried to settle myself down and fired one more time. This time he flew over sideways. Well, to be accurate, he just fell straight down. Finally, and to think I gave Bob grief about his Herter's shells.

Amazingly, Bob had been able to watch the entire circus. After my second shot, a bull stepped out briefly where Bob could see it and then stepped back in. He had a chance for a quick shot at it, but he just assumed it was the one I shot. *That close,* he thought, *there's no way Chaz could've missed.* It ended up there were two bulls in that small clump of trees. We could've each gotten our bulls in the first ten minutes.

Bob walked over to me and asked what all the shooting was about. I told him what happened.

"Well, it's a good thing that cannon tipped him right over," he said with a smirk on his face.

When we opened the elk up, we noticed that both lungs were mush. The impact must have shocked him in frozen position. He was standing there dead.

Bob made a smart-ass comment about how my 338 Magnum tipped the elk right over, and he might even trade in his trusty 7mm for one.

I got the hint.

We got ready to skin and quarter the bull when Bob said, "Wait a minute. We're right off the trail. We have Jughead at the truck and I have a rope."

"Brilliant idea," I said.

As I cleaned things up, he went to get the horse. The smell of a dead animal didn't seem to bother Jughead at all. We tied the rope around the antlers and, with just enough snow on the ground, Bob pulled him right down the trail to our truck. The ideas kept getting better. We never had it so easy. Maybe this was why people hunted down low by their vehicles.

We found a strong game pole near our truck that someone had made.

"Why don't we just hang the whole elk up to skin and quarter him," Bob said.

"Great idea, but Jughead could never pull up that kind of weight."

"We'll tie the rope to the bumper and pull ahead," Bob said.

Brilliant. Everything went according to plan. I couldn't believe it.

Bob went out several times over the next few days, but the snow was getting deeper, and he had a hard time walking around with his ankle hurting. The last morning, he stayed in the camper. We stepped outside to take a leak by the camper just as a herd of at least thirty elk came running out of the woods less than 100 yards from us. There were a few bulls in the group also. By the time Bob wondered "how in the hell am I going to jump up in the camper, grab my rifle, load it, and shoot," it was too late: they were gone. But what a show we got. Front row seat

The herd headed down towards the main road and went right behind a pickup that was parked back in the woods. Apparently those two guys must have thought they had a chance. They started their truck and raced towards the road, but we never heard a shot.

We headed towards Bob's place where Noris met up with us. He helped cut and wrap my bull. We split the meat up, and I tied my 5x4 antlers on the hood of my Jeep, said my goodbyes, and I was off.

It sure made my Dad happy when I stopped to show off my bull. He was as proud as I was. By the way, while I was in Bismarck for a few hours, some asshole broke into my Jeep and stole my new 338 Mag. I hope it kicked the hell out of them like it did to me.

Next Year ⟶

Chapter 13

Let's Buy More Horses?

After talking it over with Bob, I purchased two more quarter horses. They were flatlander horses and had never been in the mountains. They were both very good riders and didn't seem to mind small packs.

For a change, the trip to Arvada was uneventful. I met up with Bob, Noris, and his brother, David. As always, since he was the new guy, Bob made David swear his life away that he would never disclose where we were hunting. Like his brother, David was a great guy. We found out later he could really cut and chop wood. That certainly took some pressure off of me since I did most of it – NOT!

We got everything *orekenized* for the trip and, naturally, Dear Marie was out getting our groceries while Tom cleaned up my chickie bones and cans. The weather was pretty nice as we headed out. Once we crossed over Eisenhower Tunnel, Bob got to show David his mountain driving skills. By now, some of the other travelers recognized Bob's truck and trailer and moved out of his way, especially on the curves. I noticed David was gripping the armrest next to him very tightly. Me? I just relaxed and told him it wasn't bad unless it was snowing heavily.

"It's an easy way to check on the horses when the trailer swings around to the front of the truck," I told him.

He didn't think that was funny.

We made our typical stops for food and drink. Since we had a new guy, I thought I would enrich him with my knowledge and help raise his IQ.

As we drove by Toponas, I said, "David, do you know what that means?"

He had no idea, and before Bob could spoil it for me, I laid it on him like I was a tenured teacher. "Well let me tell you," I said, using my deeper instructor's voice. "It means 'Sleeping Lion.'"

He asked me how I knew that.

I just responded by telling him, "You stick with me, and you'll learn lots. Yep, uh-huh. Would you like a piece of chickie?" I pulled a lint-filled leg out of my shirt pocket.

Bob sighed. "You'll get used to the Chaz; he grows on you."

Rich was in the parking area when we got there. He said he took one of his loads in already. He had an old ornery mare named Pricy and a little burro I called #7. When Rich saw our horses, he took a liking to Gilby. (Our other horse must have just been called Horse.) Rich always told us that if we needed help, he'd be obliged. We did use the burro on occasion. That ass and I had a lot in common, except that I was the dumb one. The trail up was good, and we got to camp in good time.

Once we got camp set up, I noticed it was getting easier and more *orkenized* each year. While the guys went to find firewood, I *oreknized* the groceries and supplies. My hand just didn't fit the saw or axe handle!

Each of us brought a dish we had premade at home to help with the cost of the groceries. After all, they were costing us $100+ back then. We didn't realize what a deal that was.

We had a couple days before the opener, so Noris took his brother around and showed him some areas he could hunt. Bob and I reminisced about the past, especially about the crazy experience we had the year before. Since it was nice out so far, we dug out our fishing gear for later.

That evening, we sat around a beautiful campfire. Naturally, I was doing most of the talking, trying to increase their IQs. Best of all, it was the perfect time and place to have our annual Christmas in the mountains as we shared our camp gifts. I couldn't wait to get another handmade, beautiful "Graybeard" knife.

As we were handing them out to each other, Bob walked over to me.

Yes! I was as excited as a little kid getting his first BB gun. He handed me a paper bag. I opened it up, full of anticipation. There it was. A beautiful box of Levi Garrett and some Anise candy. With a fake smile on my face, I said, "I say, 'Tank You!'"

It's amazing how fast a five-day hunt goes by. Our system was a morning hunt and an evening hunt like we'd done in the years before. The only exception was if someone was on the elk and the odds were in their favor, they were to keep after it. As long as there weren't a bunch of other hunters around, this worked quite well for us each year. It seemed to us this helped keep more elk in the area. It's true we didn't kill elk all the time, but at least we were seeing them, which to me was and always will be an amazing sight.

Noris and David headed towards Porcupine's opening morning, as Bob and I ventured up to Boob's Meadow. I went up and over to Tom's Meadow while Bob nestled in his usual blind. Bob started a streak this year that went on for a few years to come. Five minutes after opener – BANG!

We still didn't have any means of communication yet, so we just relied on our instincts and how well we knew each other. I could hear a few bugles occasionally. A shot or two would echo off in the distance throughout the morning.

As I peacefully sat in my blind, losing a battle with an irate squirrel. The more sticks I threw at him, the louder he got. Obviously, he was telling every elk in the area where I was, what I was wearing, and how big a gun I had.

I had only heard the one shot that sounded like it came from Bob. I decided to slowly walk through Kit Kat and peek over towards Bob to take a look. As I peered over the ridge, sure enough, there was Bob working on his elk. I ran down to him in jubilation. He killed another spike bull.

We processed him out and went to get the horses. After breakfast, we all shared our morning stories, then went up for Bob's bull.

Like I said earlier, our horses were flatlanders and certainly hadn't ever been around a dead elk. There were several obstacles to get through in order to reach the meadow, but both horses did great. We slowly led each horse up to the smell of the dead elk before packing them. Other than Gilby letting out a big snort, they were fine. It was amazing and very unusual to me to see this, but we certainly appreciated it.

After hanging the quarters up, we sat around camp. The guys returned and said they had seen some elk, but they were either too far or there were no bulls. Our license was for bulls only this season.

It was such a beautiful day, I decided to do some fishing. I promised we'd have fresh trout for a snack before going out on the evening hunt. Noris told me I'd have to catch them first. *Smart ass.* Then the competitor in me shot out of my mouth.

"Tell you what I'll do," I stated. "I'll catch a decent Brookie, clean him, and have it back in camp within two minutes."

Since Bob and Noris were in the meat business, they said I had a bet, but it had to be to federal meat inspection standards.

Whatever.

I had an ace in the hole. Remember my little honey hole over by the old camp? The only stipulation I asked for was to bait my hook in camp before I took off. That's fine they said.

Ready, set, go!

Off I went. Only had to run (limp) 100 yards to my secret destination. I snuck up to the creek so as to not scare any fish away. Just as I was ready to throw the hook in, I noticed the bait had fallen off. I quickly put some bait on and let it float downstream.

Bang – I had one instantly. As I lifted it up, sure enough, it fell off back into the stream. *Damn it.* The bait was still on my hook, so it went back in again. Just like that, I had a nice one on. By nice, I mean eight to twelve inches, which was normal for these smaller streams. I left the head on, pulled the gills and guts, washed it out, and ran back. Tick, tick, tick.

As I ran into camp, Noris said, "You have 15 seconds left."

I handed the fish to Bob for inspection. He inspected it thoroughly and kept saying, "I don't know."

"Come on," I said.

"Okay, it's passed."

I had two seconds to spare. I went and caught several more that I cooked in foil with onion and lemon over our open fire.

Delicious!

I hate to admit this and many hunters probably went through the same thing, but during my early years of hunting (starting at 14), I felt that if I didn't get my so-called limit, I was a failure. I was more of a killer than a hunter. Sure, there was peer pressure from friends and coworkers, but that really shouldn't have even entered into the equation. Unfortunately, I had this feeling for a few more years while hunting all kinds of birds and animals.

Even though Bob's bull would be the only one we got that year, all of us had seen plenty of elk and, of course, had a great time.

I didn't tell the guys at the time, but I had actually passed up on a shot at a couple of spikes that year. Yes, I know the meat is delicious and that was probably foolish, but I was just hoping to get a bigger one. Maybe I wasn't just a killer after all, or maybe I was just stupid.

We stopped by Rich's camp to say goodbye on our way down. He told me if I ever wanted to sell Gilby, he was interested.

"You'll be the first to know," I said.

As I left the guys in Arvada, I told them the food was good this year, and I'd bring fresh chicken for an even better feast. They just smiled, probably hoping I was just going to put the broasted chickie in a box instead of my pocket.

By the way, the knife I thought I was getting at camp ended up under my Christmas tree a few months later as a gift from Bob.

Next Year ——————▶

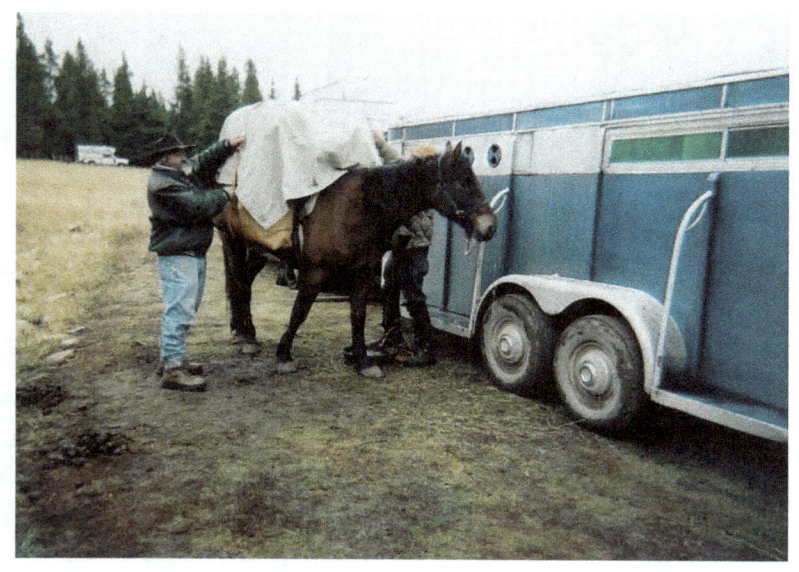

Charlie & new horses - 1986

Chapter 14

Goodbye Horses... For Good

Hauling horses all the way to Colorado was starting to be a major issue, especially when driving alone. I had sold one of my horses but kept Gilby. Since my daughter still had Rusty, I made a call to Rich to see if he still wanted Gilby.

"Absolutely," he said.

I asked him if we could use him to take our stuff up.

"No problem," he said. "You can even use #7."

Again, this year, Bob and Noris had set up camp early. Rich had given them a hand taking things in. I was to bring up Gilby, my pack, and some fresh chicken.

I got to the parking area early, so I was able to get a good start for the trip up. There were a lot more vehicles parked around us now. Hunters were walking around all over the place. I sure wasn't used to seeing this. I had Gilby mostly packed up with my things before I secretly put the fresh chicken in a gunnysack and tied it. Yes, they were alive. After all – I said fresh chicken!

As I started up the trail, there were camps here and there along the way with people standing around and waving to me. I held my breath, hoping those damn chickens didn't start crowing. There were a few times I had to give them an attitude adjustment along the way, so no one really knew they were there.

Rich wasn't in camp as I hurriedly led Gilby by. I didn't want to have to explain the prank I was pulling on the guys. Not really a prank… this <u>was</u> fresh chicken.

Camp Arrival

When I walked into camp, the guys were out somewhere. I took the restless chickens out of the sack. Now what? There was no chicken house up here. I couldn't just let them go. I guess I hadn't thought about this part. I was just thinking that fresh fried chicken would be a pleasant treat and definitely a surprise for the group. The only thing I could think of was to hobble them together with rope around their legs and tie them to a tree. It worked perfectly.

I unloaded the rest of my things and, as I turned around, Noris walked towards me. He held out his hand to greet me, but before that happened, he noticed the three chickens.

In his typical raspy voice, he said, "Shiiittt." He couldn't believe it. We both got a chuckle about it as Bob got there.

"What in the hell?" he said.

"Nice to see you too," I stated.

"Are you crazy, you dumb ass?" he said, as he finally started to laugh.

As we were sitting in camp strategizing our chicken butchering, a young pine marten strolled in and literally stopped a few feet from these 3 roosters. He was bobbing around, looking them over. Just like that, he ran off. I could just imagine him telling his mom and dad that he'd seen three of the biggest grouses ever and they were all white. They were each big enough for a meal for a week. I bet the dad told his son to stay away from the red berries from now on.

Naturally, I named the chickens. They were Fred, Clyde, and Sam. Clyde was the orneriest of the three and gave me trouble all the way down. The guys decided that I would butcher them the next day. Wait a minute. You guys are in the meat business!

That night, Sam got untied somehow and disappeared. We never saw or heard of him again. We didn't hear anything during the night either. He must have just walked away. That damn Clyde even crowed the next morning. Too many things to get ready – I'll butcher the other two tomorrow. That night, I elevated Clyde and Fred to keep them out of the reach of the pine martens.

What an idiot. They climb trees!

Sure enough, the next morning, Fred's rope was hanging there, and he was gone.

I decided I'd better butcher Clyde before it was too late. He was the last one left and, besides, I hated this one. I knew I had the upper hand when I laid his head on a log and swung my hatchet down on him. I had butchered enough chickens to know that you throw them away from you after cutting off their head. Well, ole Clyde got me in the end anyhow. I threw him at least 6 feet away, and with blood flying all over the place, he made one last leap right at me. I slipped and fell as he landed near me. By the time this ordeal was over, I'm the one that looked like I was on the chopping block. The guys got a big laugh out of this. To make matters worse, I cooked him to a crispy gold perfection, but he was still so damn tough, we couldn't eat him. Clyde won again.

Enough chicken talk. It's opening morning.

We each went our separate ways. Sure enough, shortly after shooting time, as I was sitting in Hog Pen, that all-to-familiar bang rang out from Boob's. I was still preoccupied because I had elk all around me. My heart was just racing. There was a small spike near me, but he looked like a yearling, so I didn't even think about it. The cows were chirping to each other, and the calves were playing Who's Tougher as they jumped in the air and pranced around.

This was a sight and thrill that never would leave me. There was just something about elk. They were my addictive drug. The wind switched and there was no way I could approach that bull. *Maybe tonight.*

Bob wasn't back in camp, so I just grabbed some snacks and headed up to help him. Sure enough, as I entered his meadow, there he was again, working away on another bull. This one was actually a 2x1. We worked out butts off on this one. The body was much bigger than his last one. As I was sweating away, I could hear the wife saying, "Have fun!"

We got it all packed down to camp. Noris came in later than usual. It was such a treat to listen to his stories and see the excitement on his face each time. He truly loved elk hunting.

I was the youngest, but it was amazing how walking around in that altitude would take so much out of a guy. We actually started taking cat naps in the afternoon. That made a heck of a difference for all of us, even me in my early forties at the time.

Noris and I didn't get anything that evening, but it was always the anticipation of a bull stepping out that kept you going. While walking back to camp each night, the stars would sparkle like diamonds. They weren't this close to me in North Dakota.

That night while lying in our bags, Bob and I were just talking about the day. Noris had fallen asleep. I finally quit talking and told Bob goodnight.

"Good night, Charlie," he said.

I was just starting to fall asleep when I heard a faint cluck, cluck, cluck.

"Bob, do you hear that?" I whispered.

"Yes," he said. "I think he's saying chuck, chuck."

You've got to be kidding me – it was Fred. I'll be damned. All of a sudden, there was a loud rapid burst of cluck, cluck, clucks. As we laid there in the dark silence, I said, "Say goodbye, Fred."

Then he clucked closer to us. I jumped up to save him. Actually, I followed Bob out for moral support. There was Fred caught between two dead branches. Bob grabbed his head, and the pine marten grabbed his tail – the tug-of-war was on! I was cheering Bob on like it was a high school wrestling match. The marten was winning. Finally, Bob was able to beat this 4-legged Bigfoot varmint off with a stick.

"I knew you could do it, Bob."

"Thanks for your help," was all he said.

Unfortunately, Fred didn't make it, but on the other hand, I didn't have to go through all the trouble of frying tough chicken. As for the marten, I'm sure he had a story to tell for many generations.

After the morning hunt, Bob and I were going to take his elk down to the truck. I went back to Hog Pen, but the wind was coming from a different direction, so I sat on the other end of the meadow. There was a bull around 200 yards away up on top just walking into the timber. The wind was perfect for me now, but I had to cross the open meadow. It was right at daybreak, so I hunched over and hurried as fast as I could.

I figured if I had eyes on me, I would maybe look like some kind of animal to them. Sure enough, a whole damn herd stepped out into the meadow between me and the bull. I knelt motionless, only moving my eyes. A couple of spikes and many cows and calves were within 100 yards of me. A curious calf came within twenty yards. Again, the thrill was overwhelming.

Naturally, as often happens in the mountains, the wind shifted. The lead cow walked right towards me and gave out her warning bark and they were gone. The calf closest to me seemed confused and hesitant as it trotted off. I bet he got an ass-chewing from his mom.

On my way back to camp, I heard a shot in Noris' direction, but it sounded way too far away to be him. I didn't figure in that the wind had changed direction. Noris wasn't back at camp when I got there, so Bob and I packed up his elk and headed down. We stopped by Rich's camp on the way down. He had a cow permit and had filled his tag. He was also taking his last quarters down.

With only a few days left to hunt, he offered to come up and help us pack down. Little did we know how helpful that would end up being. We arrived back at camp just in time for my evening hunt. There was Noris – blood on his pants. He had shot a 3x2 bull. Turns out that shot I had heard was his. Congratulations went all around.

I didn't see anything that evening in Hog Pen. I was sure I scared that herd off.

Tomorrow was the last day. Rich came up and took a load down with Noris. Bob started putting camp away. No one liked to get an elk on the last day because it was a lot of work and we all had jobs to get back to. It had snowed a little bit that morning. I told the guys I would only shoot at an elk if it had antlers back to its ass.

Like a damn fool, I went back to Chuckie's Mountain. I've got to be crazy – either that or I hate myself. As I reached the base of my mountain, there were tracks from a lone elk. It certainly looked like bull tracks, but there just wasn't enough snow for me to tell. I followed the lone track slowly, always looking way ahead and stopping often to listen.

I ended up following this thing almost to the top of my miserable mountain. The guys are going to kill me if I shoot one up here on the last day. After all, I have been known to lose a dead elk up here. Suddenly, I could see a part of the body of a large elk. I was so excited and proud of being able to track this elk that I almost didn't notice how dark the hide was. *'There are no moose up this high!* I could only see part of the chest, so I leaned against a tree and got ready.

We were only 50 yards apart. He's going to step out with antlers back to his ass and he'll be mine. All that work ahead of me, but that's okay – I'm here to get an elk. Quietly, he stepped out. He was a she – the biggest damn cow I've ever seen. She just stood there, looking at me as if to say "Gotcha." Even the elk were pulling pranks on me.

Back at camp, I could tell the guys were relieved I didn't get one that far up. I helped pack things up before the last evening hunt. I went to Hog Pen that evening just to picture all the elk I had seen earlier. As with any type of hunting, you need a lot of good luck along with your skill.

When we got down to the truck, I asked Rich if he wanted Gilby now, which he did. He paid me and we all said our goodbyes. Bob took his trailer back to Arvada – empty this time. Now he can really fly through those mountains.

Just as we were ready to part ways, I yelled out, "I'll bring fresh pork next year!"

"No!" Noris exclaimed.

Then I could hear Bob say, "Dumb Ass."

Next Year ⟶

Chapter 15

A Little Help
from My Friend

This year, a friend of mine (Les) decided to go with me. I picked him up in Bismarck, ND, along with my broasted chickie. My mother sent the cookies again and Dad couldn't wait to see what we got when we returned home. Each of us had decided to bring a meal for supper again. From soups to hotdishes, we were eating well.

We met Bob and Noris up by Rich's camper. Rich had another guy with him and an extra horse. Thanks to him, my ex-horse Gilby, and #7, we got everything up to camp again. I talked and sang John Denver songs to #7 the whole way up. Rich said he'd ride up once in a while during the season to see how we were doing.

As far as walking up, it had been raining for a few days and the trail was extremely slippery. Les was a bigger guy and was having difficulty walking at this altitude. The fact that he was a heavy smoker didn't help him any. Unfortunately, he slipped on one of the many rocks on the trail and fell with his gun and scope hitting the ground very hard. We never shot our rifles up there before the season had started, so we just hoped for the best. I told him if nothing else, he could use my gun. Les loved to hunt, but this type of hunting just wasn't his style. He struggled through the whole trip, but he still helped with all the camp duties.

Other than the campsite being very wet and muddy, everything went together quite well. Of course, we were all soaked and had to start drying clothes out as soon as we could. We had a difficult time finding dry firewood again. This would be the last year with the small barrel stove.

Everybody was tired from the trip, so we hit the sack early. We had two days to finish things up before the season anyhow. Do you know what else didn't like the rainy weather? You guessed it. Those damn killer mice. I swear they were having their mouse convention in our warm tent. They hadn't even reserved it. This time I had a plan. I took them little bastards personally and the war was on.

The rain had quit by opening morning, but that cool damp chill just went right through you. At least now I had one of those new fancy down-filled jackets that all the other guys had for years. I had pointed out the general area of Hog Pen to Les on the way up, so he knew where to go on opener. Noris headed to Porcupine's, I went up the draw, and, as usual, Bob went to Boob's Meadow. A half hour went by and no shot from Bob. That was unusual for him. Just then – bang, bang, bang! The shots sounded like they came from his direction, but I thought he either missed or we'd have to tail one.

I didn't have any activity that morning, so I met up with Les on the way back to camp. He had some cows close and personal and was pretty excited about it. I told him we'd grab something to eat and head towards Bob. He couldn't believe the climb up there. He never had a chance to go through the torture of hiking up my mountain.

At first, we didn't see Bob. Ended up, he was around the corner in a draw. Sure enough, he had another young bull

158

down. I still maintained the buckle for largest in camp so far. Les found out firsthand how much work it was to process these large critters. He had killed many deer, but this was definitely a different experience for him.

"Wait until we carry this thing down to camp," I said.

Noris showed up with his backpack, so we were able to get most of it down the first trip. Les did okay, except for his cigarette breaks and stopping several times to catch his breath.

The good news for the remainder of the hunt – it had quit raining. The bad news was that it started to sleet and snow every day.

That evening in a warm tent with our bellies full, we talked about the day's happenings. As all the *shoulda-coulda-wouldas* went around the room, I was devising a war plan for the mice. The guys were getting ready for bed as I was setting up my master plan. Small rope – Check. Small stick – Check. An empty large pork and beans can. It had to be a pork and beans can. Don't know why; it was just an engineering decision stuck in my head. Every mountain man type knew the technique. Since I was Tom's mountain man here, I had to live up to the expectations.

I gently tilted the can up on one end and placed the stick under the open end. I had tied the rope to the bottom of the stick and ran it all the way over to my bedroll. I laid down and pulled the slack out of the rope, then jerked it. Down went the pork and beans can – perfect.

The little disease carrying varmints only started running around after the lights were out. Since I was always the last one talking and getting into my sleeping bag, I said, "I'll get the lantern." I couldn't sleep, anticipating an attack at any moment. Sure enough, through all the snoring, I could hear the scratching on the poly flooring. Then I heard it chewing on the piece of Snickers I had put under the can. I reached for the rope in the dark and pulled it towards me. I didn't have to scream like a little girl, but I was so proud of my brilliant plan, I shouted, "I got the little bastard!"

The guys weren't quite as overjoyed as I was. The next morning, sure enough, the can was moving a little bit. He was pissed. "Now what?" I said. I wasn't going to get near it. Noris just said, "Shiiittt," with his raspy voice, opened up the tent flap, slid the can over, and threw him out.

"What the hell?" I said. "Now I have to do it all over again."

The elk were few and far between. There wasn't much shooting around us either. We were lucky Bob got one.

On the second to last day, I asked Bob if Les and I could go up to his meadow.

"No problem," he said.

I asked him if nothing came out, would he mind if I went towards the top after posting for a while.

"Go ahead, just make sure it falls back down the mountain if you get one."

As Les and I sat in the blind on this cold, snowy morning, we could hear a bull bugling up towards the top. After a few hours of nothing, I said, "Follow me."

It was almost straight up and at least a half mile to the top. Les was having a hard time. The mistake I made was telling him we were "almost there" quite often, to which he would reply, "That's what you said way down there." The higher we went up, the more elk signs we saw. I could hear the chirping back and forth with an occasional bugle now

160

and then. I turned to Les one more time and said, "We're almost there, just another 50 yards."

This was the toughest. You literally had to pull yourself up. I could smell them. I peeked over the top and sure enough, I could see legs and partial bodies in the pines. This was the same area I had my confrontation with the bull I lost during archery. Without turning around, I whispered, "Les, Les."

I turned around and the only sign of Les was his footprints heading back down. I never did see any bulls. The wind was starting to swirl, so I crawled back down the steep embankment thinking, hopefully they wouldn't smell me. At least I knew there was a herd up there. When I got back to camp and told the guys, Les said, "You're full of shit. You're also not a human; you're a damn goat."

Rich showed up that afternoon and asked if we minded if he hunted with us this last evening. He could after all he'd done for us. He hadn't seen many elk by his camp either.

I asked Les to come with me to Boob's and he said, "Are you crazy? I'm staying right here in this warm tent."

"Okay," I said. "Rich, you're coming with me."

Rich wore pretty thick glasses and as we were walking up, it started snowing harder and harder. We sat in the blind for almost twenty minutes when I noticed an elk had stepped out into the meadow about 200 yards away. I could barely see it with the naked eye, so I put my scope on it. It was a spike bull. With the snow coming down, it was very hard to get a clear view through the scope. I wasn't going to take him, but I knew Rich wanted an elk.

He couldn't even see it. He pulled his rifle up and I literally pointed the barrel toward the approximate area the bull was standing in. The elk hadn't moved and had no idea we were there. We were losing light fast and Rich kept repeating, "Where is he? Where is he?" When I looked at Rich, his scope and his glasses had as much snow on them as was on my cap. It's too late, we decided, and kind of had a chuckle about the incident on the way back down. Just another story Les didn't believe.

Once again, Bob was the only one that had a chance, but what another wonderful chapter in the life of elk hunting. It was a wet, sloppy trip out, but all ended up well. We said our goodbyes again and headed for home. Les and I had to drive in the snow almost all the way home. By the way, he thanked me and said it was quite an experience, but it was just not for him. "It's for mountain men and goats," he said.

Next Year ⟶

Charlie and #7 - 1988

162

A New Plan

We got in touch with JC, the cowboy who bought Jake and Spice, to see if he could take our camp in and how much it would cost. He had fishing camps up there, so he said he would take us up. The cost depended on how many pack horses or mules it took to pack in. We agreed to meet with him a few days ahead of time. Jake and Spice were long gone by now.

Just before I left home, my wife and I met up with another couple we had known for years, Rick and Sandi. That damn Rick (ex-buddy) went and told Sandi that I was shy about taking showers and going #2 in the mountains. She thought it was hilarious. I was quite embarrassed. She handed me a package that was wrapped like a Christmas gift. "Okay, thanks," I said, but I couldn't imagine what it could be.

I drove straight to Bob's this time and met up with him and two friends he knew from Oregon that were going to hunt with us. Noris wasn't feeling good again, so he couldn't go. Tom was all excited when I got there, but for other reasons than laughing at the chickie bones and cans. He was getting his first elk license and was going up with us for a couple of days before he had to go back to school.

We could still purchase a bull tag over the counter, but the new regulations called for at least 4 points on one side to be legal. Uh-oh, Bob's in trouble.

Bob's friends, Dennis and Ron, followed us up to JC's. Bob made it clear again that the only stipulation he had was for those two to never disclose where we were hunting. They sincerely assured him and said they just felt honored to even be with us.

When arriving at JC's, he told us to unload everything that was going up in a certain area while he went to get the horses. He was terrific with horses, but after all, he was a world bronc riding champion and runner-up several times. We were in good hands.

When he came around the corner with two mules and saw all our stuff, he said, "Holy shit, I'm going to need the whole string."

Nothing like getting off to a rocky start.

"What's this," he'd say. "A folding chair? Whatever happened to sitting on a log?"

Man, at $75 per horse, this could get costly. Each one of us even brought up folding camping cots. Bob bought a bigger tent (12'x15') and, of course, all the poles that went with that took another mule. I tried to help, showing him all my horse skills and rope knots. All he said was, "I can see now why you sold me your horse. Why don't you just stand there and hold this lead rope while I do the packing?"

On the way up, he definitely showed these pack animals that he was in charge. We were all following behind the packs, dodging horse biscuits all the way up. JC told me not to get too close behind "Carmelita," the mule, because she was in heat and he was pretty sure she was taking a

164

liking to me. I'm an old mule skinner, not a mule, but whatever. I found out later I was hanging out with a movie star. Jorge and Carmelita were in the movie 'Tombstone.'

We got lucky with the weather and were able to put up a dry camp. The Oregon boys cut wood to beat hell. The new tent was much nicer than the smaller one. There were pockets sewn on the inside for storage, mostly for my shit.

The weather was very warm – nice for us, but not for hunting elk. I showed the new guys where the crapper was, but never showed them my secret spot.

We sat around the fire that night and exchanged stories. Then it was time to give out our small hunting gifts. By now, I had enough surplus of anise candy and Levi Garrett to open a convenience store. Then I remembered my package from Sandi. When I brought it out, everyone sat around like little kids and asked, "What did ya get? What did ya get?"

Since I also was curious, I ripped it open to see. I had told him back home that it got cold up here some nights so I was thinking maybe some homemade blanket or something like that. What the heck? The top looked like a small umbrella. As I pulled it out of the wrapping paper, it just kept coming and coming. I held it up with a puzzled look on my face and turned around towards the guys. I reached into the opening of what appeared to be a shower curtain and sure enough, there was the handle to push up the umbrella top. As I pushed open the top, the entire thing was enclosed with a shower curtain all the way to the ground. I was standing inside of it when the guys burst out in laughter.

Sandi had painted the words "Shy Shitter" on the outside of it. She left me a note that stated I could also use it for my shy shower. Damn Rick! We all got a big laugh (at me) again. It worked great until it collapsed on my head right in the middle of doing "my business." You can only imagine the mess.

I was in pretty good shape this year, all things considered. Bob and I split the guys up and showed them the areas that should be pretty good to hunt in for at least the first few days. We also told them that elk will move overnight and even though there might not be much sign yet, they could move through at any time.

The tent was set up nicely and we were still able to get around in it, even with a fifth person. Besides, this was Tomm we were talking about. The trip was already a success for me because I slept on an elevated cot for more protection from the killer mice. I also brought up real mouse traps, not pork and bean cans. Found out later, those little shits can really scurry up things, you know, like cot legs. No wonder they've been around for thousands of years. I never did get one in the traps, but they sure ate a lot of cheese.

Since my Elk Tipping Over cannon (338mg) got stolen, I brought my killing machine (25-06) back again. Bob said when Tom goes back, I could use his 30-06, which would definitely be better for elk than my BB gun. I could shoot the eye out of a gopher with this thing, so I just figured I'd make sure to hold on to the vital areas or I wouldn't shoot at all.

The season started. The four point or better certainly made a difference the first few days. All of us were seeing cows, calves, and spikes. Tom was with his dad and at least he got the thrill of seeing the elk so close to him. I think he figured out pretty quickly why Bob and I were hooked on elk hunts. It wasn't just the killing. The thrill of it all never goes away, but if it does for me, I'll quit.

It was still very warm and dry. No snow. Several hunters would ride by from down below thinking all the elk were partying up high since it was even warmer down lower. Most of them were literally road hunting on horseback. I never figured that out. When I did talk to some of them and tell them there weren't many elk around, and that I hadn't seen any legal bulls, they would give me that "You lying bullshitter" look. I don't know what it is about so much disbelief in some hunters. I'm a bullshitter, but I'm not a liar.

Tom had to go back to school, so he headed down. I sure hated to see him go. He did get plenty of "learnin'" from me though. We were seeing less and less elk for the next three days, and we only had one more day to try and at least get one. No sign, no bugling, and no shooting. Just too nice out, we thought.

We spent some great quality time around camp, which I learned to appreciate as my years went by. Unfortunately, my shy shitter didn't work too well for shitting because it was hard to hold the umbrella handle and do your thing at the same time. However, it worked great for a sponge bath enclosure. Thanks Sandi!

This was the fourth night of the hunt. We weren't disinterested, but it was unexpectedly disappointing. We told the guys to start packing the things they didn't need for the last day of hunting. Bob was getting into his grumpy mood again, which was starting to rub off on me. My feelings were more about anxiety and the thought of going back to reality again.

We informed the guys that it was difficult if we killed a bull on the last day, but that's what we're here for, so we'll figure it out if we get one. Dennis was going to head up the draw and Ron was going to Hog Pen for the morning hunt. Not until morning did Bob and I decide to just take a slow walk up the trail to Porcupine's Meadow. "Dennis should be just west of us," Bob said as we were walking south towards the meadows.

We talked quietly most of the way, reminiscing about all our hunts. "We didn't see many this trip," Bob said. "But we sure had our chances over the past years." We weren't giving up yet, but we knew the odds were against us. There was a faint bugle call off to the west. We just stood there taking it all in. As we got closer to Porcupines, a high-pitched bugle echoed over us from up towards the meadow. Bob whispered, "A spike, let's see how close we can get to him."

When we got to the meadow, there was another bugle – the same bull. There were scattered trees in the meadow, and I had made a blind on the south end a year or two before. That was our goal – get to my blind. It was right behind a big evergreen overlooking a little open draw below. We were about 50 yards from it when we noticed a spike bull and some cows near it. Bob sent me ahead and the sneak was on.

My heart raced; I couldn't believe we might have one last chance. I got behind the two evergreens, looked back, and waved Bob over to me. He was just feet from me when a spike let out an ear-ringing squeaky attempt of a bugle. We knelt down as the bull walked by us less than 10 feet away. Then cow after cow passed by on the same trail. When they all finally walked by, Bob crawled up to where I was sitting. We peeked over to look down the draw below us.

There were elk everywhere, but no legal bulls. What a rush. Bob told me, "You better get a good rifle rest, just in case." There was a branch that was eye level in front of me that would work perfectly. We had one hell of a show for about five minutes when a 5x5 stepped out at the end of this small draw at about 150 yards. He was heading for the heavy timber. He stopped for a second and gave me the opportunity to get a good shot off. I held on the front shoulder and fired. He took off at a trot. Another opening, and I shot again. I didn't notice any difference in his cadence whatsoever. I wasn't used to this gun, but that certainly shouldn't have mattered.

He stopped broadside in one more clearing less than 200 yards away. I took a breath again, held steady, and fired. He fell straight down. The polished white tips on his antlers seemed to gleam like neon as he laid there in the dark timber. Bob gave me a high five and congrats. We were surprised and overjoyed. This is hard to believe, but as we stepped over the log we were sitting behind to head to my bull, another 5x5 ran out from a clump of trees between us and my elk, no more than 50 yards away.

We both stood there in shock. Finally, I said, "Get 'em, Bob." Bob put two 7mm reloads into his lungs and he was down. I told him it would've taken at least 4 more shots with the Herter's bullets to drop him.

We were overly excited and then realized all the work we had ahead of us. As we started to process mine, a shot rang out west of us. Nah, that can't be Dennis, we thought, that was way too far up the mountain. By the way, I had hit my bull in the vitals all three times.

As luck would have it, it started to snow huge wet flakes. It had been warm all week and now Mother Nature had to go on the attack. We didn't care – we were in seventh heaven. It took us quite a while to get both elk done. We walked back to camp to get Dennis and Ron to help us at least pack them as far as our campsite. Ron was the only one there. We had some lunch and the three of us headed to Porcupine's. We were almost there when we met up with Dennis. He was all excited and had blood on his pants.

"That shot must have been him," Bob said.

Sure enough, he had hit him but had to trail him quite far before he finally expired. At least he had it gutted out, that'll help. Now we had our hands full. After several trips back and forth, about a mile each way, we got Bob's and my bulls back to camp. In the meantime, Dennis had carried his quarters down to the main trail and brought the head back to camp. He was going to go get the meat in the morning, but we told him as long as it was right by the trail, we'd just have JC go up and pack it down from there.

We had no way of communicating with JC, but luckily a hunter had come by our camp on his way out and we asked him if he could stop and give JC a message for us. He said he would, but we didn't know if JC would get it or not.

We had the tent down and our supplies packed up by mid-morning the next day. Now there was plenty of snow on the ground and it was very cold out. We stood around a while, waiting for the horses and then thought maybe we should go carry Dennis' elk down. We were all pretty exhausted from the day before. Just then I could hear JC hollering at Jorge and Carmelita. We were relieved, but did he get the message and bring extra packhorses. Not only did he get the message, but he also brought an extra wrangler.

He was impressed that we had camp all bundled up and ready to pack down, but he wasn't too happy they had to go up another mile for the other elk. Nothing like riding a horse in cold, snowy, wet weather.

Been there, done that – it's miserable.

JC's helper and Dennis went up and got his elk while we helped JC pack all the other meat and camp supplies. I think we ended up using 6 pack horses down, that's counting Jorge and Carmelita, of course.

I don't know why, but it seemed as though JC directed most of his complaining and bitching at me all the way down. No, it didn't have anything to do with the hundreds of pounds of meat and these sets of elk antlers tied on top of the packs that he was still so puzzled and upset about.

"What the hell do you need all this shit up there for, especially a damn folding chair!" *His words.*

It might sound hard to believe, but we ended up great friends for the next thirty-plus years and still are to this day.

We got to Bob's and spent a couple days cutting and wrapping all the meat. "Where's yours?" I said to Ron. Just kidding.

"Hey Tom, thanks for letting me use your gun. You missed all the fun. Is that a frown I see on your face?"

"Next year, Chaz," Tom said.

Next Year ⟶

A Ten-Day Camping Trip

Chapter 17

I met up with Bob, Tom, and Noris again. My, how the years fly by. Tom could only hunt for a couple of days again this year, but he was excited, and I was happy to have him up there, albeit only for a few days.

Since we knew we couldn't keep up with the pack horses, we started to drop our supplies off at JC's and started walking up ahead of them at our own pace. They would usually pass by us around Rich's camp, probably because we stopped and bullshitted too long. Bob's ankles were getting worse. He said he may have to start riding up in a year or two.

Tom and I walked and talked all the way up. He was turning into a very mature teenager. Even if I was hurting or getting tired, I couldn't show it around him, after all, I was his mountain man hero.

Setting up camp now wasn't work; it had become enjoyable since we knew it would be warm and comfortable. We had lucked out on the weather so far. You just never knew when it would turn on you. Bob brought a small Zenith transistor radio this time. Great idea, did we bring extra batteries? At least now, we could listen to some weather reports.

173

Getting reception up in the middle of nowhere proved to be challenging, except when a local business would have its broasted chickie commercial on. They made the dumbest clucking sounds I'd ever heard. By the way, even though it may have been omitted, I can assure you I had pieces of broasted chickie in my pockets each year. Never did get food poisoning.

We ate like kings again. I even started cooking some fancy meals, you know, like a hamburger and fried taters. My specialty was trout over an open fire.

It was so nice out, after we had our campsite completed, Tom and I would fish a lot. We had become so close ever since he was a baby. He was more like a sun to me than just a great buddy. He was the same age as my youngest son.

He got a kick out of me constantly trying to put the big hurt on those killer mice. So far, I had killed more elk than mice and that wasn't very many. Speaking of which, once you got a couple of nice bulls and then nothing the next year, some of your idiot acquaintances back home would again tell you what a waste of time and money it was. They had no clue the feeling I would get being amongst Mother Nature's beauty and God's great gifts, especially the elk.

This was a wilderness area and the local sheep ranchers were allowed to graze their herds up here for several weeks during the summer. It appeared as though they weren't out of here that long ago, but that shouldn't bother the elk herds at all. For some reason, though, there just weren't as many elk around as there was in the earlier years.

Opening morning, Bob and Tom went up to Kit Kat and Boob's Meadow again. Noris went to Porcupine and I decided to concentrate on Hog Pen for a few days. I had only seen a few cows near the meadow and a couple on the other ridge towards Bob and Tom. Not even a spike bull to be seen. The rifle season was always after rutting season mostly, but it wasn't unusual to have a bugle now and then. Still, we didn't see or hear anything.

There would be an occasional shot up by the lake and someone was always shooting down below. Who knows what they were shooting at. Some of them were just up here for the weekend and probably just having some fun camping and drinking.

Tom had to head back to school again, so the three of us continued to search for some elk. One of us would see a few, but nothing legal.

One morning, I decided to take a slow walk-through Ole Dad's. I hadn't been there since I last hunted during the archery season. It was definitely a dry year. The trail through Ole Dad's was mostly like a soggy bog, so I wanted to check to see if the elk were hanging out in there.

It was always a peaceful, quiet walk going through there. There was a steady incline for about ¾ of a mile before it dropped down on the other side of the mountain. There were steep ridges on both sides of me that reared up like giant steps. About halfway up this marshy trail, I could smell elk. I stopped more often and let my eyes and ears do the searching. There was some sign around me, but it didn't look like many.

Then I heard them up above me. I found a good rest and looked toward the sound that I had heard. There they were less than 100 yards up on a ridge. They were walking in a straight line. I counted at least 10 of them but unfortunately, all I could see were their legs. They were in the pines and there were no openings ahead of them. I had no shot. After the rut is over, most of the bigger bulls, especially the herd bull, go off in small groups or even by themselves. The odds were this group was probably cows and calves, with maybe a spike tagging along. I guess I'll never know.

Ole Dad's ran down into Porcupines in a roundabout way. That evening, I told Noris there were some elk above him – I just couldn't see what they were. Bob hadn't been seeing anything in Boob's either, which was very unusual.

I went back to Hog Pen the last morning while the guys went to their regular spots. After three hours or so, I got up to head back to camp, when I noticed movement up on top. I sat back down and got a good rest before taking a peek through my scope. As it stepped out, I could see it was a bull. He was in no hurry.

To the naked eye, the antlers appeared very small and probably not even legal. I pulled my scope on him to count his antlers. He had 4 on the right side and a goofy looking 1 ½ antler on the other. Even though he was legal, the antlers weren't much bigger than a medium sized mule deer. His body wasn't near the size of the other elk we had gotten either. My guess was that he was a very young bull.

I'm not saying I could've killed him, but I certainly would have had a nice 150-yard shot. I decided to let him go. After telling the guys what had happened, I didn't get my ass kicked, but I sure got it chewed off. Nobody else saw anything that morning. We sat around camp cleaning up and eating all we could, so we didn't have to carry it back down.

It was still a great hunt. The weather had held, and we were able to pack up a dry camp for a change. Wouldn't you know it, JC came up with a whole string of packs again, and we only needed two. There was no way to know at that time unless one of us walked down 6 miles to tell him and then back up again.

By the way, we didn't have extra batteries, so I came up with the brilliant idea of wrapping the old ones in tin foil and placing them by the fire for a few minutes. I don't know how safe that was, but it worked.

We all had a safe trip home and couldn't wait to return.

Next Year

Charlie & Tom (Speckmouse)

Chapter 18

We've Got Neighbors

There were four of us again, counting Tom for a few days. Tom got out of school a day or two earlier, so we took off right away. At least I had more time to spend with Tom and camp.

The only additional items we brought for JC to haul up were our thicker foam cot pads and two more folding chairs. "What the hell, Charlie," was part of his "Hi, how ya doing." I was going to offer to help again, but I figured I'd get enough ass-chewing when he arrived at our camp.

He told us he was charging a guide fee this year.

"A guide fee?!" I said jokingly. "Did you forget where you're going? Besides, I'm the one who had to show you where our camp was in the first place."

It was something he charged his hunters in his camps. We were fine with it and were just glad he was able to take us in. He was just like me – stubborn, quick-tempered, but still had a sense of humor.

There were many more vehicles and campers packed up there this year. They were from all over – Wisconsin, Pennsylvania, Minnesota, and Montana. Lots of horses also. The weather was decent, so I was sure some of these hunters would be going up high, maybe to the lake. The lake was a couple miles past our camp and as far as we knew, there usually was elk up there.

We got the tent up and I *oreknized* everything inside as the guys gathered wood. I only set four mouse traps up this year. I sure hoped the guys didn't step on any barefooted.

We had supper and then just sat around taking all the sights and sounds in again. The camp robbers greeted us as always. There had been no martens for the last couple of years. Maybe no chickens equaled no martens. Just before dark, we stood by the trail listening for any bugles. There were a few right towards two of our regular spots. It looked and sounded promising.

As we were sitting in the tent that evening with me doing all the talking, I thought I heard a horse. We stepped outside and people were going by on the trail towards the lake. We were hoping they would keep going up the trail, but we lost sight of them.

We got up at daybreak so we could finish up everything in camp. Tom and I went to get water from the stream over by our old campsite. The rushing stream was quite noisy, so we didn't notice anything out of the ordinary until we started to head back to camp. I could have sworn I heard people talking. We sat our water buckets down and walked up to a little knoll.

"Damn it," I said in disgust. There was a big camp less than 100 yards from ours right around the corner. They had five horses walking around in the open meadow by the main trail. I'm not much for meeting new people, let alone hunters right beside me. We went and told Bob. He was a people person.

All I could think of was all the years and miles we put on to find decent spots to hunt just to be overrun by these city slickers. We were in a wilderness area and it was open to the public, even people who weren't from North Dakota.

It took a lot to get Bob excited about *sitcheations* like this, so after a nice breakfast, he walked over to their camp. When Bob got back, he had somewhat of a smile on his face. Turns out they didn't know each other, but Bob and their leader, Pat, were from the same area in Wisconsin. They both knew the same people back home. Thankfully, they asked Bob where we were hunting and said they'd stay out of our way. Now that's the hunting ethics I was taught. They also asked if it would be alright to camp there.

It wasn't ours to say, but of course it was okay. They'd never been elk hunting before and were having the time of their life. I eventually met a couple of them and they assured me they would stay out of our way. This was to be known as Pat's Camp from now on. They also said, if we got one, they'd help with their horses to pack it down to our camp. We thanked them but said that wouldn't be necessary. I think, no, I know, Bob didn't want them seeing his meadow.

On opening morning, there was nothing moving. It was very quiet. Not much sign again either. There were starting to be more and more standing dead trees everywhere. Bob went over to Pat's to tell them to be careful if they were out in the woods when the wind picked up (which was often). Every once in a while, you'd hear a loud crack followed by a thunderous bang when one of those huge trees would fall.

Tom couldn't catch a break. It was hard enough to find a bull during the 5-day season, let alone only a couple of days.

Naturally, as luck would have it, the next morning after he left, Bob headed up to Boob's only to find a herd of twelve or so right at the entrance of the meadow. He had to wait until legal shooting time, but he had already noticed there was one legal bull in the group. As I was sitting over in Hog Pen, that familiar bang from his 7mm rang out. I listened for the second and third shots but heard nothing. *I'll be damned... one shot.*

I just smiled. I felt as though I was right there beside him. The only excitement I had was a coyote, a faint bugle in the distance, and a small mountain wren of some sort that sat on a branch, inches from my head. It kept tilting its head side to side, looking right at me. Now that's what I call birdwatching. I left early to go help Bob with what I was sure was a kill. I grabbed two backpacks and a saw and headed up. Couldn't believe it – he had shot him 75 yards away from the tree line on the edge of the meadow.

Thankfully, we were in the meadow because that wind Bob told Pat about came up and dead trees were falling now and then all around the woods. The echo was clear as could be when one fell on the mountainside way across from us. Pat's group also got to experience this dangerous episode. His group had a cow permit and had gotten one.

That evening we celebrated by having a Hemingway. What is a Hemingway, you ask? Rich told us it was a tradition to have this drink after an elk kill in the mountains, however, it was his tradition to have as many as he wanted with or without an elk kill. The drink was a shot of Crown Royal mixed with cold, clear Rocky Mountain stream water. So tasty.

I'm not much of a beer drinker, but every time Rich came up to visit us, he would bring a 6-pack of Schlitz. After a couple of those, I felt like I had a buzz on. *It has to be the altitude.* It's a good thing Gilby knew his way back to his camp because sometimes Rich left our camp not knowing which way to sit on his horse. He was a character.

That night when we were in bed and I finally quit talking again, Bob said, "Listen."

We could hear a faint rumble. It got louder and louder until it started to sound like a freight train coming.

Bob said, "Watch out, it's a straight-line wind coming down the valley right at us."

The only protection I had was to cover my head with my sleeping bag. Brilliant. I can't believe our tent didn't end up in North Dakota. The dead trees were crashing all around us again. Our camp was fine the next day. Pat's camp, however, had several of those giants fall near their campsite. They thanked us for our hospitality and headed down lower to finish their hunt. It had scared the hell out of them.

During the day, Bob and I practiced our hatchet throwing skills. Over the last seventeen to eighteen years, I had yet to beat him to twenty-one. It would never fail; I'd be up to seventeen or so and he'd have a score of eight. Every time I was ready to put him away, he would say, "Don't let the pressure get to you, Chuckie." Damn it if I wouldn't mess up then. Final score this time – Bob 21, Chaz 17. I was damn good, but he could hit a target the size of a quarter twenty feet away.

One day a couple of Mexican sheepherders stopped by when we were throwing. They were impressed. To really show off, I stood by the target and placed my hand over it and opened up my fingers with two on each side. As Bob started to throw his hatchet, I noticed those two guys turn whiter than me and their eyes got really big.

Mama didn't raise no fool. Sure, Bob was fantastic at throwing, but I'm not that stupid. I pulled my hand away right as he let go of his hatchet. Naturally, bullseye. What a chicken shit. I would have been fine. We all had a good laugh in the end.

With only a couple of days left, I couldn't decide whether to go to Boobs or Hog Pen. It was a ton of work bringing one down from Boob's, so I chose Hog Pen.

Lady Luck had blessed me again. I was sitting in Marly's blind waiting to talk to my bird friend when I heard something in the timber to my right. With my eyes glued to that area, sure enough, a bull stepped out. I knew better, but I got into the habit of looking at and counting the antlers first, before I ever thought about shooting at them.

It wasn't really Trophy Hunting Syndrome, but I was always looking for what I thought was a decent bull. Like I said before, any elk is a trophy as far as I'm concerned.

Back to the bull.

I could see the antlers were skinny from the side view, but when he turned towards me, they were nice and wide. He was right at 100 yards or so. I started a new antler counting system right then and there – Two, four, boom! I nailed him with my brand-new Remington 300 Win Mag. He was a nice 5x4. *I'll be damned… I got the largest in camp again.* Our standards weren't that high, I guess.

JC planned to arrive in a day and a half, so I quartered him and carried the quarters down towards the main trail to hang the meat in the trees right there.

JC appreciated that. He actually started congratulating us on our success. I don't suppose it had anything to do with the fact he charged $100 more for packing out an elk. He usually was guaranteed one per year from us, and now he had two again. Hey, we were happy that he was happy. We were getting to know JC and his wonderful hard-working wife, Margo, better and better each year. At least Margo would greet me with a smile and a "hi Charlie, nice to see you" instead of cussing at me first.

Eventually over the years, I would get a big welcome hug and a bigger goodbye hug, also.

How the hell d'ya like that, JC? Love ya, man.

You know the routine – drive, cut meat, wrap, pack, and goodbyes. See ya, Tom.

The drive home wasn't that bad. I had 11 hours to relive another elk hunt.

Next Year

Chapter 19

Bat Attack!

Bob called me several times throughout the summer as he always did. This time thought, he was telling me about a bat problem in the mountains, especially right where we were hunting. It wouldn't be so bad, but bats were known to carry rabies. That's all I needed – killer mice, mean chicken-killing martens, and now rabid bats. I had no idea how to protect myself from these blood suckers.

Marly came with me again. I told him about the bat problem in Colorado. He said he couldn't stand bats either and that I should be extra cautious.

"Thanks pal," I said. "Remember how we always have each other's backs?"

"Oh, yeah," he said. "Where were you when those three Mexicans were going to attack me?"

"I was hoping you forgot all about that," I responded.

"I still owe you," he reminded me.

"I have some good news, Marly," I said.

"What's that?"

"I won't be singing Merle Haggard to you this year," I said.

"Good," he replied.

"I'll be singing John Denver all the way down and all the way up the mountains," I said with a grin.

Then Marly pulled a Noris on me, "Shiiittt."

Tom was a senior this year and was able to get a couple more days off. Marly and I met up with Bob and Tom in Arvada again. We loaded up our supplies and headed to JC's.

"Hey, Marly, see that sign 'Toponas' – what does it mean?" I asked.

"I don't know," he replied.

"I told you a few years ago! Think!"

"Dead Cat or something," he said.

Oh my God, he hadn't been around me for a while and now his IQ was going to hell. Bob, Tom, and I knew there was going to be a jackass standing in a small pasture when we rounded a specific curve, so we all said at the same time, "Hi, Marly." I got a sock and a smile from him.

JC was happy to see Bob, Tom, and Marly.

"Hey, JC," I said, "I'm right here."

"Oh dammit! Hi Charlie."

Here came Margo. No cussing, just "Hi Charlie" and a big hug.

"How ya like 'er now?" I boasted to my ex-hunting partners. Not you, Tom.

After JC bitched about the packs again, we loaded up to start walking in. Bob's ankle had gotten worse, so he ended up having it fused. We all agreed he should ride up with JC. He instantly said, "Okay." They passed us near Rich's again. Rich wasn't there yet – must have been running late. He could only hunt for a few days also, so he was going to give Tom a ride back to Arvada.

On opening morning, the weather was very cold. Not much snow, just damp, windy and cold. Bob had all he could do to make it up to his meadow. Tom went along and went over to Kit Kat. I went to Hog Pen with Marley and sat down over a ridge below him. We couldn't see each other. I had seen some elk way off in the timber, but that was it. Nothing up in Boob's either.

The wind picked up throughout the day and evening. Bob didn't go out. "No sense spreading my scent around," he said. I think his foot was bothering him. I went up with Tom and sat in the cold. We sat there talking about how fast time had gone by. "And now you're a senior," I said. There weren't even any birds around.

The next morning, Tom and Bob headed up to the meadow. I went towards Porcupine and Marly went back to Hog Pen. I didn't know it at the time, but Bob had gone back to camp earlier than normal. It was still quite windy outside.

As I made my way back, half daydreaming, walking on the trail, a damn legal bull jumped right in front of me and disappeared into the timber before I could even think about raising my gun. What a rush! He had to have been standing right by the trail watching me.

Seconds later, a shot rang out. In that wind it was hard to tell where it came from. When there was shooting, whichever way you turned your head seemed to be the direction the sound came from. When there were two of you together, each person would point in a different direction where they thought the shot had come from. Then the arguing would begin.

Anyhow, I couldn't tell which direction the shot came from in that wind, so I headed back to camp. Bob was at camp and said he didn't hear it at all. When Marly went there, he said it sounded like it came from Boob's. Tom finally came in and said he got a quick shot at one going through the edge of the timber. He said he had checked for blood, but unfortunately, Tom was also color blind like me, so he came down for help.

Bob couldn't go anywhere, so after having something to eat, Marly and I went up to help Tom. In other words, probably just Marly. At least I could see the antlers, especially if it was dead. We spent a couple of hours up there looking all around. Absolutely no blood or hair of any kind. "Ass-kicking time, Tom," I said. We got back to camp and told Bob. "Bend over, son, it's part of elk hunting."

I had noticed Bob and Marly were spending more time in the tent one day. *They must not be feeling good.* That night, everyone was in bed except me. I was the one to put the last log in the stove and, as always, turn out the light. Naturally, I kept talking in the dark. I wasn't getting a response from anyone, not even my pal, Tom.

A few minutes after I finally shut up, I was just lying there, thinking about the bull that jumped up in front of me. So close, yet so far away. All of a sudden, a screeching noise rang out and something with glowing red eyes rushed at me from the center roof brace. I can't remember what came first: the heart stoppage, the shit in my shorts, the shock, or grabbing my flashlight. All I remember was ducking in my bag, swinging at it like a madman, and screaming like a little girl. I was able to shine my super mini light right at it somehow. Bob was right; there were bats!

It sat inches from my face. I could see his vampire teeth and was sure it was going to grab me by the throat. I imagined blood all over my new expensive sleeping bag. *What about rabies?* That's if I lived through this life-threatening ordeal.

Then, a moment later, it flew back towards the roof of the tent and then back at me again with the accuracy of a laser. *Why me?* I made lots of promises to God about what I'd do if he got me out of this horrible *sitcheation*. I never thought to try and make the sign of a cross.

Wait a minute! All that screaming and knocking everything over with my karat e moves and no one woke up to save my ass. Then all their flashlights came on. They couldn't say anything during the ordeal because they held their hands over their mouths trying not to burst out in laughter. The fits of laughter started after this killer bat was hanging above me all limp. It was some kind of Halloween vampire bat but in the dark, I certainly thought it was a bat.

Marly said, "Now we are almost even for your Mexican stunt."

The assholes had spent that extra time in the tent putting fishing line over the top pole and practicing swinging it at my bunk until they had it just right. After an hour of exuberant laughter, they went to sleep. Not me.

After Tom had left and I got my heart working normally again, we continued looking for a bull. Each year, more trees were dying, and it was starting to look like salt and pepper in some areas. Instead of the thick dark timber we had hunted in years before, it was opening up more. You could actually see up to the top of some of the mountains.

As the last few days were approaching, Bob went out when he could. Marly and I walked up to Porcupine's a couple of times. There was a camp about ¼ mile from ours. It was up on a knoll overlooking the stream below. We talked to three young guys from Missouri that were camped there. They had never been here before and weren't seeing many elk either. I named that camp the Missouri Camp.

We ended up seeing several spike bulls, but not many cows or calves. We were questioning whether they had moved out of the area or if there just weren't that many elk around anymore. There were no wolves or bears around at that time. You would hear of a mountain lion once in a while, but we hadn't seen or heard any up here.

Bob stayed with our packs in camp to wait for JC while Marly and I headed back down. We couldn't wait for Heart Attack Mountain. Yeah, right. Actually, we still made it up that monster in pretty good time. Sadly, no elk this year, but a bat memory I'll never forget.

"My turn, Marly," I snickered to myself.

Next Year ⟶

Broken Oath?

Tom graduated high school, and Bob moved back to his home state of Wisconsin. Tom enrolled in college but delayed his first semester so he could go on one more elk hunting trip. We had a fourth guy with us this year. Since we had a scheduled date to meet up with JC, we decided to leave a day earlier and stay at a motel in Colorado the night before. It was nice to get a good night's rest before walking up. Bob was able to walk with us again and we had him set the pace.

It was a dry summer and quite warm again when we arrived. You just never knew how to dress for the hike up or what clothes to bring. Eventually we learned lighter was better and to bring quality down-filled and rain-proof outerwear.

JC was waiting for us. He didn't have as much to holler about this year because we didn't bring as much stuff.

I bought all the groceries this time and made some meals at home to simplify camp a little bit. I did a lot of "fancy" cooking at home and was going to treat the boys to a Rocky Mountain Gourmet meal one evening. I wasn't about to share the broasted chickie in my pocket though.

There were still fall colors all around which made the trip up even more picturesque. We noticed the grass was very short in the green meadow areas on the way up. Dry weather or a lot of elk – that was the question.

We had such a good system down for setting up camp, it was getting easier each time, especially when there wasn't a foot of snow. After everything was set up, Tom took the new guy on a venture to get him familiarized with the area. We didn't notice much elk sign on the way up, so Bob and I were trying to come up with some kind of plan. "They'll definitely be looking for water with as dry as it is," he said.

On opening day, we went our separate ways. I showed the new guy the wet marshy area above camp. He was to watch that area for the morning hunt. I went to Hog Pen for a while and then I went up a bit looking for sign. No bugling and very little shooting anywhere. This is why they call it hunting instead of shooting. How many times has a guy heard that? It ended up that none of saw anything the first day.

Same schedule for day two. The morning hunt was uneventful. Just before quitting time that evening, the new guy shot at a bull in the marsh area. I met up with him at dark and we looked where it had run into the timber. Even though it was warm during the day, the nights still got plenty chilly. I told him if the elk was down, he'd be fine until morning. Going through that marshy area was tough enough in the daylight, let alone in the dark.

We decided to all go up there in the morning and look for any signs. After four or five hours of searching like Sherlock Holmes, there was no sign of blood. Bob said he either didn't have any blood in him or you missed. He agreed on the latter consensus.

When we got back to camp, Tom said, "Bend over."

"For what?" the new guy said.

"You'll see, just bend over."

Three swift kicks were delivered to his rear end; he had received the lesson of the day.

Tom told him, "I've been there, done that."

For some reason, I started to do most of the cooking. I loved to cook at home, so it carried over up in camp. Halfway through the hunt, I made the boys a salad, a bowl of homemade "mamata" soup, fried pork chops, mashed "badadas," and sweet corn from my garden. That was the start of what would become Rocky Mountain Gourmet Fixin's. The only problem was that I did all the cooking after we came in for the evening hunt, usually around 7:15 pm. It got awfully late some nights. For those of you that don't know, cooking in this high altitude takes quite a bit longer, especially if you're trying to boil something.

The boys cut a lot of firewood up. We sat around on two huge deadfall logs that had been there since we started the camp. We placed some larger river rocks in a circle for our fire pit in front of these two logs. *'There you go, JC, we're sitting on logs instead of folding chairs.*

They caught plenty of brookies. Most of which they let go but brought back enough for a nice snack. I'd wash them up, throw some onion and lemon in the cavity, wrap them in foil, and place them on the hot coals. It doesn't get any better than that. I even brought up a homemade frying pan that I made out of an old washing machine that had the square lid. You old timers know what I'm talking about. I fried "badadas" and burgers on it at the same time. It was so large though; we could only use it on the open fire. It was great for bacon, eggs, and hashbrowns also.

195

There were other camps up there again. The three Missouri boys were back again. They even brought us over some Saw Mill Gravy they had made. Damn good, nothing like southern cooking. We pointed out areas we thought would be good to hunt around them. They appreciated the information. Even better, luck and skill combined and they got a bull on that hunt.

We were finally seeing cows, but not even any spikes. Occasionally, riders would come up from below looking for elk up high. The reports from down low were worse than up here.

Towards the end of the hunt, Tom and I took the new guy up towards Porcupine's and showed him several smaller meadows and draws that usually held elk in them. We even pointed out the way to our beautiful mountain lake up the trail another mile or so. None of us ever dreamt that showing this person our honey holes would change our hunting area forever in years to come.

As we were walking back to camp, just enjoying the scenery, I reminded the guys to always be alert. I showed them where that bull had jumped up right in front of me. Then a shot rang out and startled the hell out of us. That sure sounded like Boob's area. Arriving back at camp, there was no Bob. We grabbed some food and I said, "We better take some packs and head up and check. As we entered the meadow, there was that all too familiar sight – Bob standing over his bull elk. Everything went fine packing it down to camp.

It took a few years when I first went with Bob before I even got to see his meadow, let alone hunt in it. Unknowingly, we just took a new guy up there and he got to see everything. Again, we had no idea how troublesome this would end up being.

We followed each other as far as Cabella's in Nebraska. Naturally, we had to buy things we didn't need for next year. They headed on to Wisconsin and I headed for North Dakota.

Next Year ──────────▶

One of My Favorite Trips

Bob and his brother, Benny, met up with me in North Dakota. I got to know Benny on the long trip down. He was a character. Strong as a bull, but real quiet like Bob. Didn't talk much, but then again, who could when I was around. He had a great sense of humor albeit a little dry. He was quite a woodsman and looked forward to getting up to camp. Bob told him about all our past hunting trips and since he'd never hunted elk before, he was excited. After driving for nine hours, we decided to stop at a motel and get a fresh start in the morning. I knew it would be a lot of work with only the three of us.

The weather was just right – not too cold and not too warm. We got to JC's early in the morning. He was impressed that we didn't have all that shit as he called it. He said, "I think I only need three horses this time." I sensed sarcasm in his voice. We told him to have a safe ride up and we headed out to get our backpacks ready. I carried the heaviest stuff.

Yep, uh-huh.

The walk up was very pleasant. I sang John Denver to Benny and Bob most of the way. Showed him all my rest areas I had to stop at most of the time walking up and back down.

"What do you mean, rest areas?" Benny asked.

"Well," I said, "I have a problem with the ole brown eye. When it wants to *meischt*, it *meischts*."

"What the hell does that mean?" he asked.

Bob just shook his head. He'd heard it all a million times before.

I said, "That's German for shit."

"Oh my," replied Benny.

He liked our camping spot and was a great help putting it up. Bob and he found a perfect downed log and started sawing and splitting it. He was good. I guess when you live in the lumberjack capital of the United States, you have to be good.

We had a couple days to kick back before the season started, so we took Benny fishing, showed him our hatchet skills, and played cards. I even showed Benny how I could catch a camp robber (Canadian Jaybird) with my bare hands. I would put a piece of bread on my lap and when they came to get it, I grabbed them. I caught a couple that way.

I set up my kitchen the way I liked it. Bob couldn't believe it. He told Benny that just a few years ago (it was at least 10), The Chaz couldn't even boil water and now he's a gourmet chef. "Hey, wait a minute. Just because I put on a chef's hat doesn't make me a chef," I said.

Our special meal this year was an eight ounce ribeye steak, French fries, and a pea and pearl onion mixture for our veggies. Of course, we had homemade borscht soup and salad first. We started bringing up packets of oatmeal with fruit or brown sugar in them for a quick breakfast before we went out hunting. They were actually pretty good, but we had to make sure we ate it before the Levi Garrett or we risk confusing the two.

I showed Benny the draw to go to for opener. Bob asked him to go with him, but he thought the odds would be better if we all split up. I was going to work Chuckie's mountain for a couple of days. Benny had hunted deer in the Wisconsin woods for years. The average shot there was probably 50 yards. He had a difficult time judging the distance here in the mountains.

By now, you know what the odds are for hearing a shot from Boob's meadow. Pretty damn good. It happened this time too. The three bangs from that 7 mm were very recognizable. Around 10:30 am or so, I hooked up with Benny and told him we have to grab our packs and go help his brother. He was as excited as me. Bob had a nice 5x5 down.

Benny got to experience a little heavier backpack now. That wasn't the issue. The problem was stepping over all the dead timber and going down the steep terrain. We got it back to camp and started cleaning the meat all up. The camp robbers helped us also by removing a lot of the fat.

There were more elk around as well as more hunters, at least for the first few days. Something happened to me the second afternoon during the 5-day season that had never happened before. I got very sick – mostly stomach flu and diarrhea. I was plenty familiar with the diarrhea part, but the stomach flu took me down. It only lasted twenty-four hours – thanks in part to Benny.

We had a small bottle of brandy with for our evening tug before we went to bed. Before Benny left for hunting, he heated up some coffee. He poured me a cup, added the sugar from the oatmeal packet, and a shot of brandy.

"Here you go, Chaz, this should help."

Bob threw a fit. "Don't baby him, for Christ's sake," he'd say as I sat there smiling.

It did help me. I told him I bet two more of those would cure me right up.

Earlier my secondhand wood cot had broken, so I was sleeping on my pad on the ground with the killer mice again. Just so Bob and Benny wouldn't be afraid at night, I placed my pad right between the two cots. We were lying in our bags that evening with the light still on. I was feeling much better and my talking skills started up again. My diarrhea wasn't a factor anymore, at least for the day anyhow.

As we were lying there, I felt a slight pressure in my stomach. *Must be gas.* I was going to be very careful and just let out a silent fart. *Oh no, I feel something wet and mushy between my butt cheeks. This can't be! Now what?* I had no choice but to face the facts and come right out and tell the guys the truth. I sheepishly looked at Benny and said, "I think I shit in my bag."

I can still hear him and Bob laughing to this day. They damn near fell out of their bunks. As I unzipped my bag and crawled out, I said, "I wouldn't have had to tell you guys."

Benny instantly choked while laughing. "That's for sure," he said, holding his nose.

I grabbed a new used pair of shorts and went outside. "Throw me some more wipies," I hollered.

Bob searched for those shorts for a couple of days. He said something about showing Tom. Now I had to check my sleeping bag. I opened it up all the way and it was fine, but the guys kept screaming, "Zip it shut quick!"

What would a guy do without hunting buddies?

With a couple days left, Benny went up to Boob's and I headed toward Hog Pen area. Two shots rang out that morning in Boob's again. Damn, did Benny get one? I had seen some, but the wind was wrong for me to go after them. By the time I got back to camp, Benny was there. I asked if that was him that shot. "Yep." Did you get him? "Nope." He described to us where he was standing and where the elk was. He said it was about a 200 – 250-yard shot.

Remember, he was used to the woods of Wisconsin, not the open mountainsides. He was only off with his distance estimate a little bit. Where he shot from towards a lone tree that was on the hillside where the elk stood was 410 yards. We knew because Bob had shot one from the same spot.

Benny said, "That explains it. I could see dirt fly below him after each shot which I thought couldn't be my bullets because he wasn't that far away."

Yep, uh-huh.

I told him I didn't think there was a 410-yard open are in the Wisconsin words. He laughed until we told him to bend over.

We had packed most of our things away before the last day to make it easier for us. Benny hunted close to camp the last day and I went back to where I saw the elk the day before. It was still dark except for a little light from a partial moon. As I was sneaking up to the blind, I could hear them. They were just over a little knoll in front of me. I had to change my direction to get to the blind, so I headed to my right to get into the wooded area. I worked my way up. There were several elk still in the meadow. They must have slept there overnight.

There were three spikes, a few cows, and one legal bull. It looked like a 5x4 at least. He stayed right in the middle of the others, and I had no shot. As daybreak came, they started to head into the timber. His antlers were glistening from the sunlight that just peeked over the mountain behind me. Several had already disappeared into the woods, and he was still between two cows. It was 200 yards (for sure, Benny) and all I had was a headshot. Yes, on paper, I could put five shots in a one-inch group, but I wasn't about to shoot at his head. The cow between him and I walked ahead and the cow on his other side turned to the left. I had an opening on his shoulder with only seconds to decide. I laid my rifle on a good rest and squeezed. Down he went.

I couldn't believe it. The young kid in me came out again. One thing I realized as I was walking toward him was that I had whispered "sorry pal" just before I shot. I had never said that before. I've always had respect for all the animals I've hunted, but now my emotional respect must be starting to show. I was happy, but I also was sad in a way. I think that's respect, at least in my mind.

We worked our butts off getting everything packed and ready to go down. I had skinned him out and quartered him myself. I just laid the quarters on some dead logs by the trail, hoping the coyotes wouldn't eat it all overnight. I had gone back to camp to get some game bags to put him in which should help a little bit.

After JC had everything packed up, we cleaned up our camping area and followed him down. We met a lot of second season hunters this time on the way down. Colorado had started boasting to the world that they had more elk than any other state. That became part of our overcrowded hunting spots down the road, but the crucial intrusions came from the people that broke Bob's ethical oath and trust.

We were tired and definitely needed a shower, so we drove for a few hours and then stayed at a motel. Bob and Benny were in one room, and I was in an adjoining room. I kept the adjoining door open so I could talk to them for several hours. I think they were faking all that snoring I was hearing. You get so used to living in a tent for days, I forgot I didn't have to walk across the room to turn the light off when the switch was right by my head.

That's not the worst of it. It's embarrassing when you catch yourself half-sitting on the coffee table in the dark, looking for the toilet paper. Just kidding, but it is a different habit to break.

Yep, uh-huh.

Next Year

Bob, Charlie & Benny - 1994

Chapter 22

The Army Invasion

Bob asked if I minded if his nephew came hunting with us. He was a chiropractor and hadn't done much hunting. It was fine with me and Marley as long as he understood Bob's oath about secrecy.

Marly and I met up with the guys at the same motel in Colorado. We had a day to get everything ready to pack up at the motel. I showed the guys my new scope I had put on my 300 mg. I wanted one with a little more power since I was so persistent in counting antlers before I decided if I was going to shoot or not. The brand is irrelevant, but it appeared to be a very good scope. I know it was expensive. By now, I even had up-to-date warm clothing.

We had prearranged the date we would meet up with JC to pack us in. We bullshitted with JC a bit that morning then started our walk up along with several John Denver tunes. I had had another hip surgery that summer and was still a little gimpy.

Camp went together nicely again. The nephew was taking it all in. When I would see the excitement in the new guys, it would always refresh my appreciation that I had been able to be here as many times as I had. One evening with just one day to go before opener, we heard talking and horses go by on the trail. It was already dark out.

The next morning, I walked out to the trail to look around. I could hear some kind of rumbling. I walked up on top of a little hill by the trail and couldn't believe my eyes There was a huge green Army tent between our camp and Pat's – literally 50 yards away. The rumbling was from the guys' snoring. There had to be lots of them. There were mules and horses all over the place. The invasion had begun. They even had a confederate flag up on their tent.

Turns out it was a so-called company elk hunting trip. I certainly wouldn't have called it that. They were from down south, alright. There were at least twenty of them. So much for this year. The elk usually passed through this meadow where they were set up. For sure not this year. We could smell the horse shit clear back to camp.

On opening morning, we just hoped for the best – after all, we knew the area better than they did. Marly went to Hog Pen, the nephew up to TD's, and I went with Bob. Lucky for me, Bob couldn't walk that fast with his ankles still bothering him, so I was able to limp along with him.

As Bob and I walked by their party tent, the lights were still off. All we could hear was snoring and farting. I told Bob I should tear down their flagpole. He said, "Chaz, I think they've got you outnumbered by about 19 guys. Let's just go hunting."

We stayed in our blinds longer that morning, partly to let them see where we were if they came up this far. On our way down, almost back to their tent, there were two guys standing on a high point just off the trail. I'm not saying that there couldn't have been an elk come by then, but the odds were probably one in 10 million.

I didn't feel like talking to any of them as we walked by. Their party lasted all day and halfway through the night. We walked by them again the next morning. Same scenario only there were a lot of beer cans and whisky bottles by their fire pit. Again, we stayed up there longer, hoping to see something. I'm sure all that noisy ruckus that echoed through the valley coming from their camp didn't have anything to do with the fact that we hadn't seen any elk yet.

Yeah, right.

When Bob and I came down, we were shocked again. They were gone. Every last one of them – horses, mules, tent – everything was gone. Some minor garbage was left behind, but we took care of that. We found out later from guys down below that they intended on bringing some women up there and the boss found out. That was it; he pulled the plug. I'm sure it was an expensive long trip up with three semis full of horses, mules, and all those guys. At least we were relieved. We felt kind of bad for the two guys we saw up on the hill. At least they had a rifle and hunted one day.

Since we weren't seeing anything, Marly came up with the brilliant idea to walk down about 5 miles and work out way back on a trail that went cross-country towards our camp. All the walking I did over the years, I had never done this nor hunted in the lower areas. As I was hobbling along with my gimpy hip, he'd turn around and say, "Come on, old man." He was a year older than me – what the hell.

We came across a narrow meadow that was near Rich's camp that was full of tracks and droppings. Rich was hunting the second season, so we wouldn't be bothering him any. It just looked too good to pass up. We picked out a spot where we both could sit and decided to come right back down here for the evening hunt. Instead of continuing over the mountain tops, we angled back to the trail, so we knew where to go up that evening. We had already put on about 10 miles that day. We got back to camp and had something to eat, took a little nap, and headed back down.

We sat in our makeshift blind facing each other so we would see if anything was coming from either end in this long narrow meadow. There seemed to be more birds down there. They were serenading us all afternoon along with the chipmunks harmonizing in with their constant chatter. It was a warm evening, and we were very relaxed and half-awake. It had been a long day.

I whispered to Marly, "Here they come."

The herd hadn't made a sound. They just appeared. At least a dozen or more. They were heading right towards us when I noticed something flash across from my right. It was a ground squirrel that came between us and ran right up Marly's leg. You talk about a little girl gasping for air. Marly's eyes got as big as an owl's and his panic-stricken arms stiffened right out. I held my hands over my mouth as I was silently laughing my ass off. Funniest damn thing I'd ever seen.

Of course, Marly thought I'd done it on purpose. In the meantime, I whispered to him again, "There's a spike 10 feet behind you." By now, he was so damn upset at me that he didn't believe me. He turned slowly and got a closeup view of the bull as it walked right past us. The whole herd came right by us. Three spikes and the rest cows. We had to wait until well after dark to sneak out of there so as to not spook them.

I had to assure Marly on our way back to camp that there was no Bigfoot that was going to attack us.

Yep, uh-huh.

The other fellows hadn't seen anything, so Marly and I went back down early the next morning. Not an elk around anymore, but at least now we knew we had another place to hunt as long as Rich wasn't there.

That afternoon, Marly's neck went out. He was in a lot of pain. What're the odds that we had a chiropractor in camp. What I didn't know is that Marly couldn't stand to go to them for treatment. After I assured him that he wasn't going to break his neck and he was licensed, Marly finally sat down. T

he doc kept saying, "Relax, Marly," and then SNAP.

I couldn't tell if he looked relieved or shocked. He was so tense; I don't think it even helped him.

Here's another odds maker – having a chiropractor in camp in the middle of nowhere and his back goes out. That's no shit. I told him to lay down – I knew what to do. What a trip.

The weather turned on us; it got cold. Marly hunted closer to camp the last evening. Bob and his nephew stayed in camp, and I went up to Boob's meadow. One hour left before it was over. At least I saw some elk and had plenty of fun, I said to myself, when just like that, a nice 5x5 stepped out into the meadow all alone. He was standing at 200 yards. It had started to sleet – rain and snow at the same time, just as he stepped out.

I got a good rest and pulled my gun up with my new very expensive 4x12 scope to take aim. Damn, I could hardly see the elk through the lens. It must be covered in snow, I thought. I went to wipe it off as fast as I could, but there wasn't any snow on it. I pulled it up again and it was like looking through a thick fog. I turned it down to the lowest power because I knew the bull was legal and was standing at 200 yards. Still, I could barely make the animal out. It had to be the snow and the fact that I was losing light, but when I looked at him with the naked eye, I could see him clear as a bell. I just couldn't get the crosshairs on him for a good shot. I headed back to camp very disgusted at the weather and myself.

That evening sitting in the warm tent, Bob said, "Let me see your gun." It ended up the scope had a foggy vapor inside of it. The damn thing went to hell in the colder weather. Good thing it wasn't expensive.

After having several discussions with the factory representative when I got home, they offered me a new scope and a pair of binoculars. I told them I appreciated that, but it would never replace a very nice 5x5 elk. Needless to say, I was beyond upset.

Ironically, Bob and I were the ones in pain when we started the hunt and ended up the two who were in the best shape when we were done.

Take your skirts off, boys. No offense to you wonderful ladies out there who probably hunt more than I do; it's just camp talk.

Next Year ——————➤

Chapter 23

A Long Overdue Trophy

After consulting with Bob and Marly, I was able to bring a good friend with this year. We'll call him Donk. Big, strong, baby-faced kid. Bob came to my house and the three of us headed to Bismarck to pick up Marly. We stopped by my folk's house and picked up Mom's homemade goodies. Of course, we had to make one more stop for fuel and broasted chickie. They all liked it very much. Now they knew why I carried it in my pockets for days.

I kept to the same routine at the motel in Colorado. I introduced Donk to JC, and we were on our way. Both Bob's ankles were bad again, so he rode up. Marly and I showed Donk all the high points on the way up. He was curious why we called a mountain we were going down Heart Attack.

I said, "You'll see when we come back out."

He was in awe with all the fantastic surroundings but had a hard time breathing in this high altitude. At that time, he was a smoker – WAS a smoker. I swear he could have carried me and Marly in his backpack though. Very strong kid.

We set up camp and started to put our things away. I reached over and handed Donk his bag and said "Man, this is heavy, what the heck do you have in there?"

He just gave me that baby-faced smile.

The guys went to collect wood. Normally, they'd cut the larger ones in 4-foot lengths to bring them back to camp, but now we had Donk around. He just carried the whole damn tree, well just about.

That evening, we shared our past experiences with Donk and told him we'd give him some options where to hunt tomorrow. I showed him which pouches on the tent were his so he could put his personal things in there.

The next morning, we got up bright and early to finish up camp. Marly set the portable cook stove up so I could make us a big breakfast. Bob and Donk split some more wood. I went back into the tent for something and as I turned to go out, I noticed Donk's pouches were full, all 6 of them. Bags were bulging out the top of the pouches. After taking a closer look, I yelled, "Donk, get in here!"

"What's wrong?" he said with a sheepish look on his face.

"Holy shit," I said. "Your pouches are full of bags of candy."

"Well, you said I could bring my own favorite candy bars and they're all my favorite."

I grabbed our water jug and a small kettle and told Donk to come with me. I took him to show him how to get water from the stream. As we knelt down by the rushing water, I pointed out the little particles that were floating by our camp. I told him how important it was to take the kettle by the handle, skim it across the top of the water into the current, and fling it out three times. Then we could dip the kettle and start filling the jug.

With a puzzled look, he asked what good would that do in a moving stream? I stood up and headed back towards

214

camp to hide my laughter and then I said, "Just do it each time you fill the jugs it gets rid of the amoebas."

We all watched him do this several times over the next few days. One afternoon, we were sitting around camp and he said, "Chaz, what good does it do to fling off the top to get rid of the amoebas when there's got to be more rushing by from upstream?" We couldn't take it anymore. We all started laughing. His baby-faced smile turned into a frown.

"Easy, big fellow," I said. "The same thing was pulled on me years ago."

The day before opener, two people walked into our camp. They seemed to know who we were, but I didn't know them. I asked them if they were up here before and how they knew about this area. They said they'd never been here, but an acquaintance had told them how to get here and where to hunt. This was our first encounter as a result of someone breaking Bob's oath. Telling other people. In several of the following years, it got quite a bit worse. This all started with a person none of us thought would do something like this. This wilderness was federal land and open to the public, but ethics are ethics in my opinion. There was nothing we could do but hunt the way we hunt and hope for the best.

Opening day, we had Donk hunt the draw and TD's mountain. He had seen some cows the first few days, but he also had those two newcomers walk through a few times when he was posting. That is the problem. Someone who hadn't been here or even hunted elk before read something in a magazine somewhere and then goes out and gets amongst them. As if they're going to lay right there waiting for you to shoot them. No magazine can give you the information I received from Bob and my own experiences over the years. All these two had to do was ask instead of telling use where they were going to hunt.

Marly and I hunted Hog Pen the first three days or so. There wasn't much sign around. We had only seen a couple of spikes and a few cows so far.

Bob was up in his meadow, and he too had only seen a few cows. He said the grass in the meadow was short and there were many more trees that had fallen over on the mountain side.

We got lucky again this year because the weather was holding out, but that also made it easier for people to come up from down below.

Bob had hinted to me a couple of times that he didn't know how many more times he thought he would be able to make it up here.

With only two days left to hunt, he asked me to go up with him that afternoon to his meadow. That was always a special treat for me. I had damn near walked through the entire area over the years, and it was just nice to sit in this meadow and take it all in. We took Donk up with us and had him post at the entry, which was a blind spot for us further up the meadow.

Instead of sitting in his normal spot, Bob decided we'd sit up on a ridge overlooking the meadow. I sat right beside him like I had done when I shot my first archery bull. We laughed and joked and talked about all the good times we had over the years. The evening breeze was blowing in our faces, which was perfect when the elk came out. *If there's any elk left.* I sure hadn't seen many during this hunt.

With maybe an hour or so of daylight left, Bob let out a fairly loud fart (I'm pretty sure it was him). We both started laughing, then just like that a spike popped up in front of us. He came from our left side and was grazing right in front of us, maybe 75 yards, if even that far. As luck would have it, the wind shifted and blue right towards this little guy. He jerked his head up and looked around, then just started grazing again.

Bob whispered to me, "What a dumb ass."

I pulled my gun up and told Bob I got him right in the neck. It was just another exciting story to tell.

After about five minutes or so of watching him, Bob pulled his gun up and said, "Several years ago, you would have been mine."

I turned to look towards Donk and thought I was seeing things. Right behind the blind Bob had always sat in, I could see several white tips that stood out in the dark timber. Then I noticed the wide dark outline of his magnificent antlers. In a calm voice, I said, "Bob, now that's a bull." He was still looking at the spike in front of us and said, "This little guy?"

"No, look down there," I said.

Then the beautiful heavy rack 6x6 stepped out in the clearing 200 yards away. "Take him, Bob," I said.

"No, you saw him first, you take him," Bob replied.

"Bob, you've waited all these years for a trophy like this. You take him." I insisted.

He shot and it bolted right towards us. He fired two more times with no reaction from this huge animal.

"Are you shooting Herter's shells again?" I asked.

Less than 100 yards from us, he finally fell to the ground. What a beautiful bull. "He'll score 300 easy," I said

217

in jubilation. Donk heard our hootin' and hollerin' and hurried over to us. His eyes got as big as saucers. He helped us gut him out, but we only had a couple hours of light left. I sent him down to camp to get some game bags. By the time he got back up, we had it quartered. We decided to just bag him for the night and bring the packs up the next day. It would be our last day and we had all day to pack him down.

Donk headed down ahead of us while we wrapped things up for tomorrow. As he went around the far corner of the meadow, we lost sight of him. We didn't realize it at the time, but there was about 15 minutes of shooting time left. All of a sudden, two shots rang out in front of Bob and I as we were walking towards Donk. Did he fall or what the hell happened?

I hurried ahead of Bob to check the *sitcheation* out. When I went around the corner, Donk was just standing there on the trail with a dumb look on his face. I nervously approached him and asked what happened.

"Was that you that shot? Did you fall? Are you hurt?"

"I just couldn't pass it up," he said.

For an instant, I thought he had maybe shot a coyote. He pointed up on a little knoll and there laid a beautiful 5x5 bull elk. My God, this isn't real. Way to go, Donk. Bob caught up to us and the hootin' and hollerin' continued. What a day! Bob went on down ahead of us. He was beat. Donk and I gutted his elk out as it got dark. I decided we'd skin and quarter it in the morning.

Back at camp, Marly couldn't believe all the excitement. Yes, we each had our Hemingways. I don't think any of us got much sleep that night. Marly went to Hog Pen the last morning and I went back up to Boob's. I told the guys I was going to post for a while and then start skinning Donk's elk, and they could come up there in a couple hours after daybreak.

It ended up being another long day, but we got everything back to camp. Donk ended up carrying two quarters, one on each shoulder and two bags of burger meat tied together that we put around his neck. He made it about 100 yards and down he went. The rope had cut off his blood circulation.

I hurried up to the big lummox and said, "Is that too heavy for you?"

He gave me a dirty look and took off again.

Marly and I didn't get one, but what an unbelievable trip. We were very tired out the last evening, but we were still able to get things ready for JC. We decided to all stay with Bob and wait for JC to arrive. You never knew if he had any help or not. I told Donk if JC is short a horse, you can carry two quarters down. Just kidding, but I'm sure he could have.

When JC got there, he couldn't believe it either. Biggest bull he'd ever seen came out of this area. Bob definitely has the biggest in camp now. Goodbye buckle, I thought. When JC finished packing the head on his pack horse, it was the most picturesque moment I'd ever seen, just like in those magazines. The antlers draped over each side of the rump on the very large pack horse and there was room to spare; it was so wide. What a sight as the pack horses headed across the stream with Bob riding right behind his bull. I swear there was a glow around Bob's head as he rode off.

Every camp we went by on the way down and every hunter we met that was going up for the second season had to check this bull out.

Everyone asked the same question. "Where'd you get him?"

Bob would just answer, "In the shoulder."

Then they'd see Donk's bull and just shake their head. "Two great bulls," one guy commented.

Bob and his bull were the talk of the area for years to come, rightfully so.

I just kept thinking to myself, 'I hope this doesn't help finalize his decision to hang up his spurs.' It just wouldn't be the same.

We had a good trip home. It didn't seem as far heading home when you have two nice bulls in the back. We stopped by my folks' home on the way through. My dad was so excited, he had the whole neighborhood come over and look at the elk.

I looked forward to every upcoming elk hunt and after this fantastic hunt, I couldn't wait until next year. By the way, Donk found out why we called the last mountain out "Heart Attack." He was really panting, and I noticed he hadn't smoked on the way down either.

Next Year ⟶

Bob's Trophy – 1996

Chapter 24

Another New Guy

Bob asked Marly and me if he could bring a friend this year. I initially thought it was just going to be the three of us again. Noris was doctoring, and Tom was in college. No problem, we said, extra help is always welcome. Bob and Dave drove down separately to meet up with us at the motel in Colorado.

I was personally well-stocked with candy bars (learned from Randy), Levi Garrett, and toilet paper. I bought all the groceries and planned for several gourmet meals this time.

We got into a routine to go out for supper at a favorite restaurant near the motel the night before we headed up to hunt. Bob and Marly told Dave that he better enjoy this meal because it was the last good one for the next eight days. The Chaz is the camp cook. Dave didn't comment.

We got to JC's and dropped off our supplies. Dave and Bob were about the same age – eleven years older than me. They both had talked about riding up but decided to walk with us. We took our time, the trail was good, but Bob was having a hard time again.

We got all settled in that first evening after having a bowl of soup and snacks. Dave found out right away that I was the last one in bed. I turned out the light and I talked everyone to sleep. That night, a bull bugled right up in Hog

Pen. I woke Marly (which, by the way, was always a treat) and told him to listen. Another bugle bellowed out and I said, there's your bull, Marly. We were hopeful now.

The next day, Marly and I caught several little brookies for a snack later on. I finished *oreknizing* the tent for my benefit, of course. More pouches equaled more room.

I decided to cook one of the more difficult meals on the night before season opener because we always got in so late during hunting. We had homemade "Mamata" soup, salad, North Dakota walleye filets, Rosie's bean dish, and fried taters and onions. As we sat around eating, Dave never said a word. I hope he liked it.

On opening day, I went up with Bob, Dave went to the draw, and Marly to Hog Pen. I was sure I'd hear a blast from Hog Pen sitting up in Kit Kat. Bob and I heard a few bugles and several shots up by the lake, but that was it. Dave had seen some cows. Marly hadn't seen anything, so he went up on top just to check for some sign. He told us just as he got into the timber, there he was 35 yards away. At least a 6x6 with white tips looking right towards him. The breeze was from the right direction, so Marly had a chance to get ready.

The problem was, he was behind a thick brushy area and all Marly could see was the antlers. He couldn't see his head or body at all. He thought he had to step out eventually. Marly said he didn't even see it happen, but the big bull disappeared without making a sound. He was sure the bull didn't even know he was there, so he didn't think he spooked him. Needless to say, Marly was very excited.

Bob surprised us that warm afternoon by making us homemade donuts and I threw the brookies in a pan and we had a wonderful brunch.

The evening hunt was uneventful for Bob and me for a while. I sat with him so we could watch both ends of the meadow.

Just as we sat down in our blind, Bob said, "There's a hunter sitting up by Kit Kat."

Damn, he's in my spot.

We sat there watching him fidgeting around. I suppose it was to make sure his scent got all over the place. *Idiot.* About an hour before quitting time, he stood up and with a loud scream, yelled, "Hey, Bill, let's go!"

Another guy walked down the draw where the elk usually would come out. I swear it wasn't 15 minutes after they left, that a herd of twenty-five or so elk walked down the same path Bill had been on. Undoubtedly, there were cows, calves, and a couple of spikes. We could see other elk in the timber, but we were losing light, so we snuck out of there.

That evening, the boys had soup and salad while I was making us elk burger, corn on the cob (from my garden), and French fries. French fries sure take a long time in the high altitude. Dave was still silent, but at least he was eating everything.

The next morning, bob and I heard a shot, but couldn't tell if it had been Dave or Marly or some other hunter. We got back to camp around 11 or so and neither of them were back yet. We had only heard one shot. Marly showed up and said he heard the same shot also. To him, it sounded like it was up towards the lake. We were having breakfast when Dave showed up. He was all smiles.

He had shot a younger bull right in the neck. He said it came from behind him and stepped out in front of him broadside at 75 yards. It was up in the draw so packing it down to camp wasn't so difficult as most of the other elk we had killed.

Dave stayed in camp to work on his quarters and head while Bob and I went back up to Boob's and Marly headed back to Hog Pen. We saw a few cows that evening, but we were all glad to see that Dave had gotten his bull.

For supper, I warmed up the soup and made the guys a salad. The special tonight was seafood fettucine. I put scallops, crab, mussels, and shrimp in with the fettucine noodles and homemade sauce. I sat right beside Dave as we were eating.

I couldn't take it anymore, so I said, "Dave, if you don't like the food I'm cooking, you don't have to eat it. I can make you something else."

He just smiled as he wiped off his mouth and said, "Chaz, I take my wife out on our anniversary each year and we go to very nice restaurants, but I have never eaten food as good as this."

I didn't know what to say. I just assumed he was eating it so he wouldn't hurt my feelings. I told him so.

He laughed. "I don't know if I'd have hurt your feelings, but I just wouldn't have eaten it if I didn't like it."

That made me feel pretty good. We had our Hemingways and went to bed.

Two days to go. The weather was still good. A few hunters here and there, no problem. I went with Marly to Hog Pen and Dave walked up with Bob. I sat down below Marly again to watch the lower meadow. A shot rang out and startled the hell out of me. *It had to be Marly.* I sat for a while and then walked my way back up to him. He wasn't in his blind and I couldn't see him anywhere. I walked over a little knoll in the meadow and there he was, working on his bull.

It was a young 5x4 – perfect. I could taste the steaks. The excitement just never ends. It's such a privilege to just be here and I considered getting an elk a big bonus. We worked on it for a few hours and hung it up by the trail since we only had a day or so before JC came back up. That was Marly's first bull and, needless to say, he was overjoyed, as was I. The other two heard the shot also and figured it was one of us.

That evening we had two Hemingways. It was a perfect night to serve the boys barbeque ribs, mashed taters, and steamed candy carrots.

Neither Bob nor I got an elk, but once again, it was a fantastic hunt. Another chapter in my elk hunting memories.

Next Year

Chapter 25

Two New Greenhorns

During the following summer, Bob called me and said he wasn't going elk hunting anymore. He said his ankles were just too bad. I felt lost and devastated, but I understood. I told him he couldn't just up and quit like that. He had to at least tell me when we were up there, not when we were back home. We could have done something special up there. I didn't want him to get upset with me, so I let it go for the year.

He said he had something for me before I went hunting. My wife and I had started to meet up with him and his wife every summer since they moved back to Wisconsin. We would meet halfway and spend a weekend together. He had a beautiful camp flag embroidered with a bull elk in the middle, right below the words 'Graybeard Camp.' On the left side, he had the names Bob, Tom, and The Chaz and on the right side, he had Noris on top and Marly on the bottom. He left room for another name in the middle.

"I'll hang it in front of the tent every year," I promised. I was and am proud to be a part of Graybeard Camp.

He said, "You have to carry on the tradition now."

I told him, "Those are big shoes to fill. We'll toast to Graybeard Camp and especially to you, my dear friend, every time I'm up there.

This time, I took my neighbor, Dean, and my brother-in-law, Chuck, with me. Marly had other obligations.

We stopped in Bismarck as always to see my folks and fuel up. Naturally, I had to stop and get my broasted chickie. I picked up a 10-piece box. They said that was a lot of chicken for the road trip. I told them that was mine, they'd have to get their own. Afterall, it had to last me 10 days. Both of these guys had hunted elk in the past, but never stayed in a tent in the wilderness before, so they were quite excited, especially after all the stories I told them on the way down.

Dean and I had purchased five sets of custom panniers — four sets were mine. They were well-made and the corduroy material was super durable.

Our trip down started out with strong crosswinds through North Dakota and South Dakota. As we entered Wyoming, it started snowing heavily. I got through the road closure gate, but we should have stayed in Sundance. The Vikings were playing the Packers that night and my goal was to get to Musk, Wyoming where I had made a reservation at the motel.

There was a lot of snow on the narrow road all the way. I had to zig-zag around huge drifts most of the way. We got to the motel with a couple of hours to spare before the football game. I went to check in and told the attendant I was glad we made it in time. He told me then, "There's no heat. The power went out. We're waiting for the National Guard to bring us generators if they can get through."

I didn't care about the heat, I just wanted to see the game. What an idiot – no power means no TV. I asked how far away the next town was. He said it was about an hour away, but he didn't think we could get through. 'No problem,' I thought to myself.

I told the guys the *sitcheation* and took off. They were not happy with me. I could hear them muttering, "He's crazy!"

We stopped at the nearest motel, but they were full because of the storm. The game just started, and they had it on the big screen in the lobby. Chuck and I watched it while Dean went to find us a room somewhere else, hopefully. I did a lot of loud cheering for the Vikings that night. How was I supposed to know Wyoming was full of Packer fans? It got a little ugly. Luckily, Dean managed to find us a room. We were able to get back on the road early the next morning.

We got to our motel in Colorado around noon and started to pack the panniers. I knew how much weight we could put on each side, and this would help out JC. We had our last "good" meal and called it a night.

We got to JC's and unloaded the panniers. Of course, he had to rearrange them, even thought I had them packed perfectly.

Yeah right.

As we walked up, I noticed way more elk sign than last year. I always held my breath when we got closer to Graybeard Camp, never knowing if someone else would be there already. Especially since there were many more vehicles parked by the road this yar. Our camp was empty, but sure enough, there were two people camping in Pat's camp. Ended up, they were two more oath-breakers, trickled down from the first one. We set up camp, hung the camp flag up, and gave a toast to Bob.

231

The weather had completely turned around. It was in the 60s during the day now. We were sitting around the camp the day before opener when four young guys came barging into camp.

The first thing their so-called leader said was, "We're going to hunt over there and there and up there and there," as he pointed to everywhere that we hunt.

I asked him where they were from. They were from down south and the older fellow in camp was from the Midwest. They were camped in the Missouri camp. I simply told them the places he pointed to were where we hunted and asked if they had been here before since I didn't recognize any of them.

"No, it's the first time for all of us," he answered.

"Well, how do you know about this area then?"

He said a good friend of his back home was here a couple of times and told them where to hunt. I probably shouldn't have said this, but I told him that my good friends wouldn't have come up here without me and they sure wouldn't have told five other guys about it. They just walked out of camp.

I sent Dean and Chuck up to Hog Pen just to sit and watch the night before season to get familiar with it. I went up to check on Boob's for the first time on my own. There was good sign up there. The guys had some cows and calves walk by them just feet away. They were really excited and optimistic for the upcoming hunt.

On opening morning, I left early for Boob's because of all those other hunters around. I got to the entrance of the meadow in the dark, so I stepped aside from the trail to wait until I could see through my scope. Many times, the elk would still be in the meadow from the night before and I didn't want to spook them away.

All of a sudden, I could hear talking and saw damn flashlights coming up the trail below me. It was three of the guys from the Missouri camp. Two of them came right by me with their flashlights still on. They had no idea I was standing right there beside them. They walked into the meadow with their lights on and sat right in my blind.

The third guy that came up was the elderly gentleman. I stepped out and startled the poor guy. I told him, "Your buddies had no idea I was here and they're sitting in my blind." Then I gave him my opinion on their damn talking and using flashlights all over. He apologized and said he was going to go elsewhere.

I said, "It doesn't matter now – those two scared away any elk that might have been here."

I walked over to Tom's meadow and sat for a while. As I was sitting in the blind, there one of the guys walked right by me again. This was ridiculous. They had no idea what they were doing. Disgustedly, when he was out of sight, I walked up through Kit Kat and came out on top. As I looked down towards Bob's blind, I could see someone was still sitting there. I never looked at him. I just started to walk across the meadow to head back to camp. I was so optimistic after seeing all the elk sign around. Now, with these guys prancing around, who knew where the herd would go.

I met up with Dean and Chuck back at camp. They had two guys walk right through Hog Pen right after daybreak – the peak hunting time. These guys didn't realize they were wrecking the hunt for everyone, not just us.

To make matters worse, the two from Pat's camp shot a small bull on TD's Mountain. People came out of nowhere and started walking the woods in every direction. I more or less told the guys we're screwed, and we'll just have to keep trying the way we had been and just wait it out. "If there were any elk here, they were certainly gone now," I told them. Everyone was disappointed. I told them, I've never confronted so many hunters right here with the exception of the Army tent guys, but they weren't hunters.

Since the Missouri guys were all over Boob's, I took Chuck way up and around another area I knew of. Dean worked the Hog Pen area again. Chuck and I were just below a ridge when a bull bugled right above us. It had to be just over this ridge, but it would be very difficult to get straight up it. We slowly headed up the ridge when it bugled again. "He's really close," I whispered. By the time we got up there, he had disappeared. "What a thrill," Chuck said. So close – a little luck would've helped.

Finally, by Monday morning, most of the other camps had left. I was trying to figure out where to send the guys. Dean was going to try Old Dad's, Chuck went way up again, and I went back to Boob's. As Dean was heading up Old Dad's, he noticed a bull down by the stream. He could see it was legal, but it was still too dark to shoot. By the time it was shooting time, it had disappeared into the timber. Chuck and I didn't see anything.

The next morning as I approached Boob's, there weren't any elk out, but I just wanted to sit in the blind and reminisce. I was about 200 yards from the blind when suddenly, a bull started trotting up the hill behind the blind. I pulled up on him through my scope. He was definitely legal. I took my small pack off and tried to get a good rest. The wind was from my left, so I had to compensate for that. He stopped and I fired. Nothing. I fired two more times. Again, no reaction whatsoever.

My rifle only held three shots, so I had to load again. I was starting to panic. Was it that windy? I knew the yardage. The bull was just walking. I don't think he knew where the shots were coming from. I fired two more times. Something was wrong. I'm no Buffalo Bill Cody, but I could shoot. I only had one shell left. I'd never shot over three times, so I didn't carry that many shells. I got the yardage at 400 yards now. I adjusted for the wind and fired. Finally, over he went. Last shot, for heavens' sake. Three shots had hit him in the lung area.

It ended up when I got home, I fired my rifle to check. Somehow it was two inches to the right. Between that and the wind, that must have been what caused it.

After two and a half hours, I had him all dressed out and ready to pack down. I figured the other two must be on some elk or they surely would have come up. Then I realized I hadn't shown them how to get up here. I lifted the head and cape of the nice 5x5 onto my shoulders and headed down. It's amazing how heavy the head is. As I came into camp, the guys were just sitting there. They looked up and were shocked to see me carry this bull. They hadn't even heard me shoot – I just couldn't believe it.

As we packed the meat down, I stopped to pull a big branch away from the trail so Dean could get through. As he knelt down to get by, the large branch slipped out of my hand and pinned his hand right against a tree. Dean's a big boy and he was pissed. I couldn't take his screaming like a little girl anymore, so I pulled as hard as I could to get his hand out. It swelled up immediately. I felt terrible, but I didn't do it on purpose.

Dean wasn't feeling very well so he stayed in camp the last night. Chuck was having trouble with his brown eye, so he hunted nearer to camp.

Sadly, we started packing things up to have them ready for JC the next day. The hunt seemed to go by faster and faster each year. I was upset there were so many hunters around and there was nothing I could do about it. Several of the new hunters to come were all due to one person telling another about my sacred place. Then they would tell 5 others and the chain reaction was unstoppable. I just had to learn to accept it. At the time, I had the advantage of knowing where all the draws and meadows were, but future electronics would take that away from me also.

JC brought up an extra riding horse so Chuck asked me if I minded if he rode down. Not a problem, but I wondered what would be worse on his brown eye – walking or riding.

The guys had a good time. Plus, the roads were better on the way home. Life was good.

By the way, I fed the boys Rocky Mountain Boil (lobster, crab, sausage, corn on the cob, taters and onions), fried chicken, turkey legs, shrimp New Orleans, and Swedish meatballs, along with all the fixings.

Next Year ————————▶

Chapter 26

The Return of My Mentor

I had called Bob several times during the summer asking him to at least consider going hunting one more time for old times' sake. We all met up with Noris and his wife that summer. Noris had a growth from his throat to his ear removed earlier. That was part of the reason for his raspy voice. Only took ten years to figure that out. Later on, towards fall, I begged Bob to go one more time and maybe bring Noris. It would be the four of us again, like during archery. He caved and said he and Noris would meet us at the motel in Colorado.

Marly and I had another windy trip down, but at least there was no snow yet. I told him about the tough trip last year. We met up with the other two in Colorado. Bob was impressed with my new panniers. We got everything packed and went to our favorite restaurant to have out last "good" meal.

JC was happy to see Bob and Noris again. What about Marly and me? Bob and Noris told him that this was definitely their last year. Bob rode up with JC and old Noris walked right with us all the way up. He was now in his early 70s, but in good shape. As always, Marly was in great shape also. As for me, I was so banged up, I wasn't sure if I was in good shape or not. I just kept walking.

I wrapped up a couple of folding chairs for Bob and Noris so JC wouldn't know what they were. He would have hollered at me. Everyone made it to camp okay. I noticed our sitting logs around the fire pit were withering away.

We were awfully tired again. After setting camp up and putting as much stuff away as we could, we had some soup and snacks and went to bed early.

The next day was beautiful. Some hunters had gone by and kept going towards the lake. We finished the camp and had a big breakfast. Bob and I decided to go for a short walk. We were looking around at all the higher mountains when I said, "Remember when I first came up here with you, I had said, there ain't no mountain I can't climb? I think I'll have to retract that statement, Boob. They're getting bigger and I'm getting smaller and older."

We decided right there that this trip wasn't just about killing an elk, it would be more about all the memories we would cherish. Like I said before, an elk is a bonus.

The day before the season opened, Bob saw seven legal bulls in his meadow – wow. Noris went to look around Porcupine's while Marly and I checked out the Hog Pen area. There was plenty of sign everywhere.

On opening morning, Bob's elk had vanished. Noris didn't see anything. Marly heard a bull bugling, but that was it. As for me, apparently you can't outgrow dumbness. Yes, I went back up Chuckie's Mountain. The wind was in my face as a bull bugled quite a ways in front of me. I slowly worked my way towards him. The bugles were getting louder. I was gaining ground.

After two hours, I finally got a glimpse of him. He was a nice 6x5 walking in the trees ahead of me about 150 yards. I didn't have a shot yet. He went over the top of my mountain, and I lost sight of him. I didn't want to push him too hard, even though I don't think he knew I was behind him. Almost ½ hour later, there was a single shot down the other side of me. It ended up two guys from New York had shot a bull up there that morning. I don't know if it was the same one, but you guys are welcome.

Noris continued to hunt Porcupine's the whole trip. Marly never gave up on Hog Pen. I went with Bob for a few days up to his meadow. We talked and talked about all the great times we had albeit some were a little crazy. We wondered where all the years had gone.

We were a little rusty at hatchet throwing, but we played a lot of cards when the weather was this nice. We played a game called Thirty-One or Screw Your Neighbor. You started with three quarters each that you had laying by you. We didn't take any change up with us so the guys used M&Ms or candy bars or whatever they could find. I picked up three bigger pieces of tree bark and used those. Whenever you would lose a hand, you had to get rid of one each time. I lost a round and threw one bark piece over my shoulder.

Chip and Dale were always running around camp eating every crumb that dropped. They were sure chattering today in this nice weather. I lost another hand, grabbed another piece of bark, and flung it over my shoulder. Bob looked at me and said, "You killed Chip."

Noris just said, "Chaz, what did you do?"

It didn't make any sense to me until I turned around and saw poor Chip lying there on his back. I rushed over and picked up the little guy and set him on the table. I couldn't believe that little piece of bark nailed him right in the head.

I felt terrible. It didn't help matters any with the guys treating me like I was Al Capone.

All of a sudden, Chip spun around, looked right at me, and leaped off the table. I think I saw him raise his middle toe at me as he ran over to Dale. Boy, the story he must have told her.

Bob had one stipulation for me when he decided to come on this last trip. He didn't want me to make so many gourmet meals.

"You didn't like them?" I asked.

"Of course, I did!" he replied. "But it gets too late and it's too much work for you."

So, this year, all we had was meatloaf with mashed taters and gravy, pheasant strips and fries, biscuits and mac 'n' cheese, burgers and hot dogs, and homemade soup. Bon Appetit.

On day four, Bob and I spent a lot of time in his meadow. When we left for camp that evening, he turned around and said, "I'm not coming up here tomorrow – this is it." Then he looked over the meadow and said, "Thanks for all the memories."

I felt a lump in my throat and sick to my stomach. We had an emotional friendship and still have that to this day.

The last morning, I decided to go with Marly to Hog Pen. He didn't want to go too early in case they were out so we could see them. We were walking quickly on the trail. We were still a few hundred yards from where we went up to Hog Pen and out stepped a beautiful bull at 100 yards. He was standing above us on the ridge. There was nothing around us by the trail to rest your gun on and Marly would move his gun around while shooting if he didn't have a good rest.

We had just come around some evergreens and the bull hadn't seen us. I quickly got down on all fours and told Marly to shoot over my back. He knelt down and I could feel his elbow resting on my back. I took a deep breath and said OK. I swear, thirty seconds went by. I couldn't hold my breath any longer. I whispered, "Wait, wait." I took another deep breath and gave him the okay to shoot.

Come on, Marly, I'm going to pass out. I guess he was having a hard time getting him in the scope at that angle. Finally, he fired.

I got up to congratulate him and the bull just stood there looking at us. I went down again. "Shoot him, Marly!" He fired again.

The bull ran straight towards us. Marly fired his last shot at him, but he still kept coming.

Marly said, "You take him!" I fired at about 50 yards and down he went.

Marly said, "Nice shot. He's your bull."

"No way, Marly, you had to have hit him," I said.

Bob was right behind us. He was going to check a lower meadow near Hog Pen that morning. He heard the shots and came over right away.

Marly was very disgusted with himself. Bob and I walked towards the bull. Marly said, "I'm going up to the top of the ridge to see if there's any blood there."

As he headed up, I whispered to Bob, "If there's no bullet hole on his left side, make one there with your knife. That bull is Marly's."

When we got to the bull, Marly hollered down, "There's blood up here!" He came back down, and we both shook his hand.

"Nice bull, Marly," we said in concert.

We were happy for him and, needless to say, he was overjoyed. It was a beautiful heavy 5x5 trophy that he eventually had mounted.

We were able to quarter and hang him right there by the trail. Doesn't get any easier than this. None of the guys really drank, but we all enjoyed a couple of Hemingways that evening.

We had leftovers for supper and started packing things up. Another adventure was over. It never hit me until the morning when we took camp down that Bob and Noris would never be up here again. It was almost like losing a friend to me. Just a sick feeling all the way down the trail. It sure helped seeing Marly's bull up on Carmelita.

Two of my favorite pictures over the years were Marly and Noris sitting by the open fire and Bob riding behind the string of pack horses on the way down. This was a great, yet sad ending to this chapter for me.

Next Year ⟶

Bob's Return – 1999

Chapter 27

Five Amigos

We rarely had more than four guys in camp; this year was an exception. I had asked Randy, Dean, and Linus if any of them could go with us. Marly was already a go. Turns out, each of them could go so, rather than pick and choose, we decided to make room for five guys. Linus ended up flying down while the others rode with me. Linus met up with us at the motel in Colorado.

Since all most of us had been here with me before, we all knew what to do when we got to JC's. I could see JC counting the dollars with all the pack horses he would need for five of us. Just kidding. There weren't nearly as many vehicles in the parking area this time. We were hopeful again.

When we arrived at Graybeard Camp, I noticed a bear had been here – fairly recently too. That had never happened before. Some idiots were camping in here earlier though. They left garbage here and the bear scattered it everywhere. A couple of the guys picked the garbage up while the rest of us set up camp. We hung the camp flag up and toasted Bob.

It was crowded in the tent with five of us, but Randy said he'd sleep by the door so he could reach the wood stove. When he would get a chill during the night, he would just reach over and put in another log with my permission, of course. During the day, we just put his cot outside. All in all, we were pretty comfortable.

Since Randy had seen so many cows the first time he was here, he sent in for a cow permit. He was the only one with a cow tag. Everyone was familiar with most of the area so they each picked the spots they were going to hunt for opening morning. Of course, now that I had seniority, I went to Boob's and Marly went to Hog Pen. Dean went up Old Dad's and Randy and Linus went up around TD's Mountain.

Other than the hunters that rode or walked up from down below for the day, the only others we ran into were two guys past TD's that were hunting Lost Meadow. They told us there were four guys from California up towards the lake also. None of us interfered with the others during the season. That's the way it should work. You were bound to bump into someone in the woods at times. When that happened to me, I would just ask them how they're doing and tell them to have a good hunt. Then I would be on my way.

This was a strange year. There was good sign everywhere. The bulls were still challenging each other with their bugles. Things were looking optimistic. Linus and Randy had seen a couple of spikes, but no cows. Marly had a small herd come out, but all were cows and spikes. I had a few cows, calves, and two spikes visit me also. I personally think that the 4-point or better was working. There were a lot of spikes around. That's great for the future.

Everyone was hunting hard, but Lady Luck just wasn't on our side yet. Ost of us were seeing cows except for poor Randy. Marly had him go to Hog Pen with him to get his cow. We could hang it right by the trail again. Piece of cake. After trying that a couple of times and only seeing two spikes, Randy went back with Linus.

The season always opened on Saturday. It was already Monday, and we had no elk. I would've bet money we'd have a couple by now, especially with fewer hunters around. Strangely, I wasn't seeing any elk in Boob's thought. Very unusual. I was in my blind Monday morning, just looking around and daydreaming about all the elk I had seen up there in the past when a legal bull stepped out at 150 yards. I looked him over and decided he was pretty nice.

I told him, "Sorry pal," and fired. He was down. He was a very nice 6x5½. *Bob's luck is with me.*

I knew the guys wouldn't be able to come up and help me, so I processed him myself. I had him ready to pack down. I carried the head back to camp that morning though. Later, a few of us went up and packed the quarters down. The rest of the guys hadn't seen anything. There was shooting around us though. Turns out the two guys hunting Lost Meadow each got small bulls.

Each morning for the rest of the hunt, I would get up early and make the boys hot chocolate and coffee and then crawl back into my bunk. They would be moaning about how early it was. I would constantly remind them, "There ain't no damn elk in this tent." It was so nice to have the pressure off and sleep in until 6 am. I told them I'd listen for the shooting.

Since Marly was second in command, he went up to Boob's. Dean headed up to Porcupine's. That was also a pretty long meadow. When he got there, he saw a legal bull and some cows all the way on the other end of the meadow. By the time he had gotten to where he could get a crack at him, they had gone into the timber.

Randy went to Hog Pen to get a cow, and Linus went back up TD's where he had seen some elk a few days before. I was getting things ready for breakfast for the guys when they got in and heard a shot ring out. It was hard to tell from camp which way the shot came from, but it sounded like Boob's. As the guys trickled in, each wondering who shot, here came Marly with his head down. He missed a bull and killed a tree.

We all lined up. "Bend over, Marly. Let the ass-kicking begin," I said.

Randy didn't see any cows again, but this time Linus did. Randy was going from place to place, but Lady Luck wasn't on his side either. With only a couple days to go, we were hoping someone would get another one.

The next day, I reminded the guys again, "There ain't no damn elk in this tent."

Marly went back to Hog Pen, disappointed with himself. Dean went after the bull in Porcupine's again and Randy went back up with Linus.

From camp, I noticed a smaller airplane flying beyond TD's Mountain. *What the hell are they looking for? Elk? That's not legal.*

Around 9 am, another shot rang out. This time it sounded like Hog Pen. I decided to walk down there. Marly was happy as could be. He had shot a younger bull finally. I helped him quarter it out and hang it near the trail again. This was starting to be a habit. "Way too easy this way, Marly," I said.

When the rest of the guys got back to camp, Linus told me that he and Randy had two legal bulls coming towards them in the timber. Linus was ready and said as soon as they stepped out, he was going to take one. Just as they were getting close to the clearing, the airplane I had seen flew right over them. He was flying very low. Naturally the elk ran back into the dark timber. We found out later that one of the California guys had gotten lost and the plane was looking for him. No Lady Luck again.

Dean had only seen some cows. Poor Randy. I couldn't believe he hadn't gotten a cow yet.

The last day, Dean and Linus went to their usual spots. I told Randy it would be so easy to pack out if you would just shoot a cow in Hog Pen. He decided to spend the last day there. Dean and Linus had just seen a couple of cows and a spike that last day. When Randy came into camp, he was as white as a ghost. He could hardly talk.

"Did you see any?" I asked.

All he said was, "Holy shit, you wouldn't believe it." A huge 6x6 bull had walked by him at 80 yards. They can party hunt in Minnesota where Randy lived, but not here in Colorado. He kept saying, "Linus, you should've been with me." Lady Luck just wasn't showing up this year. At least we had some delicious elk meat to share.

We were fortunate that Randy's mom sent some of her famous BBQ beef for us. Also on the menu was sirloin beef strips with rice, Rocky Mountain Boil, stuffed pheasant breasts (sorry, Bob), walleye in dill sauce, and my wife's delicious bean and burger hotdish.

Dad was sure happy I got another bull. Another enjoyable hunt.

Next Year ⟶

249

Cooking - 2000

Chapter 28

A New Guy Again

I left my place around 6:30 am for Bismarck. I only made it ten miles when the frame cracked on my little trailer. I had to wait for help to get it back to Harwood. I was able to get my mechanic to temporarily weld it up for me so I could get going. This year, a buddy of ours, Sam, from Bismarck was coming with us. Marly and I strung him along for a few weeks though.

Marly told him, "Chaz isn't sure about taking you."

When I talked to him, I said, "Marly says he hasn't hunted with you and didn't know if it would be the right thing to do."

Of course, we were both joking.

We all met in Bismarck earlier that summer. When I finally told him that if he promised that he'd never tell anyone where we're going, then I suppose you can come with, he jumped up and gave me a big hug. I never took anyone up there that was as grateful and appreciative as Sam. A lifetime friendship had just begun.

I was late picking the guys up because of the trailer hitch, but we still made it to Lusk for the evening. The US was bombing the shit out of Iraq at the time. I taped signs on my tailer letting the Iraqis know what I thought about them. After leaving Lusk, we made a regular stop at the

Wyoming State Park to look at the huge bull elk they had there.

Our next regular stop for many years to come was at Sheri's restaurant in Laramie, Wyoming. Over the years, we ended up with the same waitress, "Sandi." She was a great lady with a hilarious sense of humor. She would eventually ask us, "Would you like your same table, Chaz?" this happened every year except one when her shift had ended an hour before we got there, but they still gave us the same table. It made us feel special to be greeted like this. One year, she was so proud to be named Employee of the Year. Sam took a picture of her and me with her plaque on the wall.

Off we went to our motel in Colorado. We packed the panniers and picked up any last-minute supplies that we needed. That evening at the restaurant, Marly told Sam to enjoy his last "good" meal. My, how things just keep carrying on.

When we arrived at JC's, the trailer had broken in a different spot. He said he'd have it fixed by the time we came out. JC liked Sam right off the bat. Sam didn't drink, but it seemed like he was drunk on energy constantly. There were several inches of snow on the ground when we walked up. I put a small American flag on each of our backpacks. We told Sam all about the difficult areas as we walked up. He didn't even notice Heart Attack, but then again, we were going down it, not up. I think he kinda like "Hey, It's Good to Be Back Home Again." by John Denver and yours truly.

I noticed I was taking two steps forward and 1 step back on the muddy trail going up. My boots were full of mud when we got there.

Marly looked down at my boots and said, "You're wearing my boots." No wonder I was sliding – they were a size bigger than mine.

Sam was a busybody in camp. What's next or what do you want me to do now is all he kept saying over and over. He cut and chopped wood like a beaver. He was as thrilled as I was when I first came up here. Same thought the camp flag was something special. He helped me put up a large American Flag by the entrance to our camp. This is a tradition we started, and I still do to this day. As people eventually started talking about Graybeard Camp, they would also say "There's an American Flag right by their camp."

The same two guys stopped by that hunted in Lost Meadow last year – Vic and Brian. They seemed like good guys. They camped in the Missouri Camp this year, so we were kind of neighbors. By Friday night, before the season opener, we had 8-10" of snow on the ground and it was very cold. I told Sam to make sure he had a warm sleeping bag. Just like I had done, he borrowed one from a friend. It was a K Mart special. He got so cold he slept with most of his clothes on and we even covered him up with our pannier tarps. I thought I heard his teeth chattering a few times during the night.

Cold outside, warm inside – here came the mice again. Sam found out pretty quickly what I thought of those damn killer mice. Sam brought up some chicken that his Mama had made, so we had that for supper along with some snacks. It was a long day and walking up with snow on the trail had made it extra tough.

When the season started, Marly went up with me for a couple of days. Surprisingly, there wasn't much sign up there. Some elk had been in the meadow during the night. We could see where they pawed through for grass. Marly showed Sam where to sit in Hog Pen. I couldn't believe Marly gave up his spot, but he wanted to be nice to the new guy. Sam was excited that he had seen some cows come out by him on opening day. At least he saw some.

On Monday, Marly started to hunt more towards Porcupine's. Sam was still at Hog Pen. I couldn't pass up Boob's because there were always elk in that area.

On Monday evening, we all headed out in the very cold weather. It was much better sitting in our blinds. I heard four of the fastest shots I'd ever heard in my life. They were echoing so loud with the snow-covered ground that it was hard to tell where they came from. The last two sounded like the Hog Pen area. There must have been two guys shooting, I thought. You could see pretty well in the dark with the snow on the ground, so going back to camp wasn't bad besides being very slippery.

Marly was the only one back at camp when I got there. He said he had heard the shooting but couldn't tell which direction it came from. After about twenty minutes, we decided we had better go look for Sam.

"He's probably lost," I said.

We saw his headlamp shining up on the sidehill in Hog Pen. At least we hoped it was his. We called out for him, and he answered back. I'll be damned if he didn't get a little 4x3. He was jumping all around with excitement, then he gave me a big ole hug. It was then that we noticed he hadn't even started dressing it out yet. He said he was so excited he never even thought about it. Needless to say, supper was late that night. Since neither of those two drank, I had the Hemingways and they had a shot of Tang.

We had a portable toilet that we made. I put it down below the tent about 50 yards away. As you know, I don't care for the dark and there were bears around here last year, so I would talk to the guys as I walked toward the toilet. I quieted my voice as I was walking. Then in a faint whisper, I would say, "I'm way down here." They discovered out the next day that I wasn't thirty feet from the tent, for obvious reasons. *Oops*. I thought I had buried it good enough in the snow.

We picked up a new wood stove this year. It had side shelves for setting pots and pans on. It was much easier to put wood into and it didn't smoke nearly as much as the old one did. I had it broken in by now after a few days of hot coals. That evening, the guys were in their bunks and I decided to put a couple more logs on for the night. As I opened the door on the stove, Marly looked over and hollered at me to come here.

I started to close the door, but Marly said, "No, leave it open and get over here." Sam sat up with all the commotion going on. Marly said, "Look at the inside of the stove door." I'll be damned if there wasn't a charcoaled outline of my face, beard and all.

"That's pretty eerie," I said.

Sam said, "It's bad enough that I have to look at you and now when I put wood in the stove, I have to see you again."

I like this guy.

It was too cold to fish, but the Lord knows we had plenty to eat. Along with the chili that his Marie made, I made oofda tacos, BBQ ribs with corn on the cob, ribeye steak with garlic taters, and Pigs in a blanket. Sam was like Dave – speechless.

The weather was getting worse. Sam was the only one to get an elk this year. We packed up earlier than usual to make sure we had everything ready for JC. We met him halfway down the trail and told him everything was ready for him. We said goodbye to Rich as we passed his camp. JC had the trailer repaired for me. We said our goodbyes and started the long trip home.

We honored our tradition to stop and buy the wives something on the way home.

Next Year ⟶

Sam & Marly - 2001

Chapter 29

Tom's Return

Tom had finished his second or third degree in college and we were honored to have him back in camp. All that "learnin'" I shared with him paid off. Now he was my hero and I certainly looked up to him in more ways than one, not least of which was the fact that he towered over me at 6'3". He drove to my house and rode with me.

Sam thanked Marly and me a thousand times for taking him last year. He kept saying, "If there's an opening, I'd love to go again."

I told him I'd have to see. There were many other guys that want to go also. He didn't know it until late summer, but we had already decided he would be our third regular hunting partner for as long as he wanted. When we told him this, his eyeballs lit up and here came the hugs again. There were a lot of guys who begged to go with me. Nothing personal, but this place was something special to me, and I wouldn't take just anyone.

I started another tradition that folks appreciated from North Dakota to Colorado. I took several bags of Red River Valley "badadas" to give away. The first bag was for my folks, then a bag for the motel in Lusk, Wyoming, one for the motel in Colorado, two bags for JC, and a couple of bags for hunters we met over the years that camped down below.

After dropping off the badadas at my folks', we picked up Marly and Sam and headed southwest. We spent that night in Lusk again and the motel owners sure appreciated the badadas. We hit some road construction going by the Wildlife Park. There was a monster 7x7 ½ bull in there this year. Only in our dreams, we thought.

We stopped in Laramie and had breakfast at Sheri's.

"Same table, Chaz?"

"Thank you, Sandi."

We reached our last motel in Colorado early that afternoon and proceeded to pack our things up. It seemed like we had more stuff again. JC was be pissed, in a sarcastic way.

JC always wore a well-used cowboy hat that was given to him when he won the National Bronc Riding Championship in 1984.

I asked him for several years, "When you die, can I get that hat?" It always got a smile from him and his wife, Margo.

After helping JC with the packs, we started to head up. When we reached our camp, it looked like no one had been in there this year. No garbage around for a change. The same routine, guys. They gathered and cut wood while I *oreknized* things. We were all set by 2:00 on Thursday. We hung the camp flag up and toasted Bob.

We were sitting around camp towards sundown when bugling started all around us. That echoing Shrill never gets old. We decided to walk out to the trail to get a better view and try and hear which way the bugling was coming from. We were only halfway towards the trail when two 5x5 bulls and several cows walked right past our American flagpole.

Damn, we were excited. They didn't act like they had seen us, so we stayed in camp, not wanting to run them off. There was even a bull bugling down by the shitter.

We sat in the tent and talked quite a bit that night. At least I did. It was so nice to have Tom back. Marly told him all about my face on the inside of the wood stove.

Tom said, "Yeah, the Chaz leaves an impression on a lot of things. He sure brainwashed me when I was young."

The day before opener, we went out scouting. We didn't see very many other hunters around so far. Tom and I walked up to Boob's. It was a sad sight. A huge fire had burned almost everything all around the meadow. All those years looking at a beautiful forest — gone just like that. The meadow wasn't burned out though, and there was some elk sign.

On Saturday morning, Tom and I went back up to Boob's. We sat together in my blind. Tom was using his dad's 7mm. I was with Bob when he shot his first bull and Tom wanted me to be with him if he got a chance. Well, over 50 elk came out of that burnt timber shortly after sunup. One was a nice 6x5.

"Take your time, Tom, he's about 200 yards."

He dropped him.

I can't tell you how happy we both were. Two generations, same rifle, and I had the privilege of being there for both first time rifle kills. It meant a lot to both of us. The guys had heard us shoot and came up to help us. I told them next year, I'm going to bring up some walkie-talkies, which would help if they'd work up here.

Marly and Sam were in Hog Pen and also saw around 50 head of elk but couldn't get a shot. That evening, Tom went with me. Many more elk walked into the meadow within 100 yards of us. I passed on 5 legal bulls. I was just looking for something a little bigger. The other boys had only seen cows that evening.

We had our Hemingways that night to celebrate Tom's first bull. We laid in our bags happily listening to the radio when a news flash was broadcasted. A cowboy in Wyoming, about 150 miles from us, had gotten into an argument with three hunters in a local bar. Unbeknownst to the hunters, the cowboy followed them that night. He walked into their camp in the dark, opened up their tent door, and shot all of them. The only reason they caught him was because he had rolled his pickup later in a crash and the weapon was there in his truck. Needless to say, we didn't get much sleep that night.

Sunday morning was uneventful. Tom tagged along again for the evening hunt. We had just entered into Boob's – still 200 yards from my blind. We were talking softly and just kind of daydreaming, I guess, when a hell of a nice bull jumped and ran down a draw to my left. I knew I only had seconds to shoot, and he was a shooter. I knelt down to rest on my knee. I was too low to see him, so I stood back up. I never could shoot off hand, but I had no choice. He was just going along a small dirt hillside no more than 150 yards away when I fired.

I saw the dirt fly, but I just couldn't believe that I might have missed him. Talk about getting caught with your pants down. We went over to the spot where the dirt flew up.

I said, "The bullet must have gone right through him. There's no way I missed."

We followed his tracks for two hours until dark. Colorblind or not, there was no blood, and his tracks were far apart. He was running. Reality set in – I had missed.

We were both silent on the way back to camp until Tom said, "That's the first time I've seen you miss."

There goes my so-called hero status with Tom.

Then he said, "You're still my hero."

The next day, we looked at the dirt hillside a little more. I definitely shot over him. While we were in the woods following the bull, a couple of shots rang out over by Hog Pen. It was very dark as we got to camp and the guys weren't back yet, so we figured it must have been them shooting. I was preparing supper when they walked in. They had blood on them. Sam shot a little 5x4.

They gutted him out so I told them after the morning hunt I'd come help them quarter and hang him right there. More Hemingways. *Yeah.*

Then Tom told them what happened to me. They just said, "Bend over."

The next day when I saw Sam's little antlers, I said, "You shot a milker."

"A what?" he said.

I said, "That little guy was still feeding on his mother."

He smiled and said, "He's legal and he's bigger than yours this hunt."

We had physically gone through a lot the last couple of days, and we were worn out. Now Marly had been known to collapse the tent sides in when he snored. That boy made some noise. He watched me whittle a four-inch stick that afternoon and all he said was, "Chaz" in a don't-you-dare tone of voice.

Sam was already sleeping. I turned the light out and I assumed Tom was sleeping too. It was pretty obvious Marly was – wow, the sounds he made. I should have brought ear plugs.

The moonlight lit up the tent pretty well that night. Since I put all that work into making my smacking stick, I decided to give it a try. The snoring-relief weapon was laying by my side. I made sure that it was short enough so I wouldn't hit Marly in the head. Right in the middle of a thunderous snore, I nailed him right in the ass without even looking. Bullseye. He instantly sat straight up on his bunk and bellowed some kind of gibberish. You could see him plain as could be in the moonlight. He never did wake up.

I held my mouth so tight so he wouldn't hear me laughing and then he just laid back down and continued snoring. Then I heard Tom silently laughing. I said, "Did you see that?"

"Yeah," he said, "he never knew what hit him."

We laughed for an hour without disturbing him. We didn't tell him about it for a couple of days. He had no idea.

I was very disappointed with myself for messing up on a nice bull, but I had my chance. I passed on four more legal bulls before the hunt was over.

Marly hunted Hog Pen every day. The last night, he screwed up and missed a 5x5. *You shouldn't have told us, Marly. Bend over.*

It was very nice packing out. We said out goodbyes to JC and Margo and headed out. JC handed me his hat, and I wear it proudly to this day.

We started staying in Deadland, South Dakota on the way home for the next few years to help shorten the trip.

There was a good restaurant in our motel that served the best Rocky Mountain Oysters. Tom and I each ordered a plate of those while Marly and Sam sat there with a yucky look on their faces. Tom and myself had a few toddies before our meal.

When our supper arrived, Tom's plate was full of huge Rocky Mountain Oysters, while mine were much smaller. I certainly didn't mean for it to come out the way it did, but I blurted out to our waitress, "How come his nuts are bigger than mine?"

The poor young gal left awfully quickly with a red face.

I couldn't help but think what Bob would've said: "Dumb Ass."

Another great season.

Next Year ⟶

Tom "Speckmouse" 1990

Chapter 30

Our First Second-Season Hunt

Colorado started a draw system for the first season of elk. We didn't get drawn, what a bummer. We were worried about someone being in our camp for the second season, which was a week later. My buddy Dean wanted to put in for a cow permit so he asked me if he, his son, and a friend could hunt out of Graybeard Camp for the first season for cows. It worked out great.

JC had let his permit go for the wilderness area, so we rented 3 horses from a rancher nearby. Dean and I split the cost on the horses. Dean took my tent, stove, and poles up with him and his guys. We were able to buy over the counter licenses for the second season, but we were worried about the weather that late in the year.

I picked up Marly and Sam in Bismarck and we were off. It was in the upper 50s when we left. Soon after, my wife called me and said I had left my bag of candy bars at home.

We arrived at the Lusk Motel around 5:30 pm. Marly wasn't feeling well, so he didn't go eat with us. We stopped by the Park again on our way to Laramie. Just one 6x6 there this year. We had breakfast at Sheri's and talked with Sandi quite a bit. When we left the restaurant, we walked to Kmart to get my candy bars, etc. I had left my glasses on the table in the restaurant and Sandi wrote me a note and taped my specs on the window of my truck. *Thanks, Sandi.*

We spent that evening at the Colorado motel and put our personal things in order. Since Dean already had the heavy main items in camp for us, all we needed was a couple of horses for our bags and groceries. When we arrived at Dean's truck, he had the two horses there. This was the last day of their cow hunt. We packed the horses and headed up. It was still very nice out. There were a lot more vehicles parked in the area so there were probably going to be many more hunters for this second season.

When we got to Graybeard Camp, Dean had decided to pack up that day and head down. He took the horses with him. They only got one cow, which surprised me. His son had a memorable time though.

As we were getting ready to unpack our horses, a group of hunters stopped at the end of our camp trail. One guy rode in and said to me, "We'll just wait here until you guys are gone."

I told him we were just arriving.

He said, "Well, I saw those guys packing up to leave and we always camp here each year."

I replied, "You do? Which season?"

"The first season," he said.

That pissed me off. *Lying piece of shit.* All I said was, "That's strange because I started this camp with my buddy, Bob. I've been here since our first season going on thirty years now, and I don't remember you."

It was a good thing Dean was there for the first season, or our camp would have been taken.

As we were debating each other, another guy came walking into the camp rather briskly. "Are you Charlie?" he asked.

"Yes, do I know you?"

He was a relative of the initial oath breaker. Now we're up to eleven guys that were told about this place. It spread like cancer. None of the guys had been there before. None of them had walked hundreds of miles throughout this area over the years. They were just told to hunt here and over there without putting in any effort. Like I said before, this is public land and that's the chance a guy has to take. You just never know when you're going to be invaded.

I never understood the ethics of going home and telling everyone you could about a cherished area just for spite.

They told us they were going to camp up by the lake. *Yeah, right.* Two other guys were in the Missouri Camp and there were three guys in Pat's Camp who came and talked to us. They had heard about the camp with the American flag. They said they'd stay out of our way and asked if I could point out some areas for them to hunt.

"There are only three of us too," I said, "and we can't be everywhere."

I showed them some of our other favorite areas and they were grateful. We stayed out of each other's way, and they even had some success. It was that other crew I was worried about. We put the camp flag up and were ready for the hunt.

On opening morning, Sam went to Porcupine's and Marly went to Hot Pen. No elk, just a few hunters passing by. I was in Boob's and had ten cows and four legal bulls within 200 yards of me. One nice 5x5, one smaller 5x5, a younger 4x5, and a very nice 6x5. I was looking for something a little bigger and this was only the first day, so I let them pass. *Not sure the guys would believe this.* I told them I almost shot the 6x5. Had it been towards the end of our hunt, I wouldn't have been so picky.

That evening, we all went back to our same places. Those two didn't see any elk again. As I was sitting in my blind, I couldn't help but think of all the great times in this meadow. Nothing could beat the sight of the sun popping up over Ray Bun Mountain and hitting the tips of evergreens. The evening sunset over TD's Mountain was also an awesome sight. The burnt-out areas on the side of the mountains around me took away everything except the memories I had of that beautiful dark timber. There wouldn't be any new growth for many years to come.

When I drifted back to the present, I saw him — a bull stepping out at 250 yards. He was coming towards me. Behind him came five more legal bulls and some cows. I was sure four of the bulls were the same as the earlier ones. I watched him for a minute or so. He showed me every profile of his 6x6 antlers. He was no monster, but I couldn't pass him up. *Sorry pal.* I fired. One shot and he was expired. All the other elk left in confusion. They didn't know where the shot had come from.

I shot him at 6:10 pm, gutted him out, and partially skinned him to cool him down. The evenings got down into the teens even though it was warm during the day. I got back to camp at 7:30 and made the boys supper. They were surprised that I even shot. I think now they believed me about the four bulls I passed up that morning and the five others with the one I shot. They hadn't seen anything that afternoon. I had my Hemingway and we called it a night.

I told the boys they could hunt up in Boob's if they wanted. Marly didn't want to give up on Hog Pen, so Sam went up there for a few days. We tried my cheap walkie-talkies out, but they wouldn't work, so we still had no communication. Sam saw a spike and a few cows a couple of times, but nothing legal. Marly wasn't seeing anything.

There was plenty of bear sign around and we talked about it one afternoon. There were also two martens hanging around camp again. That night, with the lights out, I thought I heard a pan hit the cookstove outside the tent. I had hung all the fry pans on the side of the portable stove. I didn't say anything because I thought the guys were sleeping. Then they started banging together for a second time.

I woke the guys up and said, "Those martens are by the stove."

There was silence then an outburst of pans banging every which way.

"That's a bear," Sam said.

I jumped up to go smack that beast, right behind Marly as he went to check the *sitcheation* out.

He knelt down and opened the zipper slowly. As he peeked out in the dark, he let out a blood-curdling scream, "Get outta here!"

I jumped back 6 feet – it scared the shit out of me.

He said, "I think it's gone." Another sleepless night.

Neither of them saw anything the next morning. When they came back in, I was making them breakfast. They were both in the tent taking off some of their warm clothing when all of a sudden, my pans on the side of the stove started banging against each other again. *What the hell?* I looked in the tent. They were both laughing their asses off. Sam was laying on his cot pulling a rope he had tied to the pans.

"I lost a pair of shorts over that," I said. I leaped on top of Sam and gave him my version of a bear attack. "Dumb Ass," I said. *Damn pranksters.*

We had lots of food to eat and the menu kind of went back to gourmet – *Sorry, Bob.* We started with Sam's chili as always, then Rocky Mountain Stew with noodles, grilled salmon on wild rice with asparagus, ribeye with garlic taters, burgers, fries, and creamed corn, walleye cheeks for an appetizer with pan fried walleye and Bush's baked beans. Finally, on the last day, we enjoyed a bevy of leftovers. Mmm good.

The second season ran for twelve days instead of five like the first season. We decided we were only going to hunt for the same number of days as before and, besides that, I had made arrangements with a friend of JC's to come pack us down on a certain day.

JC and Margo would ride up once in a while and have lunch with us. I cooked them salmon, O'Brien badadas, brownies with whipped cream topped with hot apples and berries. They couldn't believe the menu. I loved having their company.

Sam went with Marly to Hog Pen towards the end of our hunt. Sam sat over the hill from Marly so they couldn't see each other. I heard the shot from camp. I'll be damned if Sam didn't shoot another milker. A baby 5x4, with antlers no bigger than a small mule deer. Sam sarcastically said, "I only shot him because I could see he was legal."

All I said was, "What power scope do you have to have to see those little antlers?"

JC rode up with his buddy and helped us pack down. Another goodbye and we were off to Deadwood. We stayed in the same motel. No bull nuts this year. I was still embarrassed over last years' ordeal. We bought the wives gifts and headed for home. Unbelievably, the weather was nice the entire trip.

Another memorable, terrific hunt.

Next Year

Chapter 31

Back to the First Season

We drew tags for the first season this year. Linus was going with me this year, also. He had business to take care of so he flew down later. I picked up Marly and Sam and we were off to Lusk. Without any construction, we arrived at our destination within minutes of the year before.

We had our annual supper in Lusk and then headed for Sheri's Restaurant the next morning. Sandi was on break, so we had the young gal go tell her that three bums were out there. She knew right away that it was us and came out to say hi.

We got to the motel in Colorado and packed the panniers. Linus met up with us there. JC's friend Phil had gotten some help and said he'd pack us in. Marly and Sam headed for camp while Linus and I waited for Phil. We helped him pack the horses, then we headed up. We had camp all set up with no hunters around yet. At 3:00 that afternoon, 6 guys came by and camped right around the corner from us. There were two others camped right in Porcupine's. We had shot several elk there and now they're camping in the meadow. The guys were disgusted, but I told them we knew the area and we'd just keep hunting the way we always have.

On opening morning, Sam went up with me. We walked right past the 6 guys still in their tent. Sam sat with me in Boob's but with all the hunters around, I had him go to Tom's meadow and watch there. Just as he got over the hill and out of sight, ten elk came out of nowhere and ran right past me. I looked back in the direction they had come from and here came a 5x5 bull. With all these hunters, I wasn't going to be quite as choosy.

He was 125 yards from me when I shot. He buckled but didn't go down. My clip fell out, but I didn't panic. He stopped for a split second and I fired again. This time, he dropped. Then a shot rang out from my left. It was one of the guys camped by us. He said he didn't think I had hit him, but I had hit him twice before that guy even fired.

When he came over to me, he said, "I overslept or I would've been right here."

Wonder how you knew the spot?

Sam came back and was helping me dress him out when we heard elk in Tom's. Sam quickly went back to where he just was. Now you folks don't have to believe me, but shortly after Sam was out of sight again, an entire herd of at least fifty elk came running across Boob's Meadow. I hollered for Sam. He came running and was out of breath. There were several legal bulls in the herd. I told him to get a good rest and line up his shot; they were about 300 yards away.

He fired and just like that, several shots rang out all around us. I couldn't believe it – we were surrounded by that entire camp that was beside us. I knew Sam had missed. It didn't look like those guys hit anything either. What a dangerous three-ring circus we were in.

We spent the rest of the morning packing my elk down. Marly and Linus returned and reported that they saw several spike and cows that morning. The pressure was off of me again. Now I could just cook and help pack elk down as soon as they got another one.

Everyone was seeing elk, so that evening they went back to the same areas. I told Sam that he better go up to Boob's a little earlier or there would be six guys sitting in my blind. He did, and sure enough – he shot a bull. I bought new two-way radios, and these worked for a mile or so from camp. Sam called me for help. When I got up there and found him, there was no elk.

He said it had dropped, but then went into the dead timber and disappeared. We split up. Just before dark, I had walked within 50 yards of a bull, lying in the timber, looking right at me. I slowly backed up and radioed Sam. I was sure it was his bull. Then he spooked. I watched the direction he ran and marked the sport for morning. We weren't prepared to search all night. "He'll be fine by morning," I assured Sam.

The next morning, Sam and I started the search. We had gone up and over two mountain ridges with no sign. Sam was very disgusted. Trust me, I know the feeling. After several hours, we were going to call it quits. We were working our way back to the meadow when I told Sam to go up on top of the ridge and wait there. I tried to imagine which way an elk would've gone with a lung shot. For some reason that I'll never understand, something was telling me to angle down the other side of this mountain. I can't explain it, but 300 yards later, I walked right to him.

I saw his antlers sticking up from two deadfall. I walked back up towards Sam and motioned for him to come down to me. Sam had the rifle, not me. We slowly approached him and found he was already deceased. He was in great shape and all the meat was fine. Besides that, this one wasn't a milker – it was a nice 5x4. He couldn't believe I found him. We were both very happy. Ther other two hadn't seen anything and it took most of the day to pack Sam's out with their help.

That evening, while the boys went out, I made a big supper for us. I made pecan crusted pork tenderloins with a brandy sauce, sweet "badadas," and corn on the cob. Throughout the hunt, all I cooked was Swedish meatballs with mashed taters and veggies, Swiss steak, fresh trout, and a hamburger hotdish, along with soup and salad each meal. Yes, I had my Hemingways.

I had the radio on that evening when another newsflash came across. This one was as bad as the killings in Wyoming. I don't recall which western state this happened in, but a father and son were hunting a meadow – similar to Boob's, I imagine. Apparently, they had split up and unknowingly ended up on opposite sides of the meadow. I can't imagine how this was possible, but a bull elk ran across the meadow and each of them fired at it. It's tremendously sad, but they actually shot and killed each other. I couldn't help but think about those five guys in Boob's banging away when Sam and I were in the meadow cleaning my elk. Luck is involved in every aspect of the hunting game, I believe.

Sam went with Marly a couple of times and then with Linus. They were seeing elk, just no legal bulls. The very last evening, Marly just saw one doe. "You mean a cow," I said.

"No, a muley doe."

What the heck what she doing up this high so late in the year?

Linus had a legal 5x5 come out the last evening but decided to let him go.

"I'm proud of you," I told him. That would've been an all-night job since we were packing out in the morning. Linus had brought up a satellite phone so we were able to call Phil and tell him we had two elk in camp. Obviously, we had to wait for a satellite to be near us to use the phone, but this was the way to go. I've been renting one every year since then.

Phil packed us down with 5 horses and a helper. Thanks guys! We stopped to visit JC and Margo, which is also an annual event. Of course, Margo had to see the menu. She said, "Next year, JC, you and I are riding up for lunch."

"You better," I said. "We miss your company up there."

We got Linus to the airport and headed to Deadwood. What a great year!

Next Year

Charlie Cooking - 2004

Chapter 32

Just the Two of Us

Unfortunately, we didn't make it in time for the first season. That changed things for us. One change was that Sam and I were the only ones who could go. Sam said he'd drive his older truck this time. All I said was to make sure he checked it over so we wouldn't have unexpected trouble.

No problem. Yep, uh-huh.

I left my vehicle at Sam's and transferred my things to his, including Dean's homemade large metal cooler for the elk meat. We grabbed his chili and were off to Lusk.

Sam hated chicken so he wouldn't even stop and let me get my broasted chickie. He said he didn't even want it in his truck. We checked into the Lusk Motel at 4:52, right on time. Our regular restaurant was closed, so we ate bar food and called it a night. The next morning, we were off to Sheri's Restaurant in Laramie. The park didn't have any animals in it at all this time. We stopped at Sheri's and had a wonderful breakfast at my same table. We said our hellos and goodbyes and were on to our Colorado destination.

I told Sam, "Your old truck runs good."

"Yeah," he said. "I'm going to put new tires on when we get back home."

That one got by me, temporarily.

Since it was only the two of us, we only needed two horses. I rented one horse, and Rich was going to help pack us in with Gilby. The next morning, we headed out to meet Rich and get the rented horse. We were about two miles from JC's place, driving on an extremely rough gravel road when Sam's truck started swerving a little. We got out to check. The right rear tire was going flat. We pulled the spare out and that was already very flat. Then we noticed one of the front tires was going down also.

Sam panicked. "What are we going to do?" he said.

My son and I owned a race car at this time, and I knew to start with lower tire pressure and, as the tire heats up, it will stay up. His tires didn't look like they had any cuts; they just had a slow leak. I finally answered his question.

"Sam, drive like hell as fast as you can without rolling us down the mountain side."

"Are you crazy?" he said.

"Yes, let's go."

We made it to JC's and both tires went down to the ground immediately. Lady Luck was on our side this time. Thank heaven we had a satellite phone. JC wasn't around, so we called Phil. Phil loaned us his truck – *thanks pal!* Sam dropped me and our packs off at Rich's truck. I helped Rich set up his tent while Sam went to the nearest town to get his tires fixed. When he finally got back, we spent the night with Rich. We didn't get a chance to eat much that night. It started to rain and then it poured all night.

"Your tent has some leaks, Rich," I said.

We got the rental horse the next morning and packed up to Rich's camp first and then Graybeard Camp. We got there around 3:30 pm. We usually got there in the morning so we would have time to set up.

Since it was just the two of us, I brought my 8x8 Eddie Bauer tent up instead of the big one. The tent wasn't the problem – it was the constant rain for two more days. Everything was soaked and we had very few places to dry things out. We only had a lantern and a small propane heater. We finally managed to get a plastic fly over the tent, so we could start drying things. We put the camp flag and the U.S. flag up and toasted Bob.

Friday morning, we walked back to the trail to look around. There was a group of guys in Pat's camp again. I didn't know them, but they told us later they were there because someone told them about this area. Here we go again. *Bite your tongue, Chaz.*

On opening morning, Sam saw six elk in Hog Pen. There wasn't even a milker to shoot.

I was in Boob's. Right at light, I noticed something very black just at the edge of the trees. A bear, I thought, but then this brute of the north stepped out. It was a cow – a damn Angus cow. Then two more came out. What the hell is going on? Obviously, there was a herd up here the past summer and these were strays left behind. I wondered why the meadow was grazed out so badly.

They would taste just as good as elk. Don't do it, Chaz. When I headed for camp, I tried to herd the damn things down to the trail or they would end up a meal for the bears.

The weather turned nice, so we went fishing for our supper. We caught enough for a meal that night. Our gourmet meals were hot dogs and burgers this year. We were drying everything we could. As we were sitting around camp, Sam noticed there was tape on the camp flag. I told him it had a tear in it that I had to fix first.

That evening, I was in Boob's listening to cattle mooing and shitting everywhere. That should attract a lot of elk. Then I heard a shot. I wasn't sure where the other guys were, but it sounded like Sam in Hog Pen. Sure enough, Sam radioed me that he had gotten a bull down. I told him I was tired of talking to cattle, so I went to help. We just gutted him out that night. It had bigger antlers than what Sam usually shot, but I could swear I saw some dry mother's milk on the side of his mouth.

On Sunday morning, not only did Sam sleep in, but he commented to me, "There ain't no elk in the tent."

Dumb ass.

The only thing I saw in Boob's was one of the cows, so I went back to camp after a couple of hours. I made a big breakfast and we went to quarter Sam's elk. As we were quartering his elk up, a decent bull ran by us less than 100 yards away. Of course, my rifle was in camp.

Dumb ass.

We hung his elk up by the trail and headed back. Sunday evening up in Boob's, the cattle were right beside me. They damn near shit right in my blind. I know I should never give up on Boob's meadow, but this was ridiculous. So, I decided to hunt Hog Pen for a few days. On Monday, Sam walked to Rich's camp to get a horse. Rich packed enough feed on it for a week. We only needed him for a day or so.

I hunted Hog Pen that morning while Sam went down. As I was sitting there in the peaceful blind, three of our neighbor guys walked out into the meadow from three different directions right at prime time. This just didn't make any sense to me. I stood up so they at least knew I was there, but that didn't seem to bother them at all. If their intention was to scare the elk away, they did an excellent job.

Sam got back up in the early afternoon and I helped pack his elk on our horse. It was a well-behaved horse, by the way. Sam insisted on taking the meat down that same day. I told him to ride the horse back up instead of leading him both ways. I didn't know at the time, Sam was very uncomfortable around horses. I decided I wasn't going to let those guys dictate where I hunt, so I went to Hog Pen that evening also. Nothing had come out and I could see Sam coming up the trail from down below me. He was leading the horse.

Dumb ass.

I met up with him and went back to camp. That's when he told me that he didn't care for horses.

Our neighbors had left along with the elk too, so I concentrated on Hog Pen the rest of the hunt. The only thing I saw was a guy from out east walk out of the timber into Hog Pen with his head down looking at something. I stood up again and he walked right to me. He showed me this GPS gadget I'd never heard of. It was amazing. I saw the meadow on the GPS from down by the vehicle, and I was able to walk right to it.

Damn, I hate technology, but the worst was yet to come.

We packed our camp down and left the horse with Rich. He was already packed out. JC and Margo were around so we stopped and visited with them for a while. Then we headed to Deadwood. It was another successful hunt. I should have taken that 700-pound Angus – just kidding.

Sam did put new tires on when we got home. *Dumb ass.*

Next Year ⟶

Chapter 33

Taking My Son Along

We returned to the first season again. I took my youngest son, Bobby, with me this year along with Marly and Sam. We picked them up along with some broasted chickie. I was driving again, so I stopped for the chickie. The weather was in the 50s and the roads were good so far. We got to Lusk at 4:55pm, amazingly. When we left for Laramie the next morning, it started to snow, but the roads were still okay.

I dropped potatoes off as we headed down. We ate at Sheri's again and said hi to Sandi. After packing the panniers at the motel in Colorado, we went to our favorite restaurant again and had our last "good meal."

The next morning, we talked to JC and Margo for a while and then met up with Phil and his partner. He had enough horses so we didn't have to rent any this time. We dropped off our panniers and tent and started walking up. Bobby was having the time of his life. He had hunted deer and small game at home, but nothing like this. Phil and the pack horses went by us about a quarter mile from camp. I told him to wait and we 'd help unload everything. There was some garbage in camp, so we picked it up and Phil took it down with him. With four of us up here again, we had the big tent and the two flags set up in good time. We set the stove and the cots up right away, then the boys went to get firewood.

Marly mentioned the tape on the camp flag. Sam told him it got ripped and Chaz was supposed to fix it, but apparently, he didn't. After we had some of Sam's chili, we sat around the fire. It was still pretty nice out. Marly asked me about the camp flag, so I took him over to it and showed him. I removed the tape and he smiled. I had Sam's name embroidered on there the year before, but it was such miserable weather that I spaced it out. Sam and Bobby were talking by the fire and didn't even notice. It took another two or three days before Sam saw it.

Here came the hugs again.

That night we heard a couple of bulls bugling and some coyotes yipping away. I took Bobby fishing the next day. We caught plenty of brookies for a meal. Now Marly and Sam didn't want fancy meals anymore either, so it was fast food for this trip. Well, not completely. This year's menu was soup and salad each meal, soft shell tacos, hot dogs and fries, pigs in a blanket, hotdish, BBQ ribs, and tempura-battered walleye. That's it.

We went to our respective meadows Thursday afternoon to check for sign. Bobby and I saw good sign in Boob's, but nothing came out that evening. The burnt timber was even worse this year. It went from Boob's to TD's Mountain and over to Hog Pen. It looked like a bomb had gone off – very depressing to see that beautiful forest gone. Nothing but standing dead trees everywhere. So far, no other hunters had gone by, but we had no idea how many were up by the lake.

I noticed Sam had slowed down quite a bit walking up this time. He slept a lot in camp too. That just wasn't like him. He always had trouble with his knees, but said he also wasn't feeling well.

On opening morning, Sam was able to get up to Porcupine's. That was quite a haul for someone with bad knees and not feeling well. He had seen a bull and several cows. He tried to get closer to the bull, but he just couldn't catch up to him. Marly had seen several cows in Hog Pen.

I had Bobby sit with me in Boob's. There were quite a few large areas of 5-foot-high weeds throughout the meadow. I had never seen that before. 5 minutes after the season opened, a 5x5 stepped out from Kit Kat 200 yards away. I told Bobby to get ready and get a good shot at his shoulder. He fired and the bull just spun around and ran into the taller weeds. It looked to me like he hit him, but it was hard to tell since he turned so quickly and disappeared. We just weren't sure. I told him we'd wait about an hour or so and then go look.

All of a sudden, an entire herd came into the meadow from the opposite direction. There was a nice 6x5 in the group. He came within thirty yards of us. I told Bobby, "Let's get this one for sure." Our shots were bang, bang about a millisecond apart and down he went. We walked over to him and he was definitely dead.

I said, "We'll come back to this one, but let's go check on yours."

We went to where we last saw him and we split up. I ended up finding him dead in the middle of those high weeds 75 yards from where he was standing. He was a nice 5x5. This was amazing – two bulls, ten minutes apart. We had good radios this time, so I was able to get a hold of the guys. We also brought up a couple of sleds this year to try out. There was no snow on the ground, but they still worked pretty well. We still had to lift them over all the dead logs.

We had one all quartered out when they got up there with the sleds and game bags. They took one down while me and Bobby started on the other one. Sam did not look good and I told him not to come back up. Marly brought the sleds back up, then Bobby and I pulled and packed down the second bull. What a day. Hemingways all around.

On Sunday, it turned from rain to heavy snow. Sam was still sleeping quite a bit during the day. He went up to Boob's that afternoon. Both he and Marly saw nothing over the next couple of days. I took Bobby for a walk up to Old Dad's all the way to Porcupine's. That was quality time together.

That evening, I slipped and fell and hit my head. It hurt. Sam gave me a couple of pills he said were for pain. After I took them, he laughed his ass off. He had given me sleeping pills.

Dumb ass.

I was going to kick his ass, but I fell asleep.

Marly saw a herd on top of Hog Pen and he went up and got as close as he could. There was one small, but legal bull in the herd. It still had milk on its face, he said. Sam would have shot him. Sam went up to Boob's and had a whole herd come out. It was raining, sleeting, snowing, and lightning all at the same time. He had a hard time seeing through his scope. Then he said it thundered louder than hell and the entire herd scattered back into the dead timber.

The wood was so wet, the chimney plugged up with soot and smoked us out a couple of times. A pine marten got into one game bag and helped himself to some fresh elk meat. Other than that, we had no major problems.

The next day, Marly had seen some cows again, but that was it. Sam was up in Boob's and had elk all around him, but nothing legal. He said they were bugling up higher constantly. He was having the time of his life. He finally believed me now about all the elk I told him I'd seen up there over the years.

I called down to Phil about the two elk we had. He and JC came up and packed them down on Tuesday. They said they'd be up to get us out Thursday morning.

Sam didn't go out Tuesday morning. He said it was his knees. Tuesday night, he said quite a few had made an ass out of him up in Boob's again. Bobby and I heard four shots that sounded like Marly. We waited for the call. Ended up it was someone in Lost Meadow. It was snowing and blowing the last day and the guys didn't see anything. Even the elk needed cover in this crap.

JC and Phil packed us down Thursday morning in the snow. It was a slippery walk down and up Heart Attack. We settled up with Phil and headed out. We made it as far as Laramie before we called it a night. We were beat, and Sam just wasn't Sam. The next morning, we headed for home. What a trip. Bobby had a great time.

Next Year

Bobby and Charlie - 2006

No Sam

Dean drove for this year's hunt, and we also used his utility trailer. We stopped in Bismarck and picked up Marly. Sam had some tests done since last year's hunt. It wasn't just his knees. He had a rotator cuff and his blood pressure was way out of range, so he couldn't go this time. I already missed him. He still gave us his chili though.

Then, I got some sad news: my old friend, Noris, had passed away. RIP, my friend.

It was raining when Dean and I left Harwood, but it ended up sunny all the way to Lusk. Dean's truck was sucking up the diesel fuel. We got to Lusk at 5:40 pm. A little later than usual, must have been the diesel. We spent the night and then headed for Laramie for breakfast. Sandi had our table ready. *What a gal.*

We got to the motel in Colorado around noon and the weather was in the 70s. There was a black bear sow with a black and a brown cub right behind our motel. We packed the pannier and went for our last good meal again. The next morning, we stopped to visit JC and Margo. They asked about Sam. For some reason, they liked him.

Phil and a couple of his buddies packed the three of us in. We started our walk. It was still a little warm out, even up this high. Rich wasn't in his camp yet. He must have the second season this year. It looked like no one had been in our camp over the summer or fall. For some reason, we had difficulty putting the big tent up this time. Must have been because there was no Sam. We put both flags up and toasted Bob.

We hadn't met any hunters on the way up or around camp so far. We had pretty much everything set up before dark. That evening, we had Sam's chili and snacks. Sam missed a good menu, which was burgers with garlic taters, chicken fried steak, sausage and kraut, trout and beans, ribs, and hot dogs and fries.

On Thursday morning, three guys rode by then four more a little later. Then Vic and Brian came by. They camped in the Missouri camp again. We walked out to the trail later on and sure enough the first three guys were camping in Pat's camp. Ended up they certainly weren't very friendly neighbors. Marly decided to go on a long walk from our camp to the upper lake and all the way around to the Ray Bun lake and back up to camp. At least twelve miles or so. He was tired.

There were bulls bugling on TD's Mountain and in the Hog Pen area during the night. Friday, a pine marten came by so we could take pictures. Marly stuck a marshmallow and a piece of a hot dog on two different sticks and stuck them in the ground. What a picture-taking show we got. The camp robbers were trying to get the marshmallow off while the pine marten wrestled with the hot dog. He finally figured out how to just push the stick over. He was beautiful.

Vic and Brian walked down to visit with us. Turns out, I'd be meeting them at a sports show in Denver later that year.

On opening morning, Marly headed up TD's and Dean went to Hog Pen. I headed for Boob's meadow earlier than I normally do because of the camp next door. In the dark with no flashlight, I damn near walked right into one of three guys standing on the trail halfway up to Boob's. He was the friendliest of the three. He said, "Go ahead of me, I'm having a hard time in this altitude."

As I thanked him, he said, "The other two guys are ahead of me." I wasn't too happy. By the time I got to the entrance of the meadow, there they were, walking towards my blind with flashlights blazing away.

Since I came up this far and they were in my blind, I went to Kit Kat instead. Amazingly, the elk were still bugling all around me. Right after daybreak, the two guys in my blind fired several times. I waited for a few hours, then started to head back to camp. They only had a cow permit and had shot one in the meadow.

That night, Dean wasn't feeling well – I think that he had altitude sickness. I didn't want to compete with those other two guys, so I went to Hog Pen. None of us had seen any elk that first day, but there was good sign everywhere.

By the way, when I mention "my blind" in Boob's meadow, I am referring to a clump of dead trees that I rearranged into a blind years before. I always put it back the way nature had it at the end of each hunting season.

As we had supper that night, the pine marten came right into my kitchen area to see what was cooking. I think he wanted gourmet food.

We still heard bugling during the night, along with some coyotes singing their tunes. I must have been upset about those guys being in Boob's because I was dumb enough to go up on top of Chuckie's Mountain. I hadn't been up there for years. Right when I reached the summit, it started snowing pretty good. Marly had gone the other direction this morning. Dean was going up TD's, which was south of me. I sat on top for a while and then decided to slowly walk towards Dean, which was at least a half mile away.

I had just started walking when a cow and calf popped out of nowhere 50 yards beside me. We all went in the same direction. It was so quiet with the snow on the ground that they hadn't even noticed me. I waited and let them go ahead of me for a while before I continued. I had gone quite a way on top and then I saw the body of an elk in front of me about 100 yards in the woods. The only green timber left in the area because of the previous fires was on the very top of the mountain, and I was in it.

When I stopped to look, it lifted its head. It was a smaller 6x6. He had no idea that I was watching him. I had mixed emotions about whether to shoot or not. I decided to take him.

I talked to him for a second, the fired. It was snowing heavily as I pulled the trigger. I saw him drop in his tracks. I talked to him for a second and fired. He didn't drop, he bolted to the right towards the opposite side of the mountain.

I wanted to wait for a while, but it was snowing so heavily, it was getting serious. I walked to where he was standing. I could only see a couple of drops of blood on a log. There should've been blood everywhere. I know I should've waited for a while before I continued my search, but it was getting very hard to see anything, let alone elk tracks with no blood. Even I would have seen the blood on the fresh snow.

I saw some antlers moving through the trees down the Lost Meadow side of my mountain, about 100 yards below me. I marked the spot where I saw him and worked my way to it. I didn't know if it was the bull I shot at or not. I could barely see where he was standing and there definitely was no blood. As I turned around, I couldn't even see my tracks behind me. I worked my way back to the top.

The dark clouds were hanging on top of the mountain. The snow was coming down hard. For the first time in thirty-plus years, I got turned around with my direction on my own mountain. I walked the wrong way for a half an hour before I realized it. There were no signs of my tracks anywhere. I was starting to lose light and was getting a little concerned. The guys would panic if I didn't make it back. Besides, they had no idea where I was, but then again, apparently, I didn't either. I came out of the green timber right at Hog Pen. I was so relieved.

The guys were in camp when I got back and I told them what had happened. They didn't even hear me shoot. I had a hard time cooking for the guys because I was so sick to my stomach. The next morning, I went with Marly to Hog Pen for a while, then we both went back up my mountain to search again. Marly got a glimpse of a cow and a 5x5 in Hog Pen, but no time for a shot. There was at least three feet of snow on top. It was a SOB to get through.

We got to the area where I thought I'd last seen him, but of course, everything was covered in snow. We split up but kept in radio contact. After a couple of hours of misery, we had no choice but to give up. The bull could've been long gone or he could've been near us dead under the snow. I hadn't had this terrible feeling since the bull in archery season. This was the first bull I had lost during rifle season in over twenty-five years.

We didn't realize the guys beside us left sometime on Monday. Tuesday morning, Dean went with me back up to Boob's. I didn't feel like even carrying my gun, but realized how stupid that would be. There was a bull bugling in Kit Kat. He never did come out into the meadow. Normally with all this snow on the ground, I would've tried to get to him, but after my charade the day before, I didn't think I deserved another bull anyway.

I headed back to camp as it started to snow again. You couldn't even see across the meadow anymore. Dean decided to stay there an extra hour or so. Marly hadn't seen anything. This snow is going to force the elk down eventually. That afternoon, all I saw was a lonely coyote, but the bulls were still singing once in a while.

On the last morning, Dean and I went back to Boob's and Marly hunted in the middle of Hog Pen. He didn't see or hear anything. About an hour after daylight, Dean and I got caught in a real North Dakota blizzard. Boob's meadow is higher up than Hog Pen and, of course, our campsite. The elevation, even though only a mile apart, made such a difference in the weather. We couldn't see ten yards so we headed back to camp. Dean and Marly went towards Hog Pen the last evening and I had to go up and say goodbye to Boob's meadow.

There were elk tracks everywhere on my way up. They were all heading down. It was very cold sitting in the blind and all I could think about what went wrong with the bull I shot at. I left a half hour early that evening.

A herd of elk went right behind our tent 50 yards away while we were all out. Marly said a large herd ran in the middle, but they were doing about 50 mph.

We packed out the next morning. This was a memorable, but sad trip this time. Part of life and hunting, I guess.

We missed you this year, Sam.

Next Year ⟶

Chapter 35

Sam Returns

We decided to go second season again. Sam was feeling much better except for his knees. I had drawn an antelope tag for North Dakota after many years of trying. So, after I picked up Sam, we drove through my zoned area on our way to Lusk.

If I got an antelope, my plan was to take it to a meat plant in Bowman, ND, and pick it up on the way back. There were several inches of snow on the ground as we drove through the area. We stopped several times and I made a sneak on a few nice bucks. There was one I wish I had taken. I got within 180 yards of him. He was easily a 15" or better and very wide. We were seeing plenty of antelope, so I thought maybe there's a real trophy out there. We were just driving, so it was going to take a lot of luck. Besides, this wasn't the way I wanted to hunt them.

We reached the South Dakota border and that was the end of my chances. There was snow on the ground and it was very windy all through Wyoming. We got to Lusk at 5:12 p.m.

The next morning, we saw two 5x5s and one 6x6 in the park. We headed to Sheri's in Laramie and had a great breakfast and talked with Sandi a bit. Then we were off to the motel in Colorado. We only needed a couple of pack horses this year. Phil talked JC into helping us pack in. Sam and I got to camp around 11:30 am. The horses got there just behind us. We had camp all set up by 4:00 pm.

I walked out to the trail to see if anyone was around. There were 8 guys in Pat's camp from Minnesota to Missouri. They were there for the first season and had shot 5 cows. Their horses had the little meadow completely packed down and rutted up. They told us it was quite nice the entire hunt. One guy tried to tell me he'd been camping in Pat's camp for the last twenty years. Amazing – I must be blind. I walked past Pat's camp for thirty-plus years and can guarantee you, no one was there twenty years in a row. Whatever – some people are just like that.

I had shoulder surgery again that summer, but so far it was holding up. I figured, with Sam's knees and my shoulder, we were in equal pain. I brought the larger tent up this year. The small 8x8 just didn't work, especially if the weather was bad. After those guys left the next day, we walked up to Pat's camp. They had left a terrible mess. You aren't supposed to tie horses directly to any living tree, but they did. It was dug out all around the trees in several areas. A pine martin came in for lunch with us.

The day before season opened, Sam checked out Hog Pen and I went up to Boob's. Someone had horses all over hell up in the meadow. I wasn't even surprised at that. Sam said there wasn't much elk sign in Hog Pen. So far, not many hunters around. That night I showed Sam the menu I thought he'd like. It was a simple one. Chili and soup, burgers, jalapeño hot dogs, steak, ribs, walleye, and hotdish. No gourmet. The only problem was that he wanted hot dogs every day.

On opening morning, it was still pretty warm out. Just as I got to Boob's, two different bulls bugled to my right. I went up to the nearest high point to get a better look around. I was still 200 yards from my blind. Three other bulls bugled in the burnt-out timber way in front of me. Then two other ones to my left. I was surrounded by at least seven bulls. The wind was swirling, so I knew I couldn't go after any of them. I had to hope one would enter the meadow.

With all that wind whipping around, it was just a matter of time before they smelled me. Just like that, there was silence. They have a tremendous sense of smell.

I sat quite a while then headed back to camp. Sam hadn't seen anything. Two road hunters rode by looking for sign as we were having breakfast. Sam got a little altitude sickness, so he laid down for a while. *Here we go again.*

That afternoon, we headed back to our blinds. I saw Sam across the stream by us with Glad garbage bags pulled up to his knees. What a brilliant idea, but I wasn't about to tell him that. We had to cross that stream every time we went towards Hog Pen or my mountain. Sam just saw some birds that evening. I had around thirty cows come out and a decent 5x4 that just stood around for twenty minutes at 150 yards. There was a very deep-sounding bugle back up in the timber, so I was waiting to see him. At dark, I snuck out of there. Sam was pissed I didn't shoot. That night there was bugling all around us.

"Are we in heaven?" I said. "All this bugling and no other hunters around yet."

I never, let me repeat, never go all the way down to our main shitter at night. For some reason, I did this night. I even asked Sam if he wanted to come with me. I can't tell you how he responded to that. Anyhow, I'm sitting there in the dark, doing my thing. I laid my little pen light down beside me. It was on and facing towards camp. All of a sudden, there were a couple of deep-sounding huffs as a huge man-eating pine marten came at me on the log my flashlight was laying on. I don't know how experienced any of you are at running with your pants down around your ankles, but I think I'm an Olympic qualifier. That scared the shit out of me literally. I found the flashlight the next day. Sam only laughed for two days and then told everyone when we got home.

I took Sam with me the next morning. We heard at least four different bulls bugle up there. We could see the elk way up in the timber, but there was no way to get to them, let alone shoot at them. We heard two shots way off in the distance – that was it. On the way back to camp, we heard two more bugles at TD's and Hog Pen. Now I wished we had two more hunters. We couldn't be everywhere.

We hunted Boob's that evening again. They were still bugling. Nothing came out. Just before we arrived back at camp, two bulls bugled right above our camp and then another right straight across the stream. They were everywhere.

"Maybe we have to hunt by camp," I said.

Sam was confused and didn't know where to hunt. I wanted him to get one in the worst way. We went back up again the next morning. They were bugling less and less. Nothing came out, so we went part way up the draw that I used to bow hunt. There was sign everywhere, but no elk.

"Let's not spook them out of here," I told Sam, so we headed down.

After breakfast we were just going to go for a walk up to check Porcupine's out when Rich showed up. That was a good thing because it went from real nice to rain and snow like crazy. Rich headed back to his camp later in the snow. It snowed all night long. Sam went up with me one more time with the same results. We could hear and see the elk in the timber, but it was so burnt out, they would see you coming a mile away, let alone smell you with that constant swirling wind.

Mother Nature dumped a North Dakota blizzard on us again and a bolt of lightning flashed right over our heads. A huge roll of thunder came right after, testing our ear drums to the max. We headed back to camp. Sam went back to Hog Pen and was at least seeing cows by him. I was just enjoying the elk bugling serenade. I don't know if it was the lightning and thunder that kept them out of the meadow or not.
Tuesday morning, Sam was still seeing elk around Hog Pen and I was so close, but no cigar. It was snowing again and getting down below zero each night. Sam finally bought a good -40° sleeping bag that I also ordered when we got home. Tuesday night, I was sitting in a snowstorm just looking around when two quick shots rang out. It was so hard to tell with the falling snow where the shots came from.

My radio was staticky and I couldn't pick up Sam at all. Sam wasn't at camp when I got back. 'It might have been his shots,' I thought. I tried the radio again and it worked. He was on his way back to camp. He shot another milker. We were so happy I had his Hemingway too.

I went up to Boob's the next morning, just for a couple of hours and then went to help Sam. A few bulls were still talking to me that morning. We got his elk packed down by the trail and went back to camp to pack up what we could for tomorrow. That evening, I went back to Boob's one last time. The clouds moved in so heavily, we couldn't see 50 feet. There was only an hour left before dark, so I headed out. Just as I got to the edge of the meadow and turned around to say goodbye, a lone beautiful bugle rang out way up on top.

I just said, "I'll see you next year."

It got so cold in the tent that night, my fake teeth froze in their container. We got everything packed the next morning and we were so cold, we decided not to wait for the horses. The stream had dammed up and froze during the night. We had to go over the iced area. Sam was bigger than me so he said, "Let me go first to break through."

"No, I'm the camp boss around here," I replied. I stepped out a couple of feet – no problem.

"Let's go," I said.

Ten feet later, I broke through and stepped on a round large rock. I lost my balance and the weight of my backpack pulled me backwards. I fell into the rushing water and it took me downstream faster than hell. The temperature was 8° that morning. I held my gun up as high as I could as the shoulder I had surgery on was bouncing off the rocks beneath me. I tried to keep my nose above the water line so I could breathe. I got so cold so fast that I forgot about breathing. My backpack was like a bobber carrying me downstream faster and faster.

My ears were underwater, but I could faintly hear Sam saying, "Hang in there, Charlie, I'm coming!"

He hated water, but he jumped in anyhow. He sounded like he was a mile away from me then just like that he grabbed the top bar of my pack and pulled me back upstream. I kept telling him to take my gun, but he kept pulling me backwards. My repaired shoulder hit every damn rock that was in that stream. I think Sam was aiming for them.

When we reached the shoreline, he finally took my gun and pulled me out. I knew hypothermia would set in if we didn't do something quick.

Sam was more scared and nervous than I was. He kept saying over and over "What are we going to do?"

I thought about a fire, but we didn't have any matches. It's then that I realized he had pulled me back to the same side we went in. Instead of showing my gratitude, I said, "Why the hell didn't you pull me to the other side? Now we have to do it all over again."

I was joking, but he wasn't laughing. I should've listened to him in the first place.

I said, "Okay, you go first and I'll follow. Watch out for the rocks."

When we got across, he said, "Now what?"

I'm going to walk as fast as I can and maybe I'll freeze dry. I wrung my gloves out and took off. We met JC and Phil halfway down.

"Why are you so wet, Chaz?" JC said.

Sam ratted on me.

JC said, "You get to the cabin and take a hot shower."

I told Margo I'd be fine until we got to Laramie, but they insisted I thawed out in the shower so I did. I don't think I would have drowned in that stream, but I damn sure would've frozen.

When we left, a grouse flew up and shattered my windshield. I had to damn near sit in Sam's lap to see out.

We found a glass repair in Laramie, but it would take some time to fix.

We went for a walk. We came up to an old Catholic church and went in. Sam was Catholic and I wasn't. As you come in, there was a book on the table that said to write what you're thankful for. I thanked the good Lord for Sam. I didn't tell him that until later. I didn't want it to go to his head.

We picked up my vehicle and headed to Deadwood. The next morning, in a driving headwind, we were on our way home.

Thanks again, Sam!

Next Year ⟶

The Stream - 2008

Chapter 36

Foursome Again

I picked up Sam and Marly in Bismarck. Linus had to fly down again. I couldn't believe it, but Sam drove my Suburban all the way to Lusk. We even got there sooner than usual – 4:17 pm. On our way by the park the next morning, we saw a huge 8x5. So far it was very nice out. For the first time in years, Sheri's Restaurant in Laramie was closed. No Sandi, no personal table, bummer. We had breakfast at a small place by the interstate and headed to Colorado.

We got the panniers ready for the next day and had supper at our favorite restaurant. After all, this was our last "good meal." Linus got in late that night, but he was ready to go. We dropped our stuff off with Phil and JC again. They had to pack 5 horses this time. Who brought all that extra candy?

It was fairly nice out and we walked up to camp in about 3 hours. JC and Phil met us right at our stream crossing, which was almost my death bed. Sam had to show everyone how he saved my ass. Hell, I would've floated down to the vehicles if he had let me go. It was starting to cloud up, so we put the tent fly on right away. We put both flags up and proudly toasted Bob.

I started to cook the boys some chili while they went out to check around. They came back with some fantastic news. There were three guys right around the corner and two big tents in Pat's camp. They didn't see how many guys were in that camp. All I could think of was here we go again. Three of the guys were the ones that shot cows on the first season last year. They knew where we hunted so they didn't bother us at all. The others knew of our camp and that there was a grumpy guy in it, so they went their own way also. It all worked out for everyone.

Good thing we put the fly on, as it started to sleet that night. We heard a few bugles that night also.

On opening morning, Marly went above camp, Sam went to his kill-zone in Hog Pen, and Linus and I went to Boob's. We got to the meadow just before shooting time. We could hear a bull bugling very close by. Then we saw him. He was on the left edge of the meadow with three cows and a couple of calves. We snuck along the edge of the dead, burnt timber until we got a good look at him.

Linus was shooting a Ruger single shot rifle. I had no idea about that. 'A single shot?' I thought to myself. I knelt down and Linus was in a prone position. I told Linus he could take him if it was legal. Right at shooting time, Linus asked me if it had enough points. He was seeing too much background behind the bull to really tell.

I whispered, "Four for sure," then immediately he shot.

He scared the hell out of me. Somehow, he reloaded and shot two more times in seconds, with a single shot. We walked up to the dead bull. It had at least four points all right. It was a beautiful wide 6x6. *Congrats, Linus.* I guarantee you if I would've been there by myself, I would have taken him too.

The other two hadn't seen anything that morning and none of us saw anything that evening either. At least we had one down. That evening, I cooked the boys a nice hot meal. It was fried chicken. Sam hated chicken. He'd rather go hungry, he said. I told him I made a special meal just for him. I kept it covered so he wouldn't see it. All Marly and Linus knew was they were supposed to have their cameras ready.

I served Marly and Linus first, then I brought over the covered plate for Sam. If you could have only seen the look on his face. I uncovered a whole rubber chicken. We all had a good laugh, then I gave him his hot dogs. We had our Hemingways and then it was bedtime.

On Sunday morning, it was snowing and sleeting pretty good. Sam could barely get up, let alone go hunting, so he stayed in camp. His knees and shoulder were hurting even more. I was so upset that he would never go to a doctor. He always said, "There's nothing they can do." For Christ's sake, I've had surgery done all over me, I know it helps. He was very stubborn.

Marly and I didn't see anything in this crappy weather. Our neighbors weren't having any luck either. They were hunting all around us, but we hadn't run into each other yet. Marly went with me that evening and Sam was able to make it to Hog Pen. Nothing again, but there were a couple of shots in Lost Meadow – part of the oath-breaker group.

By the way, the menu this year was pretty much stew, hotdish, and fast food.

After supper, I could tell I was getting a little chafed from all the walking. Crotch crickets were setting in. I had a technique for a cure for them. I would pour some powder down the back of my shorts and smack my ass with my hand and PUFF. That technique was called puffin'. Marly couldn't stand it. He said I was crazy. He would pull his sleeping bag up over his head to get away from the fog.

I outsmarted him though. I brought up a small piece of vacuum cleaner hose and stuck it in a small opening by his head without him noticing. PUFF. Damn, he would cuss. Hey, half the trip was to have fun. It was sure funny to everyone, but Marly.

We were getting wind gusts that night well over 50 mph. You would hear a dead tree fall every once in a while.

Monday morning, Sam came with me. Several cows walked into the meadow to feed, but that was it. Marly didn't see anything in TD's. Poor Linus was tinkering around camp since the pressure was off of him. Now he's the one saying, "There ain't no elk in the damn tent."

We called JC and they came up and took Linus's elk down after they had lunch, of course. Sam went back to Hog Pen that evening but didn't hear or see anything again. Marly went with me to Boob's. We just got settled in when thirty or more cows walked out along with two spikes, a small 5x5, and a pretty nice 6x5.

We got quite the show then. A cow was ten yards in front of us when a young bull came up behind her. He had lovin' on his mind, but she turned around and slapped at him with her front legs. This went on a few times and then he just laid down on his back and rolled around like a little puppy. The elk were literally surrounding us on all sides of my blind. What a thrill!

The 6x5 bull came within 100 yards of us and Marly smoked him – dropped him in his tracks. We gutted him out and went back to camp. Supper and Hemingways – life was good. Marly even forgave me for puffin' him. The guys were sure happy we got another bull. We called JC again and told him to bring extra mules when they packed us out.

On Tuesday morning, Sam went into Kit Kat and I went up Boob's draw after we sat for a couple of hours in the blind. I saw a nice 5x5 up near the top. The wind was right, so I worked my way towards him to get a better look. My plan was working great, but then the wind shifted. Suddenly, two cows barked and ran out just to the left of the 5x5. I didn't even have time to get upset when a huge (at least a 6x6) bull bolted from behind some trees and disappeared. I had no chance to even raise my rifle.

That was the major problem when you hunt in the timber – the damn wind. Hunting elk in this area was just different from other states I had hunted in. Your odds were much better just sitting and waiting. Of course, you can stalk up on a bull, but with a swirling wind all the time and dozens of cow eyes watching for me, it was very difficult to do.

I met up with Sam and told him what happened. He couldn't believe it. We went back to help pack Marly's elk down then. That evening, Sam and I went back up early. Sam was with me in the blind, but I couldn't see him because he was on the other side of a tree from me. We could whisper back and forth though. What a show we were about to see.

The bulls were bugling all around us and thirty or forty elk ran out into the meadow. It was identical to Marly's *sitcheation*. There was a nice 5x5 amongst the cows. I'm sure Sam was still hurting everywhere, plus the fact that I was putting pressure on him to get ready to shoot because he kept whispering to me that he couldn't get the bull in his scope. He told me to shoot.

"No, he's yours," I said.

It didn't matter though because someone fired a shot on the other side of the mountain, and they scattered like bees. So close. Sam was shaking and apologizing all the way back to camp.

"Hey, I told you I see a lot of bulls," I said. We got the guys all excited that night. I told them we almost had another Hemingway.

The next morning, up we go again. Sam stayed in my blind this time while I went up the draw. I was surrounded by elk again. For once, there was no wind. I could see plenty of cows, a few spikes, and a 5x5. I'm sure it was the herd from last night. I certainly didn't want to spook them out of the area. Then I saw a nice 6x6, but he wasn't the big one I had seen yesterday. If I could get a clean shot, I was going to try and get him. He came within 150 yards of me, but every time I pulled up on him, I could see way too many branches between him and me in my scope. I just didn't have a decent shot. When they walked away, I went back to Sam.

Nothing came out by him. I told him I saw the herd, maybe tonight. Before we went back up that afternoon, we helped the guys pack things up for the trip out the next day. It had started raining and snowing again. Linus asked if he could go up with us so the three of us headed up that afternoon.

They were bugling, but not much action. With only ½ hour to go before we were done for this season, Sam said, "We may as well go down."

I said, "Let's give it ten more minutes."

Just like that, all hell broke loose. There were more elk than before. There were several legal bulls everywhere. The big 6x6 wasn't here though. We were losing light quickly. I would point out a bull on one side and Linus would point out a different one because we couldn't see each other. Poor Sam was so confused, he couldn't get any one of them in his scope. We ran out of light, and it was over.

Sam kept asking me why I didn't shoot. I told him it was because the big boy wasn't out there. We could have filled all four tags.

What a year and what a hunt.

Next Year

A Tough Hunt

Dean and I left for Bismarck to pick up Marly and Sam. We had missed the first season, so we had the second season again. The outlook for the weather looked pretty shaky. We talked with my folks for a while then headed for Lusk. So far, it was quite nice out. We got to Lusk at 4:45pm – amazing. We dropped off the bags of taters along the way, as always.

The next morning, there wasn't much activity in the park. We stopped in Laramie and Sheri's was open again. After breakfast and talking with Sandi, we proceeded to Colorado. The weather was still nice when we got there, so we packed our things right away and went and had our last "good meal."

Bright and early the next morning, we dropped our panniers off with Phil. Dean rode up with Phil since he had back issues. We started walking up around 9 and arrived at camp at noon. The trail up was good, but Marly was struggling for some reason. Someone had left an old stove in our camp. I sent it down with Phil.

There was a camp beside us again. It was Joe, who we had met last year. He was here for the first season, and he was packing out now. He got a nice 7x6 bull in Boob's meadow. It probably was the one I saw on the last day of last season.

315

We put the flags up and toasted Bob. The guys gathered wood as I prepared supper. Chili and snacks tonight, then the menu for later was as follows: camp stew, crab burgers, steak, brats, and Sam's hot dogs. It started raining that night and continued through Friday. I hadn't noticed for a couple of days, but Marly had put up a picture of an Alaskan Puffin with a sign under it that said, 'No Puffin' in this Tent.' Good one, Marly.

On opening morning, the good news was that it quit raining, but the bad news was it started snowing heavily. Dean went up Old Dad's and followed some tracks but didn't see anything. Sam went up to TD's and didn't see anything. Marly had just seen some tracks in Hog Pen. Up in Boob's there were a few bugles up high and that was it.

Saturday evening, we heard a few shots in the distance, but none of us saw anything.

I brought up a new watch this year and I had Sam set the alarm. I rarely even need an alarm, but it had one, so he set it. It worked perfectly on Sunday morning, but it was only 2:30 am when it went off. He had set it for Eastern Time.

Dumb ass.

That morning, Dean saw a legal bull 75 yards away, but it was still dark out as it walked into the woods. Sam was up on TD's and saw several bulls above Dean up high. They haven't all left yet. I didn't see anything in Boob's. Marly had a small bull in Hog Pen poking around. It was still snowing pretty good. That evening, Sam and Dean saw some cows. Marly and I didn't see anything.

It was snowing so hard you couldn't see across Boob's meadow. On Monday morning, Marly and I went up

Old Dad's and it started storming so badly we headed back right away. Everybody's guns were freezing up – it was getting worse. By the time we got back, there was so much snow on the tent, it was damn near down.

That evening, Dean said it was storming up in Boob's, but he did see two cows. The rest of us didn't see anything.

Tuesday morning, none of us saw anything. Around noon, while we were all in camp, there was a shot that sounded like Hog Pen. Sam and Marly went to check it out. Sure enough, a retired Ranger was just riding up to look around and a heavy 7x6 crossed in front of him. He said he got off his horse and shot him 100 yards away right towards Hog Pen. Lady Luck again.

Tuesday night, I saw a spike, but the blizzard was so bad, I had to head down before dark. Dean and Sam hadn't seen anything. The weather wasn't quite as bad for Marly in Hog Pen, but it was still snowing. He saw some elk running down below him, so he ran up on the hill. It was the whole damn herd heading down. It was snowing, he was out of breath, and had no decent rest to shoot from. All he could do was watch 75 elk run by him 150 yards away. It still was a thrill.

Wednesday morning, it was still snowing. "I think we're going to lose our elk, boys," I said.

On my way up to Boob's, I noticed lots of tracks went through below the meadow. I sat in the blind for a few hours. A cow and calf walked right by me without any idea I was there. It could have been a bull, I thought. That was it. Sam had slept in; his knees were really hurting. He caught hell again from me. Marly didn't go too far from camp. He said he was having a hard time breathing. Dean didn't see anything in Old Dad's.

Back at camp, we had to constantly knock the snow off the roof of the tent, day and night. Everything was damp and cold. It was a miserable trip especially for Sam with his knees, Marly with not getting enough oxygen, and Dean with his back. Me – I was just a partially healed up wreck that wouldn't quit.

Dumb ass.

"Well," I said, "this is our last hunt this evening. Good luck, boys!"

Marly saw ten cows in Hog Pen, Dean saw nothing, Sam saw a cow and calf 50 yards from the shitter laying in the snow, and I went to Boob's for a quiet snowy evening. We packed everything we could for the trip down, had supper, and went to bed.

I made a point to make sure I had my miniature Snickers candy bars in the pocket right above my shoulder, so I could have a snack during the night. We were laying there in the dark talking – at least I was – when I realized they were all sleeping. I turned in my bag and felt a lump under my back. A Snickers must have fallen in my bag, I thought. I reached under my back with my left arm and that Snickers had fur on it. Jesus, did I panic. I grabbed it and threw it towards the door in the dark. It hit the center pole and made a ding.

The guys didn't wake up until they heard me scream like a little girl. Lights came on and I had my flashlight right on the beady eyes of that killer mouse.

Everyone jumped up and said, "What the hell is wrong?"

I kept saying, "Get him, Sam, he's right there."

I threw my shoe at it and its tail lifted. Sam went after it.

I said, "Get a knife; he's a killer!"

Sam said he couldn't find it as he bent over. He walked back to me and opened up his hand and said, "Is this what it looked like?" It was the most realistic mouse I'd ever seen. Those assholes had this planned the whole trip. They never were sleeping – they were waiting for me to notice. More heart pills. We didn't get any elk, but we sure had another memorable trip.

Next Year

Sam and his mouse - 2010

Chapter 38

Sam and the Chaz

No Marly this year. He said he was done, but I refused to believe that. He said he felt good now, but I remembered how hard it was for him to go down the mountain the year before. I've said for years and still believe it to this day that Marly was the healthiest of all of us. I guess if you can't breathe, it doesn't matter how healthy you are. I honestly thought he'd be back, but the type of hunting we did was a lot of work. Still, he seemed to love it. He'll be back, I hope.

Sam was driving again – unbelievable. He even put new tires on. We got to Lusk at 4:50 pm. The next morning, on our way to Laramie, a wrecked car was on the shoulder of the road and a 4x4 bull elk was lying there, dead. I'd never seen that before. There wasn't anything in the park, but as we were driving out of it, there was a pickup parked on the side of the road. As we drove by, there lay a second dead elk. *What the hell?*

The weather was decent, but we had a 15-minute delay due to construction. We ate at Sheri's again. Sandi was glad to see us, I think. She wondered where Marly was. We got to the motel in Colorado that afternoon. We packed the panniers for three horses.

JC couldn't help Phil, but Phil had a couple of other people to help him. The trail up to camp was extremely muddy and very slippery. It still only took us two worn out guys a little over 3 hours to get there. Phil met us at the stream. We had everything up before dark. We hung the flags up and toasted Bob.

I warmed up some chili and we called it a night. It's a lot of work with only two guys. The remaining menu consisted of Swedish meatballs, bean and burger hotdish, fish and chips, hot dogs and mac and cheese, and burgers and fries. "Are you happy now, Sam?" I asked. That man could live on hot dogs.

Sam had a sore spot on the top of his foot before we started walking up and that night, we noticed the skin had rubbed off. He said it really burned. Thanks to Bob years ago, I always had a first aid kit in camp. I cleaned it and put some mole skin on it. "What the hell is mole skin?" asked Sam.

At least I didn't give him sleeping pills for the pain.

The next morning, we both slept in until 7:00 am. We finished up camp and gathered up firewood. Damn, I miss the other guys. I don't cut wood. No choice now.

After finishing things up, Sam walked out to check around us. He saw human tracks, so he went towards Pat's. There were two guys camping there. They said they found this spot during the summer when they were out here. Sam told them where we were camping, and they said they saw the flag on their way by. He told them I'd been hunting this same area for almost forty years. He also told them that I was touchy and could get very grumpy. They said they understood that. They came over and met me, shook my hand, and said it was quite an accomplishment to hunt elk that long. I liked them – they seemed like square shooters.

They asked us where we hunted and if we could point some areas out to them, which I did.

Sam went to get water in the middle of the day. A cow and two calves looked at him from across the stream. There were also elk tracks down by the shitter. Sam saw a couple of bulls above Old Dad's the day before season and our neighbors saw them too. I had told them about Old Dad's. That night, right on cue, Sam's knees went to hell. I went and got the hatchet.

"What's that for?" he asked with his eyes wide open.

I said, "Use the hammer side of the hatchet, lay your hand on the table, and smack it."

"Are you crazy?" he replied.

"Yes, but at least you won't notice your knees hurting so much then. Good night."

I thought I heard him mumble, "Dumb ass."

On Saturday morning, I went up to Boob's and Sam was in Hog Pen. The bulls were bugling up high on my way up. 15 minutes after the season opener, I heard a couple of shots towards Hog Pen.

Are you kidding me? Another milker down maybe.

Our plan was when we heard the other shoot, we would turn the radio on at the lowest volume. I did and, like a damn fool, I hadn't checked my batteries. They were dead. I hadn't seen anything, so I headed back before noon to help Sam. He was in camp when I got there.

"Was that you that shot?" I asked.

He didn't answer. He just turned around and bent over. At least he only had one kick in the ass. He had shot at a milker up above him. When he walked up there, he said it was pretty obvious he had killed a dead tree. He said the bullet did a good job, there were shattered wood chips everywhere.

I should have kicked him twice.

That evening, neither of us saw anything.

On Sunday morning, Sam didn't see anything. I had two spikes sneak up behind me, but that was it. There was way more shooting all around us. Sunday afternoon, Sam hadn't seen anything at all. On my way up to Boob's, I heard a good bugle up on top.

I had just entered the meadow when a shot rang out. It sounded like it came from up above me. I settled in my blind, full of optimism. Just as the magic hour was approaching, I turned to look up the draw where the elk come down most of the time and there was a hunter walking down the draw. He was walking right towards me. What a letdown. It was one of our neighbors, but what was he doing up here? They knew I was up here. Here he had heard a bull above Old Dad's and followed it all day. He ended up shooting him way up and over Boob's.

I congratulated him and told him that was a hell of a hunt, but if you would've waited in the meadow where you were, you would have possibly had the whole herd come to you. I was proud of his accomplishment, but also upset at the sore timing. Now he had to drag the meat through Boob's several times to get it back to his camp. It didn't make sense to sit in the blind anymore now, so we headed down.

On Monday morning, Sam stayed in camp because of his knees. With all the human traffic in Boob's, I went up Old Dad's. It was raining early and then turned to snow.

After getting soaked for a few hours, I headed back. I told Sam again, "Get those damn knees fixed."

That afternoon, Sam was able to get to Hog Pen, but was having a hard time in the snow with his knees. Nothing came out. After all the commotion in Boob's, I took a chance and went back up. There was still a bugle once in a while off in the distance. I was getting a cramp in my leg, so I turned to relieve it and there was a bull standing 100 yards behind me. I looked at him through my binoculars and could see he was just a young bull. He stopped twenty yards from me. It was a little 6x5. He gave me a good show for a while and then winded me and was off. When I told Sam about the little guy, he got pissed.

He said, "I would have shot him."

Yes, I know.

On Tuesday morning, I spooked a cow right at the entrance of the meadow. She barked and let the whole world know I was there. I sat for a few hours anyhow, but there was nothing around. Sam had gone up Old Dad's and didn't see anything either. The weather was a little nicer for one day at least. That afternoon, the bulls were bugling all over the place. Then a shot rang out from Hog Pen. I turned my radio on, and sure enough Sam got another milker. I told him I had elk all around me so we would gut him out and quarter it the next day. On the last morning, I went back up. When I entered Boob's a couple of bulls were bugling in Tom's so I headed that way.

I peeked over the knoll and saw two 5x5's fighting. What a show. There was another young bull watching from back in the timber. Then out came what looked like a decent bull. He was around 300 yards away. I could see he had 6 points on one side, but I couldn't see the other side because of the angle. When he turned slightly, I could see he had at least 5 on that side. I hesitated but decided to shoot. To this day, I'll never know what happened. No excuses.

As I shot, I could see debris fly in my scope. He reared up like a horse and walked into the green timber. How could I have missed him? I waited, then walked over to where he was at. There was some hair and chunks of tree branches everywhere. A few small drops of blood on the snow and that was it. I followed his tracks for at least 100 yards into the woods. Absolutely no blood. What the hell happened?

Five bulls were all around me and I didn't get any of them. *Rookie.* I was just sick and very upset with myself. I had passed up many bulls and then blew it on this nice one. I went down and helped Sam get his elk to the trail, then we both went up to look things over again. We spent hours on his tracks until he mixed in with many others. We went back and I retraced everything from the beginning.

The only conclusion we could come up with was I held on his front shoulder, but obviously I hit a branch that was standing up from a dead fall laying on the ground. The bullet must have changed direction slightly and pierced across his brisket area. That explains the small patch of hair and the wood splinters all over the place. He probably healed that wound up before dark. What a dumb ass I was. Yes, I bent over, and Sam kicked my ass.

We packed things up that afternoon and I went back up to Boob's. What happened next is almost unbelievable. Sam could hardly walk anymore so he stayed in camp. I wish he would've been with me.

My intention was to go to Boob's and ask for forgiveness for what had happened. I sat in my blind in deep regret — not for missing that bull, but for hitting it with something even through it didn't appear to be a fatal wound. I just whispered that I was very sorry.

Moments later, a cow and calf stepped out. I was watching them when bugling started up all around me. Talk about surround sound. Two 5x5s walked into the meadow and then a very nice 6x5. That one wasn't the one I had encountered earlier though. Then came three cows with three more 5x5 bulls right behind them. One of the 5 pointers was wide on top. I pulled my gun up and looked at each and every bull — not to shoot but to admire. I felt as though I didn't deserve to kill any one of these beautiful creatures. I know this may sound a little crazy, but that's just the way I felt.

I put my gun down and all of them walked within 100 yards of me. Greatest Show on Earth. If any other hunter had been watching me, they'd have thought I was crazy. No comment on that. It was getting dark, and I tried to sneak out of there. I hunched over and started walking down. I stopped and slowly looked back. They were all looking right at me and just standing there. I let out a makeshift bugle with my mouth. They walked towards the trees and looked very puzzled. As I reached the tree line, I turned around to say goodbye to Boob's like I always have.

They were all gone, but then I noticed there was a lone bull on the other end of the meadow. That's right where Sam and I followed the tracks of the bull I shot at that morning. I pulled my scope up as he let out a bugle. He looked pretty nice. 'Could that have been him?' I thought. I guess I'll never know. I removed my hat, saluted him, and thanked him for the memories. I think I was forgiven.

Our satellite phone battery was dead so we just hoped Phil would bring enough horses up. We left before he reached camp. This time Sam slipped on a rock and damn near fell in that stream. I told him my pack was too heavy to try and save him if he fell in. He laughed. We met Phil by Rich's. We spent some quality time with JC and Margo, then started our long drive home. In a way, I was kind of proud of myself for what I didn't do.

Next Year ⟶

Sam at the stream - 2011

Chapter 39

A Big Surprise

Just Sam and me again this year. I went to pick him up and to my surprise, he wanted to drive my Suburban. "Absolutely," I said.

The weather was good, and we got to Lusk at 5:30 pm. We passed out the bags of potatoes on the way. Just a couple of bulls in the park this time. Sheri's was closed for good now. No more Sandi. We hit some snow on our way to Colorado. We packed up the panniers at the motel and went and had our last "good meal." JC lined us up with a different outfit to take us up this time. Now Phil's knees had gone to hell. He was getting up in age too. We dropped things off at their ranch and walked up. It was nice out and we got up to camp within 3 hours again.

Sam was hanging in there. Someone had been in our camp and left a mess.

Thanks in part to the nice weather, camp went up quickly. We put the flags up and toasted Bob! Like a damn fool, I bought new boots and didn't break them in before this trip. My feet were killing me. After having some hot chili, we called it a night.

The bulls were bugling all night long and some were very close to us. We were going to sleep in the next morning, but at 6:35 am, a deep bugle and grunt bellowed out right by our US flagpole. I whispered as loud as I could to wake Sam.

"Finally, he sat up and said, "Here's my flashlight."

"I didn't ask for your damn flashlight, just listen."

He was half awake. We threw on our sweatpants and went out in the cold. There was just enough light to make things out. The whole herd went right by us. We snuck up on a small hill by the trail and peeked over. There they were. Four bulls and twenty or so cows. Two of the bulls were nice 5x5s. Then that deep bugle and grunt sounded again. Up on the other side of the meadow stepped out a beautiful 6x6.

Selfishly, I said, "There's my bull, Sam."

I didn't mean it that way, but that was the kind of bull I was after for many years. We were freezing in our jammies. As they faded into the timber, we turned around and there was a damn tent right around the corner from ours. No one was there. They must have gone down for more supplies. We walked up to Pat's camp, and someone had left a hell of a mess there. *Damn idiots*. It was nice out now, but rain and snow would be moving in later. Several guys on horseback just went by. I sure hope they're going to the lake.

We were sitting around that afternoon when a tall guy was walking on the trail into our camp. Initially, I was pissed. I don't like company.

Holy shit, it was Tom!

I couldn't believe it. He had drawn an antelope tag for Colorado. He had just finished and was on his way home back to Montana. He just stopped by to say hi and spend a few days with us. What a great surprise! He walked six miles with a huge heavy pack on to say hi. Love that kid.

It turned out the two guys in the tent beside us were people we knew from years before. They were no problem. However, there were two more camps not that far from us that weren't as pleasant. On Friday, Tom and I went up to Boob's just to check it out. Two different fellows were following right behind us. When we got too the meadow, there were three other guys walking around like it was a convention.

All these hunters were going to screw everything up for all of us, not just for Sam and me. I wasn't in a good mood right now. Tom ran into some of those guys later. They told him they knew all about me and that they'd stay away from Boob's meadow.

Tom had to leave on Saturday, but he went up with me on opening morning. We didn't see anything that morning, but we did hear a shot that sounded like Sam, but it wasn't. We headed back to camp. Sam hadn't seen anything either. We had some hot chocolate, then Tom had to go. It was sure sad to see him leave. It left an empty feeling in me as he walked out, but it was sure nice of him to come up and see us. It was snowing pretty good now.

That evening, I got settled in at Boob's. I heard a shot but couldn't tell which direction it came from. About an hour or so later, I could hear someone talking. I turned around and here two guys were coming down the draw again, carrying a very small set of elk antlers. I mean, they were smaller than Sam's. Just before I heard them talking, a bull bugled right in Tom's. As soon as they proceeded by, that was the end of that. It was two of the guys that told Tom they wouldn't bother me.

It doesn't matter anymore, but that group of five had heard about me and this area from the original person who broke Bob's hunters' oath. I lost track of how many people found out about this area from that one person. I have no words for my feelings. It wasn't these guys' fault. I probably

331

would have done the same thing. *No, actually, I don't think so.*

Sam hadn't seen any in Hog Pen, but he did see some above Old Dad's. On Sunday morning, I went back to Boob's. When I reached the meadow, it was still a little dark, so I waited for some light. I had company in my blind. It was a cow, a calf, and a spike right beside my blind. I waited until they milled away and headed for the blind. I was still very optimistic. At prime time, here came those two guys again with sleds to get their elk out. I stood up. Now I was pissed. I know they saw me, but they wouldn't even look in my direction. All I was after was maybe a little bit of ethical respect.

I sat there for an hour or so and then headed to camp. Sam hadn't seen anything that morning. After breakfast, Sam called me over to our fire pit. I had forgotten to tell him that the rope that holds our fly up right beside our tent sounded like it got hit during the night. I woke up after I heard it but didn't hear anything else. Anyhow, there were bull tracks right around the fire pit and it had actually walked right into that rope. Ten feet from our front door. I told him with all these hunters around us, we should just post from our tent.

We went over to tell the two guys we knew next door about this. Halfway over, Sam said, "I should have brought my gun."

I said, "We're only going a hundred yards."

We got to their tent, but they were gone. We turned around as the sun came out and on the other side of the stream a cow and calf came walking down the hill. We stood still. Then two more and then four more after that came out.

They were about 200 yards away. I said, "Sam, go get your rifle."

Just as he took off, bad knees and all, a 5x5 followed up the pack of twelve cows. *Was this stupidity on our part or just bad luck?*

That evening, I headed back up to Boob's. I saw the two guys still dragging their sleds down the trail, so I walked around the other way. I was in no mood for talking. They hollered over to me and said they'd come right back and get their other sled right away. What a damn mess. I will not tell the world what my response to them was. When I got to Boob's I could see with the naked eye that they left their other sled damn near beside my blind. Yeah, that's ethical, all right.

I walked up and sat in Tom's. Two spikes walked by me shortly after. It took some tension off of me after that. I heard a shot by Old Dad's. I was hoping it was one of our neighbors, but it was one of those two guys' group members. The only thing Sam saw was hunters.

On Monday morning, Sam and I didn't see anything. That afternoon, we decided to walk up to Porcupine's to get away from these hunters. There weren't any hunters up there, but there was very little elk sign either. It was a nice walk, and we had a good talk all the way back to camp. I noticed Sam was short of breath more often lately. That evening, the only living thing we saw and killed were two mice hiding in the woodpile. Finally, after all these years, I got a couple of those killer bastards.

On Tuesday morning, Sam wasn't feeling well, so he stayed in bed. He sure slept a lot this trip. Back up in Boob's, I at least got to hear a few bugles challenging each other. It's awesome how that sound would echo down the valley.

Nothing came out this morning. The camp with the five guys in it was packing out when I came down.

Sam went out that evening and saw a few cows. The same two spikes I'd seen here before dropped by for a visit again up in Boob's. They put on a show jumping in a mud hole. That was it. It started raining and sleeting on my way down. I used my great hunting skills to kill another mouse that night.

I stepped out of the tent just before bedtime when a bolt of lightning struck so close, I was actually blinded for a few minutes. When I went back in, we could hear the roar of the wind coming down the valley. Seconds later, all hell broke loose. The local radio station said it was a straight line burst up to 80 mph. A few of our tent poles went flying.

The last morning as I headed up to Boob's, I noticed an entire herd had crossed my tracks and were heading down. They knew something was coming. I only heard one bugle then went back to camp around noon. Many trees had fallen from the strong winds. Sam hadn't seen anything in Hog Pen. I went up to say goodbye to the meadow and Sam went back to Hog Pen. Neither of us saw anything. What a trip. There were elk everywhere and we never even got a shot. So close, yet so far away. That's hunting.

This trip ended quite hilariously, at least for me. Sam went down to the shitter in the dark. When he was done doing his business, he started pulling his pants up when a mouse ran by his flashlight. He held his pants up with one hand and grabbed his light with the other. Wouldn't you know it – that mouse hit the ground and ran right up Sam's leg inside his pants. He came running and screaming into the camp like a little girl.

I called down to Steve and told him the only thing to pack down was our camp and a killer mouse. No elk.

Next Year ⟶

Tom and Charlie – Surprise - 2012

Chapter 40   I Had My Chance

I picked up Sam in Bismarck. We made our potato run, gassed up, grabbed my broasted chickie, and headed for Lusk. Linus was meeting us in Colorado again. Must be nice to fly and leave the driving to me. Actually, Sam was driving my Suburban (again). We ran into some heavy snow north of Lusk and got to the motel at 5:35 pm. You're slowing down, Sam.

The next morning, on our way to Laramie, it was cloudy, but it was in the 50s. We hit construction by the park, but we were going to stop there anyhow. One nice 8x7 and two younger bulls were there. The smallest one came right to us.

"Look," I said, "this one has milk on his face, Sam."

"It's a good thing he's in a pen," Sam replied.

Hey – we're in Wyoming, not Colorado.

We gassed up in Laramie and shoved some day-old egg and cheese gas station sandwiches down. We sure missed Sheri's restaurant and Sandi's smile. We arrived at the motel in Colorado in the afternoon again. Linus got there early and helped us pack the panniers. We went and had our last "good meal."

The next morning, we were off to the ranch. We left our little trailer at Steve's place this time. He and a ranch hand packed our things in. Sam and Linus started walking up ahead of me. I told them not to wait up for me, I had things to do. When nature calls, she calls, especially when she has a direct line to my "ole brown eye."

I caught up with them just before camp. At the present time, it was cloudy, but still nice. We didn't notice anyone ahead of us on the trail. We had camp set up and cut some wood before dark. Linus took over my wood cutting responsibilities. Thanks. Thursday, we put the fly on, and the guys gathered up more wood. I finished *oreknizing* the tent.

It started to snow, and I mean really snow. We heard bugling that night and a cow barked right by the tent around midnight. I think she smelled Sam.

Friday afternoon, I went up to Boob's. Nothing but lots of snow up there. The guys went for a walk and didn't notice any other camps around us. For the record, besides Sam's delicious chili, we also had stuffed peppers with mashed taters, Parmesan crusted walleye, burgers with potato skins, grilled cheese with homemade "mamata" soup, beef stew, and of course, Sam's hot dogs and fries.

On opening morning, Linus spent some time up on TD's Mountain. He just saw several tracks. Sam was in his kill-zone at Hog Pen. He saw some cows and calves.

On my way up to Boob's, I could hear bugling in every direction. I stopped at the entrance of the meadow and glanced around. I could hear them, but I couldn't see them. It was snowing hard up there. I got into the meadow about 100 yards or so and noticed a bull to my left along the tree line. He was in the same area where Linus had shot his 6x6. I snuck up to the nearest tree and got a better look. He was no monster, but he was a decent 6x5.

Just as I pulled up on him at 200 yards, I noticed elk out of the corner of my eye. They were all around my blind and some were even standing in my blind. I was going to take the 6x5 then out of nowhere a beautiful heavy 6x6 appeared beyond my blind just on the other side of a little knoll. I have gotten excited over the last forty years when I would get ready to shoot at these magnificent creatures, but I never got the so-called "Buck Fever" until now.

The main reason was I knew I only had seconds before this trophy disappeared. It also didn't help that it was snowing large flakes. I pulled up on him and had a good rest. No excuses there. I had a 3x15 power scope on my rifle.

Like a damn fool, I turned it up when I meant to turn it down. I corrected that, took a deep breath, and fired at the top of his shoulder. I didn't hear that whop or see any reaction from him. As he turned towards the timber, I fired one more time and watched him disappear. When I started walking towards him, I knew immediately what I had done.

I've shot at elk from every direction in this meadow. It is 600 yards long and 250 yards wide. I don't know if it was the falling snow that deceived my perception or just plain old Buck Fever. I quickly glanced up at him a couple of times before I shot. "He's 300 yards," I whispered to myself.

As soon as I started walking to him, I realized I blew it big time. He was at about 225 yards, that's it. I shot right over him – twice. What a sickening rookie mistake. I checked where he was standing, and he wasn't touched. That was the only blessing – at least he wasn't wounded. For all I know I probably shot at his huge antler.

On this, my fortieth year of hunting elk, I had my chance for the one I had been waiting for. I was very disappointed with myself right now.

I hung my head and struggled through the deep snow on the way back to camp. I bent over and told them to kick me twice. Damned if they didn't. They felt bad for me knowing that I had passed up many other bulls waiting for this one. Lady Luck had nothing to do with this.

That evening, Linus went up with me. We made it to the blind this time. Eleven cows walked out within 100 yards of us. A smaller 5x5 stayed right over the edge of the timber. Linus simply said, "He's legal," and dropped him. We dressed him out and got it ready for morning. Sam saw some cows again in Hog Pen.

I went back up early Sunday morning and told the guys to bring the sleds up around 10 or so. I was entertained by two young 5x5s for a while then they walked by me and entered their burnt timber home. We had Linus' bull down by early afternoon. Both the guys came up with me on Sunday night. Bulls were bugling up high. I told Sam to be ready. He was still pissed at me for not shooting that morning.

As luck would have it, nothing came out. We had supper, stoked the stove, had a Hemingway, and listened to mice all night. Sam was having a hard time. As if his knees, his shoulder, and his shortness of breath weren't enough, he had to struggle through three feet of snow also.

I talked him into going up with me Monday morning again. Bulls were bugling to us all the way up. The problem was it started snowing again really heavily. At 7:30 am, all the bugles went silent. I was just hoping one would come out for him, but nothing did. After a few hours, we went back to camp. We couldn't even see our tracks from just a few hours before.

The weather must have kept most hunters down below because for once, we didn't have any neighbors, just elk. That evening, all three of us went back up. Linus wanted to take pictures of the elk. The only thing we got pictures of was a giant snowstorm. We headed back down just before dark.

Halfway down, we saw a herd up higher along the mountainside running to beat hell in the trees. They sure didn't smell us. We finally got to see why they were running. There was a huge wolf right on their heels. I had heard rumors about wolves, but now I actually had seen one. I know they have to eat too, but, damn, I hated to see that.

On Tuesday morning, Sam went back to Hog Pen. It was easier for him to go there instead of climbing up to Boob's. I went to Boob's and as luck would have it, a cow and calf actually watched me sit in my blind and didn't even spook. I think they knew who I was also. Then of course, a herd of cows came out. A bit later, a small 4x4 and a 5x5 popped out together. I watched those two bulls spar with each other for a while, then three quick shots rang out, followed by two more. My show was over.

It was so hard to tell with all the snow, but it sure sounded like Hog Pen. The radios were too staticky to get a hold of him. When I got back to camp, sure enough, he had another milker down to add to his list. A little 4x3½, but he was legal, tagged, and he would sure taste good. The three of us packed it down to the trail. Another Hemingway.

We called Steve and he came up and took the two elk down. If I wouldn't have been such a dumb ass, we'd be filled up right now.

Linus came up with me that afternoon. Not sure he believed all the elk I was seeing. As we were sitting in the snow up to our necks, a herd of thirty or more came out from Tom's. They stayed up along the tree line and close to each other. There were several legal bulls in the heard. The smaller ones were on this side and there was a very nice one on the far side. His antlers stood out like a king. All you could see was his head and they were all walking pretty fast. I had no shot, but I was ready.

Linus was damn near laughing. A nice wide 4x4 left the herd and got within 50 yards of us. Linus was whispering, "Take him, take him," but my eyes were glued on the biggest one. Then the wind shifted, the lead cow barked, and they trotted off. The big boy stayed right in the middle on the other side the whole time. 200 yards away and I had no shot.

How many chances can a guy get? It was annoying.

Linus told Sam the story this time, so he had to believe it. When he told him about the wide 4x4, Sam just said "Dumb ass."

On Wednesday morning, I went up alone. Only three cows came out from Tom's. I sat there daydreaming about all the bulls I had seen and the big one I had missed. What a trip' I thought. I also worried about Sam. He was having a hard time, especially in this deep snow.

On the last evening, I went up alone again while the boys were packing up. It was a peaceful evening, but nothing around. Just as I was stepping out of the meadow, one lone bugle rang out as if to challenge me. I turned and said my goodbyes and said, "I'll see you next year."

I chewed Sam's ass all the way home. "Get your damn shoulder and knees fixed," I said.

What a fantastic trip again.

Next Year ⟶

Third Generation
in Camp

This hunt was something special both for me and Bob. Tom brought his son Drew, Bob's grandson, with him for the first time. Bob asked me if I would try and get Drew his first bull with his 7 mm just like I had with him and Tom. I told him it would be an honor. Sam and I drove from North Dakota and Tom and Drew came down from Montana.

We did our potato thing in Bismarck, then off to Lusk. We arrived at 5:20 pm. We went by the park the next morning. There were five beautiful bulls there. One was a 10x7 – *wow*! We stopped in Laramie for fuel and dried up breakfast sandwiches from the station. Tom and Drew were a day behind us. I had everything they needed for camp except their rifles and personal stuff.

Sam and I packed the panniers, then we went and had our last "Good Meal." We met up with Steve the next morning and dropped off our supplies. We started walking up right away. So far, the weather was okay. We managed to get the tent up that afternoon. Good thing too because it started raining that night and all day on Thursday.

A few bulls bugled around us that first night. Poor Tom and Drew had to walk up in this crap. We put our flags up, but we were going to wait to toast Bob until the boys got there.

Sam checked around for other camps. He came back and said, "We've got 5 guys next door again and they said they'd never been here before."

Sam said the older guy, Gary, seemed nice. He told them that I'd been coming here for forty years. He also told them, "Whatever you do, don't piss off the little guy. He gets really grumpy."

Damn, I hate being called little.

When the rain let up a little, we sat outside. Here came Gary charging down our trail right up to us. "You must be Charlie, the Grumpy Guy," he said. I was halfway embarrassed. He shook my hand and said, "I'm glad to meet someone who's that dedicated to hunting elk for forty years. I've got my nephew with me and a couple of friends. We heard about you from down below. You just tell us where you guys are hunting, and I promise you we will stay away from there."

I liked him before he ever said that. I showed him some good areas that I know we couldn't get to, and he appreciated that. He had horses and offered to help us if we needed. 'There are still some great people left,' I thought to myself.

Tom and Drew finally got in to camp at dark. They were soaked and cold. It was miserable out. I was starting to worry about them. I cooked some of Sam's hot chili for them. They asked about the rest of the menu. Here it is – soup every day, burgers, panko breaded fish, hotdish, Rocky Mountain Stew, chili dogs, and ribs and fries. No gourmet. We gave a toast to Bob, and I said, "If it wasn't for your dad, none of us would be here."

We spent all day Friday finishing up camp and getting ready for Saturday. On Saturday morning, Tom and Drew went up to Boob's with me. It was pretty quiet. No bugling and very little sign up here. Only a couple shots in the distance. I had Drew in a comfortable place – too comfortable. He fell asleep. Three cows came out by Tom's, and I whispered to Drew, "Here comes some elk."

Waking up from his sleep, he sat right up quickly. Off they ran. If that had been a bull, Drew, we would have been screwed. You have to be alert.

"I wasn't sleeping," he replied.

The kid snores when he's awake! Amazing!

Those cows were all we saw that morning. Sam struggled to get to Hog Pen. He saw a few cows. He was short of breath again also. On Saturday afternoon, me and the boys just saw one coyote. Gary's group had gotten a cow. Good for them!

We talked and laughed half of the night. It was so nice to have them up there and they liked Sam, too.

On Sunday morning, we were halfway up to Boob's when a heavy, wet snow started dumping on us and it got windy. It was getting very cold out. When we went back down, we tried to keep our stove going. The wood was very damp. We sat and talked in the tent most of the day. Sam's knees were hurting badly. Of course, I chewed him out for not getting them fixed.

That evening, the three of us went back up. It was still quite miserable out. It just wasn't worth sitting here with the wind swirling in every direction, so I had Tom and Drew head back ahead of me a couple 100 yards, just in case the elk were moving. As they left the meadow, I was walking along thinking about when Bob and I were up here, when a shot rang out and startled the hell out of me. It was the boys. I ran up to them as quickly as I could. They were walking in a circle behind some trees.

They said when they walked over the hill on the trail, two bulls were looking right at them. The bulls ran around that hill out of sight. Tom and Drew had to run back up it. The two elk were walking in the dead timber when Drew took a shot. Poor Drew, running up hill, out of breath, first elk hunt, and he was probably pissing in his pants. What chance did he have? Very little.

We looked all over for blood or hair – nothing but tree splinters again. Back at camp, Drew got another hard lesson – bend over. Sam hadn't made it very far before he had to turn back.

That night, I showed the boys my mouse killing techniques. Tom had one run right across his chest during the night. I'd still be running if that were me. Monday morning was peaceful, but uneventful. Sam stayed in this morning. When we went up that afternoon, there were tracks all around my blind. They were there during the day. *Damn it to heck.*

I just couldn't sit there that long, but I told the boys they could if they wanted to. Our time together in camp was also quality time and lots of fun. Just before dark, there were a few bugles up high. *At least there are two left.* Tom saw a herd way across the valley on the west ridge as we went down. We got to camp in the dark. No light was on. *Sam must still be out.* I opened the tent door and there he was, sleeping in his warm bag. *He must not be feeling well.*

On Tuesday morning, Drew and I saw a cow and calf. Tom had just seen that coyote again. We heard two shots from Hog Pen. *Sam, maybe?* We got back to camp, and he wasn't there.

"We better go help him," I said.

We put our packs on and were just leaving when he walked in. He was pissed. He walked past us and put his rifle in the tent. We followed him in, but he never said a word – he just bent over.

"Oh no," I thought. I would have bet money he had another milker down.

He said he was just sitting there, cold, wishing he was back in the tent and there stood a big (at least it was big to him) 4x4 on the edge of the dead timber. He had him in his scope standing there at 200 yards and he couldn't get the safety off. He said he blew on it, pushed it, and tapped on it to finally get it off safety. By now, the bull was in the trees. He said he knew better than to shoot, but he could still see him, so he shot because he was pissed. He went and looked all around for blood. There was nothing but tree splinters. He killed another dead tree.

That afternoon we went back to our respective spots. It was deathly quiet, no shooting, no elk. That evening in the tent, we sat around and talked. Drew was a very smart kid. He had no problem getting out of school for a week, but you should have seen his eyes when I said I had talked to his teacher and told her I had special *learnin'* skills and I would give him some homework up here.

"After all," I said, "look how I learned your dad and he turned out just fine."

Drew was just as shocked when I mentioned the teacher's name. Don't tell him, but I got it from Tom earlier.

I gave him a list of words and meanings the way I say them. For example, my version "mitt" means "with" as in I can't live "mitt" out you.

Badadas = potatoes. Mamatas = tomatoes.

His favorite though was "You claim-jumpin', snake-bitin', lily-livered, no account, moose breath piece of shit," which is what one says when greeting a good friend. I think he's still laughing at that. Wednesday morning and evening were uneventful again – very quiet. The weather was moving in so we packed what we could to be ready for Steve in the morning. I called him and told him we didn't have any elk. What a memorable trip this was. I wish Drew and Sam would've got an elk though.

Next Year ⟶

JC & Charlie

This One's for Sam

Chapter 42

It's very hard for me to write this, even eight years later. On November 24th, 2014, one month after we got back from our elk hunt, our phone rang at 11:35 p.m. I woke up immediately as my wife, Marie, answered it. In the dark silence, I heard the voice from the other end say "Marie." Then there was a pause and then crying.

I knew the voice – it was Sam's Marie. Then the shocking words I'll never forget: "We lost Sam," she said.

I jumped out of bed hysterically and started pacing back and forth down our hallway. I kept saying, "No, no it can't be… it just can't be."

I didn't even get a chance to talk to her before my wife hung up. I refused to believe it. *How can you die from bad knees?*

All I could think about was how I constantly chewed him out for not getting them fixed. I felt like throwing up.

An hour later, my wife said, "You should talk to her."

It was going on 1:00 a.m., but I had to know. There was no way I was going to sleep anyhow. I got up the courage to call, and all we did for a few minutes was cry. (I'm feeling that whole episode all over again as I write this.) We finally were able to talk.

She told me Sam was very weak when we came back from hunting that fall. He hated to go see a doctor, but she made him go. He had a blockage in his heart.

What I'll never understand is that he saw a doctor on a Monday and Sam told Marie that he was supposed to go in for a procedure that Thursday. If he was that bad, why the hell didn't they keep him there? I personally think Sam made that decision. He died from a heart attack the day before his appointment.

I was a pallbearer at his funeral, and I had all I could do to keep from passing out standing by his coffin. I held back the tears the best I could. This was a tough one for many people. I'll never forget him, and I hope he forgives me for constantly hollering at him.

Fall arrived again. My oldest son, Scott and his friend, Foster, came with me for the first time. We picked up Foster near Spearfish, South Dakota. They had filmed hunting shows together before, so we thought it would be a good idea to make a documentary show of this hunt and dedicate it to Sam. Foster did most of the filming and Scott filmed when he was with me. I had gone to my chiropractor before leaving home. This long ride made matters even worse on my back. I talked about Sam most of the way down.

The weather was nice, and all of our stops were right on time. The guys were extremely excited. Foster had elk hunted with his dad one time before, but this was Scott's first time. They started to realize just how much work it was when we were packing the panniers. Steve took our stuff up again and the guys filmed quite a bit walking up. It was beautiful out. The camp went up quickly for a couple of rookies.

We put the flags up and toasted Bob and I saluted Sam and said, "Rest in Peace, my friend." The guys thought it was very special and it was.

The guys cut and chopped enough wood for a week. The weather was actually hot for being up this high this late. Friday, I showed them some areas to hunt – Old Dad's, TD's Mountain, Hog Pen, and Porcupine's, etc. Foster put on 10 miles searching for the right place on Friday alone. He was carrying some kind of gadget that said how far you walked.

"What next? Just walk until you're tired," I said.

The only other hunters we saw just happened to be part of the oath-buster crew.

On opening morning, Scott was going to go to Porcupine's, but I talked him into coming up with me to Boob's. He had never seen the meadow yet. Foster said he had seen good sign up on TD's, so he went that way. He also took the camera so he could film some of his experiences. On our way up to Boob's, we had to stop several times because we had elk all around us. I told Scott I was going to have him sit with me, just like his brother, Bobby, did.

He said, "That's fine, but what if a trophy comes out? You're taking him, Dad."

I didn't say anything.

We had just got settled in my blind and several elk came out of Kit Kat. Scott was looking in that direction and I was looking in the opposite direction. Then a 4x4 came within 50 yards of us. I told Scott he was legal. He slowly turned and looked and whispered, "He's a little small."

Like father, like son. Then out of nowhere, a beautiful 5x5 came from Tom's and was walking right to us. I told

Scott to turn around as quickly as he could, but carefully. "He's a trophy, Scott." I said. The bull was only 100 yards away now and closing in.

Scott finally got turned and before he even lifted his gun, he said, "Holy shit, Dad, you take him. You've waited a long time." That sounded familiar.

I can't believe we argued for a bit, then I finally insisted that Scott shoot him, and he did. Damn near in the same spot Bobby got his – 75 yards away. What a trophy. We walked over to him, and he definitely was a beauty. Scott had the thrill of his life. He grabbed his radio and was going to tell Foster to come up and help when he was done hunting. My back was completely out.

Before Scott could even turn the radio on, a shot rang out from TD's. Foster called us instead and said he had just shot a nice 5x5 that ran right to him. Two elk down, 10 minutes apart, 15 minutes after the season opened. Talk about Lady Luck. Foster gutted his and then came to help us. I sure wasn't much help, but I did what I could. Maybe Sam was telling me to quit bitching about my back and get it fixed.

Foster brought the camera and sleds up. They got some nice filming of the whole thing. We got Scott's back to camp, then they went up and got Foster's. I tried to tell them not to overdo it, but they were young. They got everything down except one quarter, which Foster went and got the next morning.

I went back to Boob's Saturday evening by myself, but there was nothing around. Too much commotion, probably. Sunday morning, there was nothing again. I still couldn't believe Scott got that fantastic bull seventy-five yards in front of me. I was very happy, and I knew Sam would have been, too.

I didn't forget about the menu. Sam's Marie insisted I stop on the way and get her chili and I still do that to this day. What a sweet lady. Now I am not calling my dear friend Sam a liar, but he always told us he made the chili.

Yep, uh-huh.

The rest of the menu was steak and taters, Shrimp New Orleans, ribs and fries, fresh trout, burgers topped with crab meat and a cheese sauce, and the final meal was Sam's hot dogs with mac and cheese. That is the final meal we have every year. That man loved his hot dogs.

On Sunday night, Foster brought the movie camera with and we headed to Boob's. You couldn't make up a show like the one we were about to get. Scott's never going to believe this, Foster said. We tried to count the elk, but it was almost impossible. We know between 150 – 200 elk came out. We counted thirty bulls among them. Most were legal and some very nice. They were all around us.

There was a deep bugle still in the woods, though, so I didn't get too excited about the bulls that were by us. Just before dark, I saw him in the timber. It was too dark for a shot, but looking through my scope, I could see he was a 6x6 at least, and he was nice and wide. He was definitely the old herd bull. We had to sneak out of there without spooking them, which took us some time.

We got to camp late, and Foster was so excited, he had a hard time telling Scott about our episode – but at least it was on camera. Pine martens were getting into our meat. I had called down and Colton was coming up to get the first two elk tomorrow.

On Monday morning, Scott and I spooked several elk on the way to Boob's. We sat for a few hours, but nothing this morning. Colton picked up the two elk and said they were bigger than the ones their camps had killed so far. He told us they were going to be busy, so we had to pack out either Wednesday or wait until Friday. We had two already, so I said Wednesday. The boys got theirs – that's the main thing.

On Monday night, Scott brought the camera with up to my blind. We sat and talked about Sam and this hunt so far. Just like in the movies, the last hour and here they came. The same herd as the other night. They were all over the meadow again. There were several shooters, but not the big boy I had seen. The wind was in our face. Everything was perfect.

Then, the wind changed and blew towards them. At first, several jumped and raised their heads.

Scott said, "There's a monster just coming out of the trees – he's 300 yards away."

That figures. Now the wind is going to spook them all.

All of a sudden, the wind completely stopped. I was getting ready to pull up on this majestic beauty, a slight breath of air drifted slowly across our faces and stopped dead. Scott was watching with his binoculars. I didn't want him filming me shooting. It's a personal thing. Just before I fired, the bull let out a bugle and looked straight ahead. I fired, but he never moved.

Scott said, "You hit him! Get him again."

I fired again and he dropped in his tracks. We started towards him as the entire herd scattered. Scott was filming now, and he was ahead of me. As we got closer, I could hear

Scott say, "Oh my God, Dad, you did it. He's the biggest one you ever got."

When I got to him, I was shocked and started to tremble. We were losing light, so we filmed what we could. He was even bigger than Bob's. He scored 360. I just couldn't believe it. We dressed him out for the morning and headed down.

As we were walking, Scott said, "Did you get a strange feeling when that whiff of air went over us?"

I said, "Yes, I did, and I believe Sam was here."

Scott said, "He definitely was."

I shouted out that night, "I did it, Sam!"

We called down and told Colton to bring a big horse. I caped him out for a head mount and rolled the hide up to his antlers. He was very heavy. When Colton and Foster lifted him on the horse, all Colton said was, "Holy shit."

As far as we know, Steve said it was the biggest one he'd seen come out of this area. Sam would be proud. We stopped and showed JC and Margo. The first thing they said was, "Sam got you that bull, Chaz." I know.

This was the dream hunt of a lifetime for all three of us.

I retired that American Flag. The guys folded it up properly. When I got home, I made a memorial for Sam.

The upper back teeth on a Bull Elk are ivory — sometimes called "the buglers." I've saved every one of them from the bulls I have killed over the years. This Bull was special, so I had a beautiful gold and diamond ring made from one of the ivories from this magnificent animal for a lifetime memory.

Next Year ⟶

Charlie with big Elk - 2015

Scott with his trophy bull

The Hunter Invasion

Scott and I went through Bismarck on our way to pick up Foster in South Dakota. We said hi to everyone and started dropping off potatoes. We stopped and picked up Marie's chili. It was windy during the drive to Lusk. We got there right at 5:00 p.m.

The next morning, we stopped by the park on our way to Laramie. There was one monster bull elk in the park. We gassed up in Laramie and off to Colorado. Same as always, we packed our panniers the day before at the motel. We had our last "good meal" and were ready for the walk in. After dropping everything off with Steve and Colton, we headed up to camp.

It was nice but the trail was very muddy. Steve said they had 10 inches of snow a few days before we got there. We noticed my friend Rich hadn't been in his camp for a few years now. He wasn't feeling good. We had the camp set up by late afternoon. We put the flags up as always, including a new American flag, and toasted Bob. We heard bulls bugling towards dusk.

So far, no other hunters surfaced. I knew Gary was going with his friend to the other side of the mountain from us. I left his bag of potatoes in his truck down below. He was a great hunting neighbor and an all-around good guy.

I heated up Sam's (Marie's) chili for supper. Later on, the menu was as follows: soup; Foster's freeze-dried shit, I mean lasagna; fresh trout; turkey burgers; beef brisket; and Sam's special hot dogs and mac and cheese.

It was so nice the first couple of days, Scott went to the lake and caught several three-pound trout. He brought a couple back for supper – delicious. Foster put on another twenty miles scouting.

When Scott came back, he said he ran into five guys that knew who I was and where we hunted. He also talked with three guys from out east. They were all camping and hunting up by the lake. Scott told them if he ever walked up there, it would just be for fishing. He said he wouldn't even carry his gun.

Foster found some good sign, so he knew where he was going on opening day. I got everything ready to take up to Boob's. On Saturday morning, Scott went to Hog Pen for several hours, but didn't see anything.

Foster headed to where he had seen a bull the day before. He said two guys came walking right towards him with flashlights on early that morning. He gave them a quick flash with his light so they would at least see he was there. They ended up right over a ridge from him anyhow. They shot at daybreak and Foster figured there goes the bull I had scouted. He said he saw three other guys up on TD's Mountain.

Where did these guys come from anyhow. No one came by our camp on the trail.

Up in Boob's, a herd was milling around in the timber. It got windy and they were getting spooky. They

360

finally split up and headed back up in the timber. I met up with Scott back at camp. Foster ended up staying out all day.

That evening, Scott tried up Old Dad's and I went back to Boob's. It was still in the upper 60s during the day. Scott and I both heard some bugling, but that was it. When he returned, Foster told us about all the hunters he had around him. Sunday morning, Foster said he wasn't sure he was going to stay up on top all day. I told him if it was too windy his scent would just push them away anyhow, but it was up to him. I got back to camp and since it was so nice out, Scott decided to go up to the lake fishing again. He didn't take his rifle, just like he said he wouldn't. He came back with trout and one hell of a story.

One of the three guys from out east was sitting by a tree on the main trail. Scott asked him what he was doing there. He'd never hunted elk before, and his partners told him to sit by a trail. I don't think they meant the main government trail. Scott said the guy had an old military style rifle. He finally told the guy, "Come on, I'll find you a better spot."

Scott said he got him settled in in a nice area and just like that, a herd came over the hill right at them.

"There were two legal bulls, and one was huge," Scott said. "Just about as big as yours, Dad."

They came within 150 yards, then Scott looked down at this guy. He was shaking – he couldn't get a shell in the barrel and the bull kept coming. He panicked so bad, he was trying to hand the gun to Scott and said, "You shoot him."

Scott told him, "No, he's your bull." Elk fever overtook him, and the elk were gone. Later in the week, they walked to our camp and told Scott they couldn't believe what had happened. They told him that was amazing how you kept your word. They were pretty nice guys.

The other five hunters that were going to camp and hunt by the lake moved their camp to the Missouri camp right south of us. They were the ones all over up by Foster and in Hog Pen. We couldn't stop that, but at least be honest about it. Ends up, sure enough, one of them was the original oath breaker from years before and brought up four other new guys. The chain reaction goes on and on.

On Monday morning, there were shots up the draw as I was sitting in Boob's. I knew who it was. What fools with all this wind. Yeah, you might get one up there, but the rest of the herd will end up in China. That was the end of the bugling also. Scott went back over by Hog Pen. A lone shot rang out towards Chuckie's Mountain, but it could've been anybody.

Over my radio came, "Bull down." It was Foster. Scott went over to help him, and I said, "I'll bring up the sleds." We ended up sledding him right to camp. He shot a nice 6x5.

Monday evening, Scott went towards Porcupine's as I headed to Boob's. I was sitting in my blind looking around when I noticed a couple of guys sitting on the hill where you enter into Boob's. They weren't there when I went by. They weren't even wearing orange.

Crossfire again. Absolutely ridiculous.

I knew who it was and why they were doing this. The wind was swirling in every direction. With them on one end and me on the other end, there was not a chance in hell any elk were coming out. I left just before dark. I was in no mood for discussing this situation, so I went clear around them as they sat there in their camo.

Scott ran into one of their other guys coming back to camp. He asked the kid why they lied when they said they were going to hunt up by the lake. He said he'd never been here before and their leader (the oath breaker) said he knew some good places to hunt, so he had them move camp during the night before season opened. Scott told me he saw two flashlights coming down from Boob's when he went by. Things got a little heated.

The next day, they were gone. The ironic thing is, there were usually less hunters by the lake, and most of the time, there were also more elk up there.

There were no elk around for a couple of days. Wednesday morning, Scott came up to Boob's with me. He decided to sit in Tom's. Shortly after daybreak, he fired. It sure as hell woke me up. He radioed Foster to bring up the sleds. I waited until Foster arrived, then walked up there to help. He had killed a nice 6x6.

Lady Luck, common sense, and patience work the best in this region instead of chasing the elk all around or out of the area. I'll never quit learning something about the elk there, but after 43 years, I do have some idea of their movements under most situations, such as the constant weather changes and hunting pressure.

We got Scott's elk packed down and started getting things ready for heading out again. I went back up to Boob's the last evening. It was a peaceful, fulfilling evening. I said my goodbye and saluted those magnificent elk for another year.

We stopped and said our goodbyes to JC and Margo on the way home. They couldn't believe I was still wearing JC's old cowboy hat. I proudly wear it to this day.

Next Year ⟶

Coffee on the stove

Taking Bob's Advice

Three of us planned to go this year. After our Bismarck routine, we picked up Foster in South Dakota. The weather was nice, and we arrived at Lusk at 5:00pm. We left earlier the next morning for Laramie, so it was still dark when we went by the park. We picked up some fishing supplies in Laramie and headed to Colorado.

Same routine, pack panniers and have our last "good meal." We dropped everything off with Steve and started that all-too-familiar walk up. For the first time in all these years, my legs got very tired out the last mile. The guys went on ahead of me to the camp.

We set up camp and the flags before dark. The guys gathered enough wood for the evening, and we gave a toast to Bob. It was time for Marie's chili and a long overdue rest. Here's the rest of the menu for the year: Swedish meatballs; Scott's French Toast (hopefully); ribs; hotdish; camp stew; and Sam's Special.

Gary was back up here with his nephew. They were camped in the Missouri camp. Scott's three buddies from out east topped by their way up by the lake. Friday, Foster went up TD's mountain to scout and it was so nice out that Scott went up to the lake to try and get some trout for supper. I finished setting up camp. It was warm, but it was also very windy. You had to be on your toes in the dead standing wood. Scott came back with trout again and Foster had seen a herd of elk above Old Dad's.

Scott saw two guys walking up towards Boob's on his way back to camp, so he walked up ahead of them to cut them off. They were going to hunt Boob's opening morning. He told them how I had a blind for all those years and asked if they could please go someplace else. They said they would.

Opening morning, Foster went back up TD's, Scott went to Tom's, and I was settled in my blind in Boob's meadow.

Scott shot again at daybreak. I just smiled. Then there were three more fast shots. I waited for a while and then walked to him. Nothing was said on the radio. I met up with him and he wasn't too happy.

"What's going on?" I asked.

He had dropped a 5x7 100 yards from him and, while he was putting another shell in, it staggered up and went behind a clump of trees. He was ready for when it would step out. Suddenly, he said three shots were fired right where the bull went in. It shocked the shit out of him being that close. As he walked over, those two young guys from earlier were hooting and high fiving each other.

"First time hunting and one ran right us," the one guy said.

The problem was that the bull was walking dead. I can't believe what Scott did after that, but it was his choice. He said, "I don't know how you guys got here, but didn't you see me drop him? Look at the hole in his shoulder."

The one guy denied it was hit at all – he said it ran by them. The other fellow knew better. Then they said they could just flip for him. Scott told them they obviously had never heard about first blood, and he wasn't about to flip for an elk he knocked down. He told me the one guy was so overwhelmed with joy; Scott just told them to keep him, and they thanked him.

Scott and I headed down to camp. I never did see those two guys, but I guarantee you, the discussion and the outcome would have had a different ending with me. Foster said there was a camp in Hog Pen, right where we killed many elk. People must be reading too many how-to books.

On Saturday night, Foster went back up. Scott tried above Old Dad's and, of course, you know where I went. Bob told me earlier that fall, "You killed your big one now – don't be a fool and pass up on any younger ones. Get one for me."

In all honesty, that was my plan, but I wasn't going to shoot a milker – no offense, Sam. Foster had seen a pretty good herd above Old Dad's again. Scott couldn't see them because they were up much higher and over a couple of ridges. I didn't see any either.

Sunday morning, Scott went back to Old Dad's, and I went to Boob's again. Foster was above Hog Pen and all he saw were hunters combing the woods like they were hunting grouse.

I was just sitting here daydreaming again when I saw two sets of antlers coming over the hill from Kit Kat. There was a small 4x3 and a young 6x5. They topped the hill at 200 yards and stood there. The small one turned and started to walk away. I truly was undecided, but I had made a deal with Bob and there were hunters everywhere. I pulled up as he turned slightly. I held on his shoulder, fired, and down he went. When I got up to him, he was bigger than I thought.

The two young guys that claimed Scott's elk had been in Tom's all along. I had no idea. They just walked out.

I radioed Scott and he brought everything up to help me pack it out. Foster came up also and helped take him down. Scott went back up to Kit Kat that evening, but there was nothing around. Foster had seen elk on a distant ridge with hunters all over.

On Monday, I told Scott to keep watching Boob's, but they were just spooked out of there. Foster kept bumping into hunters up on TD's, but he also was seeing elk above Old Dad's each day.

Sam cursed my knees. I had banged my knee on a log days earlier and now it really was hurting. I managed to make it up with Scott on Monday night, but nothing again. Foster had a bull and twelve cows behind him on top, but never had a shot. That night, we were in bed around 10 or so when we could hear someone hollering up towards TD's. it was very dark out. The hollering got louder and louder. I said, "Someone's in trouble." I got up and got dressed.

As I went toward the main trail, I could make out Gary yelling, "Charlie! Charlie!"

Oh, my God. Something really bad has happened.

I ran down towards the stream, and I could see him coming towards me. "What happened?" I asked. I was worried sick.

"I shot a nice bull right by our camp!" he said. I was puzzled, pissed, worried, and happy at the same time. He walked cross-country through a bunch of tough shit, just to tell me this. He was so excited. I was relieved and told him I'd come see it the next day.

Tuesday morning, Foster didn't have anything happening. Scott got caught going into Boob's. The elk were just beyond the blind along the edge of the timber when he walked in, and they must have winded him and just walked into the timber. Nothing else came out.

It was still very nice 40 to 60 degrees each day. We went over and saw Gary's bull. It was pretty nice, but I told him he had scared the shit out of me. He didn't mean to – he was just excited. Scott's buddies stopped by. They were heading out. They said they saw more hunters than elk this time. Great guys, hope they keep trying. The boys didn't see anything that evening either.

The last morning, I kept telling Scott to not give up on Boob's and Foster went on top of Hog Pen one more time. Scott had heard some and Foster saw that herd again above Old Dad's. That afternoon, Foster asked me how to get up to Old Dad's. I told him it was tougher than hell. Tall grassy weeds and lots of down timber, not to mention it was almost straight up in places just to get there. He wanted to go up the last night, so I showed him how to get there.

Scott went back up to Boob's. I started cleaning things up in camp to pack down. Funny how things work out. Just before dark, I had most of my chores done and had to go down to the shitter. I was sitting there, thinking we still had a pretty good hunt considering all of the other hunters around and then three rapid shots rang out. Scared the you-know-what out of me. I had my radio on and there was Foster.

"Bull down," he said. Way up in that heavy downed shit.

What we didn't know was Scott had a big boy on the edge of the timber just going to step out. The shots didn't bother the bull, he said, and he had his radio volume all the way down, but it still made a crackling sound, and the bull was gone. We could've probably had three bulls again.

I brought the sleds up, bad knee and all. Scott was already there helping Foster. They were way the hell up there. He shot him thirty yards away. It was the same one that came out to me with the one I shot.

I told Foster, "You could've had him where it would have been easy to get him down – instead you shoot him way the hell up here."

I was proud of him, but it took us until midnight to get him down. Scott fell and hurt his knee badly too, but what a hunt.

We packed down and said our goodbyes to JC and Margo and headed for home.

This one was for you, Bob.

Next Year ⟶

Chapter 45

New Guys Again

For nearly forty years, there were many guys that had asked if they could go elk hunting with me. I just couldn't take more than a couple at a time, especially when Marly and Sam were with me. Suddenly, things shifted and everyone was too busy with life or just couldn't get away. I never dreamt there'd be a day when I would have a hard time finding someone that could go with me. Year 45 was one of those years.

I chose two guys because I wanted them with me, and I knew they would enjoy it and have a great experience.

Dean W. and I picked up Cory in Bismarck. Dean was someone I knew from Harwood and Cory; I'd known since he was very young. He was still a young man. Both of them are great guys and I was happy to have them with me. They got a kick out of me with my potato giveaways. Funny how people appreciate a simple twenty-pound bag of Red River Valley potatoes. I picked up my broasted chickie, Sam's chili, and we were off to Lusk.

It was raining when we left Bismarck and turned to snow close to Lusk. We got there at 4:30 pm. We had supper and a few toddies at the local pub and called it a night. The boys were excited and so was I. It was just slushy the next day on our way to Colorado. Now this was all new for Dean and Cory, but they were a great help packing the panniers.

We walked down to my favorite restaurant and told them this would be their last "good meal." I sure hope they didn't think I was serious.

None of us slept very well that night – too much anticipation, I guess. We got to Steve's an hour earlier than normal. He was pissed that we interrupted his breakfast.

I told him, "Steve, I've been loading these panniers for 45 years. You just finish your breakfast, and we'll get things ready for you."

We had to walk with 8" of snow on the trail. That didn't seem to bother the boys. Too bad there wasn't some color in the aspen for them to see the natural beauty up here. They weren't too impressed with Heart Attack. All I said was, "We have to come back up the mountain on the way out – you might change your opinion on that."

Someone had walked around in our camp, but it was empty. We set up best we could. Dry wood was hard to come by. We had Sam's hot chili, then I gave them the rest of the week's menu as follows; pan-fried walleye, elk steak, German hotdish, ribs, stew, and Sam's Special.

The next day we put the flags up and I told them we had to toast Bob and salute Sam. Man did these two guys cut wood then. If we could get it dried out, we would have more than enough. The problem with bringing up new blood was that I was the only one who could show them where to hunt. Getting older meant I couldn't quite climb those mountains like I used to, but we managed.

We went for a walk, and right away noticed there was a camp in Pat's. It was the same five guys that I had tangled with before. Major web of the oath-breakers. It wouldn't have been so bad, but when their leader said they were going to walk through Boob's each day and go up on top, the discussion got a little heated again. All I said was "That is going to make it tough for all of us and probably chase what's left away."

I felt bad already for Dean and Cory for having to see this. I wanted one or both of them to at least get a chance for a bull. Things settled down before opener. We did end up crossing paths, but all-in-all, it worked out. The guys got a kick out of how entertaining and noisy the killer mice were each night.

On Saturday morning, I directed Dean to Hog Pen and Cory and I went up to Boob's. Dean had a little 3x3 stand 10 feet in front of him right at daybreak. He said when it put its head down, he actually looked down at the bull to see if there was a 4th point. Now that's a close encounter. That was it for Dean that morning. Cory and I had one cow poke out. Two of our neighbors were walking up on the side of Boob's. Perfect.

Yeah right.

Later the sun came out and the snow got crunchy. You may as well use a megaphone now when you're walking through the woods.

That afternoon we noticed someone actually set up a tent between Pat's and our camp. I could damn near throw my hatchet that far. There are millions of acres up here for a campsite – come on. Dean said there were three guys camping right below Hog Pen too. It's certainly not looking too good for the first day anyhow.

On Saturday evening, none of us had seen anything and it started to snow steadily again.

It got pretty cold that night – 5 below zero. My false teeth were frozen in their container, but what pissed me off was that the coffee froze. I had to get up extra early each morning and thaw things out including Dean and Cory. On top of that, my old cot finally broke. Thank God for duct tape.

As if Saturday wasn't bad enough, Sunday morning was heavy thick fog. We went out anyways hoping it would lift. Not a thing around except a few guys in the fog, literally. That evening, Cory and I saw five elk near the top. Couldn't tell what they were though. Dean saw a small herd of twenty or so after dark.

Monday morning, more of the same. The good news was Cody and I had seen lots of tracks, but the bad news was they were all heading down. They're moving. I told the guys to watch for that. A herd could come by you out of nowhere at any given time. The sun pushed through that afternoon, and I thought we had a pretty good chance for the elk to come out that evening. We were pretty optimistic now. Unfortunately, it was deathly quiet all afternoon. No elk, no shooting. Everything froze in the tent again. I paid a lot of money for my sleeping bag that was the same as Sam's, but it paid off now – I stayed toasty warm.

Tuesday morning and evening were as quiet as a silent movie. The guys said they had heard a helicopter down low that evening though. JC rode up just to visit. He said a guy's horse had spooked down the trail a ways and ended up falling on him. JC said he got busted up pretty good. The helicopter the guys had heard was flying in to pick him up. He had ridden past our camp earlier that afternoon.

Wednesday was just as quiet. We walked towards Porcupine's to search for sign, but the snow was even deeper.

It was a very cold and uneventful hunt this time. I felt bad for the guys. We packed down the next day. I zipped up Heart Attack and when we got to the top, the guys said, "Chaz, you're not human."

The guys did say they both had quite an experience though. After our goodbyes to JC and Margo, we headed to the nearest motel for a hot shower to thaw out.

Next Year

Snowed-in tent - 2018

Camera Crew is Back

Chapter 46

Scott and I did our potato run through Bismarck. We picked up Sam's chili and headed to South Dakota to pick up Foster. We arrived at Lusk at 4:30 pm. It was sunny and in the 70s. We got our last-minute supplies in Laramie and headed to Colorado.

The boys had the packing of the panniers down to perfection. We walked down and had our ritual last "good meal" and got ready for the trip up.

We dropped our supplies off at Steve's and walked up in 70-degree weather. It was a nice walk in, but Scott wasn't feeling the best. I think it was altitude sickness. It's a good thing we got the tent up that afternoon because it started snowing big time the next morning. I told the boys how cold it was up here the year before and how hard it was to find dry wood. They found a pretty good dead tree and cut lots of wood. We started to bring up a small Mr. Heater as a backup. That worked well.

We had some hot chili and crashed. The boys insisted they didn't want fancy meals anymore, but I didn't want all the freeze-dried so-called food either, so we compromised as follows for this year's menu: soup, freeze-dried stroganoff (not bad), shrimp and crab over noodles, sloppy joes, freeze-dried something, hotdish, freeze-dried dessert (damn good actually), and Sam's Special.

The next day we put the flags up and gave a toast to Bob and Sam. After finishing up camp, we went for a walk to check around. There were two guys camped around the corner from us again. I didn't know them, but they said they knew of me. I asked them how they knew that. I guess they had heard some stories from down below. Not sure what that meant. They did ask where they should hunt and said they wouldn't bother us. Seemed like some good guys.

I bumped into a fellow I didn't know who had some kind of gadget he was looking down at. It was called OnX, I guess. He showed me how he was looking on this thing at home and had found Boob's meadow. Call me old-fashioned, but that's some bullshit. All the work a person puts in scouting over all those years and you now can just hit a button sitting on your ass in New York City. I didn't quite tell him where to stick it, but I think he could read between the lines. I think OnX could be great for private land, for calling the landowners, etc.

On Friday, Gary came by with his nephew. It was sure nice to see him. They went into the Missouri camp again. The weather had gone from the 70s to very cold over the past two days. Our Mr. Heater got a good workout. Dam mice all over again. One ran right across my beard one night. I couldn't scream because I think I was paralyzed.

On Friday Foster went up scouting. He saw three legal bulls. There was hope.

On Saturday morning, it started to get nice again. Scott and I went up to Boob's but there was hardly any sign at all. Very quiet all around. No shooting whatsoever. Foster couldn't find any of the three bulls he had seen the day before. Gary and our neighbors weren't seeing anything either. It was unusually very quiet everywhere.

The fact that there was no shooting going on anywhere told me the elk numbers just weren't as high as the Game and Parks Department might have thought they were. That evening was quiet again for me and Scott. The only thing Foster was encountering were many other hunters that had walked up from down below.

Scott's knee had started hurting him really bad now. For some reason, I was having problems with vertigo. Foster was having some physical problems also. We were all banged up. I've never had any problems with the altitude, so I didn't know what was going on with me.

The next couple of days were still deathly quiet. At least we were having a good time in camp, but we were starting to get a little cranky about everything, including me. Not sure why – maybe we just had too big of expectations because of our successful years in the past.

I just encouraged the guys saying, "Every year, every day, and every hour is a new chapter, so enjoy every minute of it – good or bad."

The three guys beside us decided to go down lower. I told them this just wasn't normal up here to not see anything and the fact there was no shooting around us was also very unusual. They asked me what I thought was going on and I told them I truly believe the numbers are not here. Just my opinion. Gary and his nephew also left early. Suddenly we had the place to ourselves. That would've normally been just great, but with no elk around, it didn't matter much. Besides that, we were all hunting in different areas and just weren't seeing elk.

Scott's knees were really hurting now and he didn't think he could make it back up to Boob's, so one morning he walked up to Porcupine's. He had made himself a blind in a small patch of evergreens up there a couple of years before, so he sat in there. He finally saw some elk. That was promising. Foster still hadn't come across any elk up high.

As for me, I was running late that morning and got in a hurry. Halfway up at a very quick pace, I completely ran out of air. I panicked. This is the first time it had ever happened to me. I laid on my back staring up at the stars and having a conversation with the Good Lord. I truly thought I was a goner. I couldn't get any oxygen in and my exhales were short. I patiently settled myself down, gave thanks above, and continued on at a slower pace. When I got to Boob's all I could see were the light-colored tan butts of several elk walking back into the timber. I was late – go figure.

That evening, Foster and I hadn't seen anything, but Scott went back up to Porcupines and shot a younger 5x4. He radioed down to us and Foster and I went up and helped him. We packed it to the trail for the horses to pack out.

That night we got the scare of our lives. By now, with the fire from the past and the damage from the beetles, the only things standing were dead trees. Big ones. We were sleeping and around 2:00 am, I could hear it coming. I woke the guys and told them to be aware, as if our tent poles could protect us. Yeah, right. When that straight line wind hit us, all hell broke loose. The thunderous booms of falling huge trees were all around us. When one crashed down right beside us, Foster had enough. He grabbed his sleeping bag

380

and a coat and headed outside. He said, "Let's go out in the open meadow to be safe" and he was gone.

I told Scott it might be over now, but here it came again, even stronger. This time trees crashed all around Scott and me. Mother Nature won. We got the hell out of there with our sleeping bags in tow. I damn near stepped on Foster. He laid his sleeping bag right on the main trail in the meadow.

I asked, "What if a horse came by and stepped on you.?"

"That's better than a giant tree," he said.

That was a long rest of the night. Trees were dropping all night long. We got back into the tent in time for me and Foster to go hunting. Nothing was around. I wondered how many elk got caught up in that disastrous wind and ended up with a one-ton tree on them.

When I walked down from Boob's, I couldn't believe my eyes. The burnt-out forest was an ugly sight to begin with, but after this, all but a few of the standing trees were flattened like pancakes. What a sad sight. It will be hundreds of years before someone will see what I cherished on the mountain years before the fires.

When we got back to camp, we realized just how lucky we were. Just feet away laid three trees crisscrossed and a huge one right by the tent. It could have been disastrous for sure. Lady Luck was with us, kind of.

We finished getting everything ready for the trip out the next day and that night talked about how lucky we were to get through that episode. This year was one of the few that I hadn't at least seen a legal bull This was such a quiet year as far as hearing bugling and shooting, but yet it ended with Mother Nature's encore, power, and noise.

Scott left early to go down because of his knees. Foster and I waited for the horses to arrive then headed down. We visited JC and Margo again and told them we had got caught in the middle of all that.

We were lucky.

Next Year ⟶

Hatchet post and Charlie - 2019

Chapter 47

Fires

I drove alone this year. Tom and Drew joined me again for another try at getting Drew his first elk. I dropped potatoes off and picked up the chili in Bismarck. I stopped by to see my folks and took my time getting to Lusk. I got there at 5:30 p.m. It was quite different with no hunting partners to sing to. I sat alone, eating leftover chickie in the motel. No sense in going to eat by myself.

The next morning, I noticed it was getting smoky as I headed for Colorado. I gassed up in Laramie and took the same route to Colorado I had taken for many years. Thirty miles down the road, a patrolman was sitting by a temporary gate on the road only 85 miles from my destination.. There was heavy smoke in the air. He stopped me and said, "There's a big fire ahead along the highway and they closed it down."

He couldn't figure out why they didn't tell me back at the station in Laramie. I'd traveled sixty extra miles out of my way. I had to go 150 miles further west then head down 100 miles to my motel. What a bummer. Another big, devastating fire in the Rockies.

The boys were already there when I finally arrived. We packed our things up and went and had our last "good meal." Ironically, this was the first bad meal we would ever have in this restaurant.

The next morning, we dropped our stuff off with Steve and headed up. Needless to say, it was extremely dry out — drier than I'd ever seen it.

My heart was heavy as I had just received more bad news. My friend Rich had passed away from cancer.

We made it to camp in about 2½ hours. Our camp went up with no problem. There were no outside fires allowed that year. For food, we ate Sam's chili, then I showed them the rest of the trip's menu. It started with "No Freeze-Dried Shit," then crab-topped burgers, Rocky Mountain stew, ribs, salmon, sloppy joes, and Sam's Special.

We put our flags up and toasted Bob and Sam.

We saw a couple of nice guys and chatted with them for a bit. On Friday, we noticed two more tents by Old Dad's and a camp at the base of TD's. These folks were camped along the natural pathways the elk take all the time. Maybe not this year.

Opening morning, I almost asked Tom if he and Drew wanted to sit up in Tom's area since the elk seemed to have shifted there rather than Boob's over the past few years. Following tradition though, I put them in my blind, and I went up to Tom's. Lady Luck sure plays tricks on a guy sometimes. The whole idea was to get Drew a bull. But Tom and Drew didn't see anything in my blind.

I was sitting where Scott usually sat in Tom's area when I saw a lone bull come along the side of Bun Mountain. *It will go right to those guys for sure.* But no, not only did it come towards me, the young 4x4 stopped ten yards from me.

Our eyes met, but it never startled him. He just stood there. There was a 50-50 chance he would turn and go into Boob's meadow once he went by me. He walked to my left, finally. All he had to do was keep going left and he'd be down in Boob's.

Just before he got to the ridge that divided the two meadows, he turned right again and faded into the woods. The guys weren't happy with me at first, but when I explained my intention, they were understanding.

Saturday afternoon, we switched places. You probably think I'm going to say it happened again. It didn't, but it wouldn't have surprised me any. We heard three shots over by TD's, but that was it. There were no elk around.

The three of us always had a great time around camp in the evening laughing and telling Drew about the old days. Tom would tell Drew how I was his mountain man hero when he was little Speckmouse. But Drew was too smart to fall for that crap.

Sunday morning, Tom and Drew had one cow and a calf come by them in Tom's. I didn't see anything.

We talked to a couple of guys I had met before – Tim and Ryan. They had seen a bear eating on a dead horse near their camp. That was ironic because the stream we crossed by our camp was called Dead Horse Crossing for years. This dead horse was a quarter mile away from the upper stream. That was the first time in all my years of traveling there that I had talked to someone who had actually seen a bear, even though I knew they were around. The bear had come through camp also. But I hadn't seen one.

Drew got ill the next morning. He was having medication issues, so Tom walked him down to his vehicle. Drew drove himself to the nearest airport and flew home.

That ended any chance of him getting his first bull for this year.

Tom made it down and back in 4½ hours. Record time.

By Sunday night, neither of us had seen anything. We heard no shooting anywhere either. That night, we were hoping Drew made it home alright; he did.

It snowed six inches overnight. We were hoping the fresh snow would move some elk around, if they were up there. There seemed to be less elk each year, causing me to wonder if the burnt-out areas and all the downed timber had shifted their patterns. This certainly appeared to be the case as far as larger herds go.

Monday morning, Tom saw that cow and calf again in Kit Kat. All I saw was a mangy-looking coyote. Temperatures were in the lower 20s. That evening produced the same quiet, lifeless results. No shooting anywhere. Near silence. Not even any birds around. The only elk we saw all day were three cows on the way down.

Three guys I had met before — Paul, Joe, and Trevor — were camped by TD's Mountain. They stopped by our camp on the way down early Wednesday. They asked me where all the elk were. I told them what I thought — that the numbers weren't there anymore. The sad part in all of this was that Tom and I appeared to be the only ones left up the area. We had the whole area to ourselves, but there were no elk around.

The wind kicked up over the next few days. On the last evening, Tom went above Old Dad's, and I went up to Boob's. Deathly silence again. I said my goodbyes to the meadow and started down. Just as I got close to where Tom was, he fired. Yes, I jumped! He went down to head for camp before dark and, when he turned around, a bull was walking right up to where he was sitting. He got off a quick shot in the timber. When I got to him, we walked back up together.

"I think I missed him," he said, "but we better double check." After an hour or so, the shattered tree God got Tom too. He had to bend over and take his butt kicking. My hopes were so high for this hunt, I felt like I had let the boys down in a way.

We packed down the next day and said our goodbye to JC and Margo again. I took Tom to the airport to pick up his vehicle and we went our separate ways. I miss him already.

Next Year

Chapter 48

Two for Colorado

All my past hunting buddies had obligations, so I searched for new blood for the year's hunt. I asked a buddy of mine, Eric, from my hometown if he'd like to go along.

He damn near jumped in my lap. "Absolutely!" he said.

I told him all the things he needed to bring as we made plans for the trip. I told him we had to make a few potato stops along the way. He just gave me a puzzled look. I introduced him to my folks in Bismarck, then we picked up Sam's chili and were on our way to Lusk. We arrived at 4:40 p.m.

It was windy all the way there due to an approaching storm, so we left for Laramie earlier the next morning. It was little more than a steady rain and very chilly out. We gassed up in Laramie and took off for the motel in Colorado.

We wanted to get over a couple of high mountain passes before it turned to snow. We had to pack the panniers in our motel room because of the wet weather. Last year was dry with fires, making this year's wet and snowy weather a stark contrast.

Welcome to the Rockies.

Eric was excited and so was I. I still hadn't lost that feeling I had since the very first trip. If I ever do, I'll have to consider just how much longer I want to continue doing this. Bob always told me that I would know when it was time. I certainly hope it's a few more years down the road. I'm only in my mid-70s and still feel pretty good (kinda).

There were eight inches of snow on the ground the next morning. We dropped our panniers off at Steve's around 9:00 a.m. His son, Colton, packed us in with help from a wonderful, hard-working young woman named Evanica. It was a tough slippery walk in for Eric and me. I noticed he wasn't even breathing hard so I pushed myself harder. I didn't want this rookie to think I was a wreck. I later learned he was pissed because we didn't stop and rest for a minute more often.

We got to camp before Colton. The campsite was just the way we had left it. Colton was a big boy but had diabetic issues. When they rode in, he was damn near blue and had a hard time breathing. I was worried he'd never make it back down. We helped unload the horses so they could get going. Eric had a couple of oxygen cannisters, so he had Colton inhale a few breaths of it before they left. We just hoped he'd make it to the ranch alright.

We struggled putting up camp in the wet snow, but that was just part of the experience. Dry wood was another challenge. My Mr. Heater saved us a couple of mornings. I cooked some hot chili to warm us then showed Eric the menu.

"Menu?" he questioned. "Up here?"

"Yep! Here it is: Rocky Mountain Boil, steak and corn on the cob, hamburger gravy with mashed taters, chicken-fried steak, and Sam's Special."

We put the flags up the next morning and toasted Bob and Sam knowing they would both love to be up there with us regardless of the weather.

It snowed until Friday afternoon. Finally, the sun made an appearance. My plan was to put Eric in Tom's while I would be at Boob's in my blind again. We went up before the official season opening to get things ready. There was absolutely no elk sign in the fresh snow.

Not good, I thought, but I didn't say anything to Eric who was busily cutting a bit of wood by himself. Five guys had come past our camp, and it looked like they were heading towards Porcupine's.

Opening morning was nice considering all the snow around. Eric and I split up and he headed for Tom's. I considered having him sit in my blind, and I would go to Tom's that morning. Am I ever glad I didn't. At daybreak, there was shooting all around us. Ten cows ran through the burnt timber behind me.

At 9:15 a.m., three quick shots rang out that sounded like it could've been Eric, but it echoed so long and loud, it was hard to tell. For some damn reason, my radio wouldn't work either. I waited for a bit and then walked up to Tom's. There sat Eric wearing a smile from ear to ear as he looked down on a beautiful 7x6½ bull.

He said, "Didn't you hear me shoot? I called you on the radio."

"I couldn't hear you," I explained, admiring his kill.

We finished skinning and quartering the elk. Later that afternoon, he brought the sled up. I told him I'd be up to help before I went hunting. That idiot went out and pulled both sleds down to the entry of Boob's before I got up there.

That evening, I saw two cows in the meadow, but with the wind swirling all over the place, they got spooked and ran away. Just before dark, I headed back to camp.

Both sleds were gone. Eric had taken the entire elk down himself. Yes, I chewed him out. I was old, but I was not helpless.

Sunday morning, there was nothing again in Boob's, but someone fired at least twelve times by my count over in Lost Meadow. *They must have caught a bull in the open meadow or they didn't have their rifle sighted in*, I thought .

Eric cleaned up the elk skull and worked on the quarters during the day. A game warden named Evan stopped by and mentioned that we didn't have the proper carcass tag. We got a chewing out, but he just gave Eric a warning. I told the warden it was my fault, explained how long I'd been coming, and told him I should've known better. The warden seemed impressed at the number of years I had come.

On Monday morning, I saw a coyote as the weather eased up a bit. A bull bugled up on top so I knew there was at least one left. It was windy when I headed down, and I saw one guy sitting above Old Dad's as I went by.

Camp was becoming a mud mess from the temperature going up. That evening, the same guy was still above Old Dad's, and I still didn't see anything. The shooting had also stopped.

When I headed up to Boob's on Tuesday, Eric said he was going to try and catch some little brookies. I decided to walk up to Porcupine's during the day. The snow was much deeper and the only tracks were human. On my way back, I talked to two guys who said they put out a campfire that was left by two backpackers. I thanked them.

Tuesday night, on my way up to Boob's, I noticed human tracks ahead of me on my trail. When I got to the meadow, those same two guys turned away from my blind, heading to Tom's. They saw me coming just before they went over the ridge. Right at the magic hour, they came walking back into Boob's Meadow like they were on a Sunday stroll. They headed down and nothing came out.

Wednesday was the same. Very peaceful, quiet, and no elks around. We packed up in the mud and watched for Colton who had ended up in the hospital but was fine now. JC had major surgery that summer and looked very weak. We talked to him and Margo for a while and headed for home.

At least Eric got his trophy.

By the way, Eric caught lots of trout, providing us with an excellent brunch.

Next Year ⟶

My Daughter's Surprise

Chapter 49

Early in the summer, my daughter and some of her friends planned to go horseback riding. She asked where my camp was. I told her that I never tell anybody where it is.

"Well then, I'll find out on my own," she said, defiantly.

I gave in and told her, but I was curious why she wanted to go there. She said that she and some of her friends wanted to go on a horseback trail ride in the area. I told her there were some very nice trails up there. Little did I know when they got to Steve's later that summer, she insisted Maggie take them to my campsite instead of taking the beautiful route along the river.

I asked Eric to go hunting again. He was enthusiastic and asked if he could bring a friend of his.

"As long as he keeps the location to himself, that will be fine," I said.

Lonny was our third guy and was a great guy to have along. He enjoyed everything and was a hard worker. And, with Lonny there, Eric had someone to cut and split wood with him.

Back to my daughter…

She called just before we left and said she hid something in my camp for me, hinting at where it was so I had an idea where to look for this surprise. I couldn't imagine what it could be or how she figured out where my camp was.

We stopped in Bismarck and did our potato thing, then picked up Sam's chili and set off for Lusk. As I merged onto the interstate, I turned the radio down because I could hear a grinding noise in the front of my Suburban. A bearing had gone out, but Lady Luck was with me this time. Right beside me was a Chevy dealership that took my vehicle in and graciously put it ahead of some others. They put new wheel bearings on the front and checked the others to be sure. They said the wheel would've fallen off after a few more miles. What a great place.

When we got to Lusk at 5:40 p.m., it was still sunny out. The next day, we stopped at the park, gassed up in Laramie, and picked up last minute items. We got everything packed and went out for our last "good meal." The next morning, we headed to Steve's.

Maggie said, "Your daughter, Dawn, was here with her friends this summer, but they didn't want to go on a scenic ride; they wanted to go to your camp instead."

"Yes, I know; she told me," I answered.

We discussed how Dawn had left something up there for me. Now I was really curious.

Lonny did okay on the way up, but he was quite short of breath. He used a couple of cannisters of oxygen on the way in.

Lonny whispered something to Eric about me walking pretty good for an old fart. To be honest, the walk in and back down felt as good as when I was twenty-four years old. Crazy!

When we surveyed the camp, it was clear that someone had been in our camp earlier. Thankfully, they didn't leave a mess. Skeletal remains of a horse that either got lost or killed laid by a tree in our camp. We got camp set up, put the flags up, and toasted Bob and Sam. Eric told Lonny the story behind all that.

Moments later, I found my daughter's surprise. She had left a picture of herself when she was young with Spice, her horse. I got the hint. I don't think she ever forgave me for getting rid of him. I never had the heart to tell her it wasn't me; it was Bob.

We had our chili, and Eric said, "Let's see the menu."

The menu that year was the same ole, same ole: hotdish, steak, burgers, soup, and of course, Sam's Special.

Over time, we saw more people. On Thursday, four guys came by right away. Later, Paul, Joe, and Trevor camped near us. Everyone seemed to be in great spirits due in part to the beautiful weather.

On Saturday morning, Eric was back in Tom's while I was watching from my blind in Boob's. Lonny was on a knoll above Old Dad's. It was quiet again with just a couple of shots off in the distance. At 8:00 a.m., I looked to my right and saw a bull coming down the side of the mountain. I couldn't tell with the naked eye how big he was, so I didn't get too concerned with him right away.

I made a terrible rookie mistake by not getting ready when I first saw him. He stepped out into the meadow all alone, almost in the same spot where I had shot my big bull. I didn't need to pull up my scope to see he was a beauty, but that was confirmed when I did. He wasn't as big as my other bull. Still, he was an outstanding 6x6. I had to lay down to get a shot off.

With my titanium shoulder, I couldn't see through the scope and reach the trigger at the same time in that position. My God, after all the elk I've had in my scope and many chances to shoot, there was no excuse for this. I panicked. I had the scope power set way too high and didn't think I had time to turn it down. *Rookie.* The bull got nervous and moved back towards the timber while I struggled to get a good hold on him in the scope. I watched as this beautiful animal walked away. Now that's the definition of a Dumb Ass, worthy of a kick in the butt from the guys.

The guys stayed out until dark. When they returned, they reported that they didn't see anything. I hated to tell them my story. I went back up there that afternoon and saw nothing. There weren't any tracks in Boob's at all – strange.

On Sunday morning, I'll be damned if I didn't screw up again, just not quite as badly; I dozed off sitting in my blind. *I must be getting too damn old.* I had never done that before. Sure, it was quiet out, but I knew I had to constantly watch in the timber for any movement — not to mention the mountainside. When I woke up, I saw that I had crossed my arms and leaned my rifle against a log on my right side. As I startled awake, I saw that I nearly missed a legal bull walking on the trail 100 yards to my left.

I slowly reached for my rifle without taking my eyes off of him. He was getting skittish and could bolt at any moment. The ground in my blind was slanted. I was using a double-legged shooting stick with the legs offset. By the time I pulled up on him, he had already gone back towards the timber and stood 200 yards away.

Because of a bush in front of me, I had to half stand up to shoot over it, putting the shooting stick out of balance.

I finally got it stable as he approached the tree line. I had to lean over to fire. I took a steady aim and fired. There was blood all over, but it was mine. I had done a lot of shooting over many years and had never been nailed by my own scope until that day.

I looked up immediately with one eye; the other was full of blood. My scope lens was also covered in blood. As the bull stepped into the timber, I could see with my good eye that he was hit just behind the shoulder. I tried to get another shell in the chamber when I thought I heard a crash. I wiped off the gushing blood as best I could and moved from my blind to get a better look, scoping where I had heard the crash.

The bull was laying down, looking towards me. I finished him right there. I felt terrible about the fact I could have lost him after making such ridiculous rookie mistakes. I knew he was fatally hit from the first shot, but that wasn't the point. I was not properly prepared for the scenario and sure as hell should have been. It was hard to be happy, which I was, yet pissed at myself at the same time. I could have dropped him on the trail right in the meadow which would've made it much easier to dress him out. Instead, he fell between three downed trees — belly first.

I approached him and saw the 6x5 antlers sticking up above the deadfall. The sound of footsteps behind me drew my attention away. It was Eric who came over to give me a hand. It was a two-man job just to turn him over. To make matters worse, the trees he fell between were scorched from the fire. Lots of cleaning was required on the quarters of meat before we packed them down.

My back and knee had been giving me trouble before this episode and now they really hurt. Eric carried a heavy quarter down to camp and brought Lonny and the sleds back up. It took us a few hours, but we got the meat to camp as Eric and Lonny talked about how they didn't see anything that evening.

I started cleaning the meat on Monday morning when the guys went out for another try that also proved unsuccessful.

Then, on Monday night, Eric came into camp white as a ghost. A bear had followed him from Pat's camp to ours in the dark. He had his pistol ready to scare it off if need be.

This was bad news. All I could think was that there was no way in hell I was using the shitter down below in the dark.

Later, JC and his son-in-law rode up to visit. I cooked them a snack – BBQ ribs and fries.

"This was worth the ride up," JC said, rubbing his belly.

Unfortunately, the guys didn't get a chance at any bulls after this. JC told Steve we had one in camp to pack out. We packed everything up for Steve and started walking down. I could see that Lonny was having a really hard time with breathing.

It was a nice walk as we approached the long, steep section called Heart Attack. Not that we timed ourselves for a contest, but we made note of how long it took walking up most of the time. When I was a young man, it would take ten to thirteen minutes to get up. Last year, Eric and I had done it in around eleven minutes. This year, I did it in ten minutes and forty seconds. I overheard Eric told Lonny that this old fart was part mountain goat.

Next Year ⟶

Dawn and Spice

My 50th Year

My 50th year. My, how time flew by. It seemed like yesterday when it all began up on the mountain with Bob, learning from a great hunter how to be a great hunter.

I prepared for the hunt on my fiftieth year with an intense hope that it wasn't my last year in Colorado. It was only fitting and an honor to have Bob's son, Tom, join me. How interesting that Tom wasn't even born when I first met Bob. What were the odds that I should stop for a cup of coffee fifty years ago, overhear a conversation about elk hunting, and end up pursuing them for the next 50 years?

I enjoyed hunting the Great Wapiti for five decades and was blessed with the best lifetime friendship a person could ever hope for. I could never thank Bob enough for taking me under his wings when I was in my early twenties and guiding me through this tremendous journey.

It wasn't just about Elk hunting. Bob and I quickly learned that we were complete opposites. Yet, we were connected — heart, mind, and soul. Soon after we met, it was uncanny how he would know if I was down or could use some everyday advice. In his soft-spoken voice, he would tell me to take a deep breath, use my head, and things would work out. I wish I would've talked to him more often back then because when I had the patience to take his advice, it always worked.

Though we live hundreds of miles apart now, we can sense a phone call coming or know instinctively if something isn't quite right with the other.

Thank you, my dear friend, for always being there when I needed you the most and sometimes when I didn't even realize I needed to hear your voice.

On this last year of hunting, it was just Tom and me. We both had a long drive alone — Tom from Helena, Montana and me from Fargo, North Dakota.

As always, I stopped by my folks' place in Bismarck. My mother had passed away last year, but I had a nice visit with my dad, age 92, for an hour before heading for Wyoming. I don't know if it was expectation or anticipation, but it sure seemed like it took a long time to get to Lusk, Wyoming for the night. Of course, I couldn't eat or sleep that night from the excitement.

I left early in the morning to meet up with Tom in Steamboat, Colorado. The weather was a balmy 60 degrees. After we checked in at the motel, we started packing the panniers for the trip in. With just the two of us, we still needed three horses. Ridiculous! I swear I bring more shit each year; but these days, it's mostly medical supplies. What's next – a walker, maybe?

It was still nice out when we started off the next morning. We were ahead of the horses for a couple of miles. The trail was dry, but I was so out of shape, I had to stop several times to catch my breath. Tom didn't even appear to be breathing hard.

Colton and Dorothy met up with us at camp. They mentioned that they were worried when the arrived because there weren't any candy bars on the post. I always left some bars to let them know we were ahead of them. I had left two there this year, but another party had taken them.

I brought up the smaller tent, which turned out to be a big mistake. The poles didn't line up because they were too small and nothing seemed to go right. *Take a deep breath and use your head, Chaz.* We managed to get camp set up partially by nightfall, though we were exhausted. As I heated up the sloppy joes and snacks, it started to sleet.

As luck would have it, we had ten inches of snow by morning. With three days to go before the season opener and the weather warming up again, this was bad. The cycle of melting during the day then refreezing at night made for hazardous walking conditions and mud in camp. I fell six or seven times, but only two were serious. My head was hard and a hyperextended knee was overrated anyhow. At least I had an excuse for being so slow getting around.

Yep, uh-huh.

On Friday afternoon, we got our hunting supplies ready for the opening morning. We sat in the afternoon sunshine, laying out our strategy for the first morning hunt. Shockingly, we were the only ones up there. But then, the hour before dark, two guys walked by and camped around the corner from us. It had taken us three days to get the camp set up; these guys showed up an hour before dark the night before opening.

We later learned the guys were Patrick from Longmont, Colorado, who shot a bull last year, and his friend, Jason. Patrick was the only one with a license.

Tom had spotted two legal bulls above TD's Mountain the Thursday before season, so his plan was to get up there and try to bag one. On opening morning, I headed for a ridge opposite Tom. I could see his green flashlight now and then as he worked his way to the top through treacherous downed timber. Then I noticed two other lights on the next ridge over from him. It was obvious Tom and Patrick had the same idea. I went up to Boob's meadow and nestled in. It was so quiet… eerie. None of us had any luck seeing or hearing anything the first morning.

"I don't think I'll be much help if you kill one way up on top," I told Tom.

"Good point. I'll hunt Tom's Meadow near you tonight."

It was a good plan in theory, but all we saw was one cow. We didn't know until we spoke with a local down below that there had been a terrible winter kill of elk in this area over the past winter. For the past several years, I noticed fewer and fewer elk; this year was no different.

We were skunked on Sunday also, but we heard a shot above TD's. Sure enough, Patrick had gotten his bull, a nice 6x6. He had several long trips packing it down. We congratulated him. I told him that, thirty years ago, I would've been up there also.

Much to our surprise, two more guys came by around 2:00 p.m. on Sunday afternoon. They were friends of Patrick's – Dan and Skipper. Only Dan had a license. They camped near us next to Patrick. As luck or skill would have it, they walked up into the toughest part of the area and shot a nice bull that afternoon.

I mentioned to them both that maybe I had been doing things all wrong all these years. Just grab your OnX, get up there late, and shoot your elk. It was all in jest, of course. They had done a hell of a job.

Oh, to be young again. I had hunted exactly where they were many times over the years. It was nice and quite rare to have quality neighbors like them.

They all packed out early as Tom and I kept trying to find a magnificent elk for ourselves. We saw two small legal smaller bulls up on top the last day, but I told Tom that, by the time I got up there, they would be dead of old age. It ended up that we were the only two left for the last couple of days.

My great friend, JC Trujillo, rode up to our camp to visit and reminisce about old times and how fast the years slipped by. Tom and I spent the remaining afternoons and evenings talking about all the stories from the past, especially our times with his dad. I don't want to treat our time together like it was the last Colorado elk hunt for me. But maybe, just maybe, it was the beginning of a new chapter.

If it was to be the last hunt, what an ending it would be having Tom with me. He was turning 50 on my 50th year hunting. All that was missing was Bob. Then again, he and Sam and Noris had always been here with me.

We didn't fill our tag, but just sharing all the memories and friendship made it all worthwhile. My heart ached when I left the area, especially Boob's Meadow, not knowing if I'd ever see it again. Nonetheless, it will always be in my mind. Who knows, maybe this Dumb Ass, Shit Shoe, Mountain Goat, Old Fart might make it up there a few more years.

In conclusion, I hope you will take away from these stories just how much I appreciated the opportunities and the magnificent beauty of the Rocky Mountains and, of course, my love and respect for the Majestic Wapiti.

We were blessed to see it all — the warm days, the heavy snows, the birds, the trees. True, the fires in that area were ugly, but that's just Mother Nature cleaning herself. As the new growth begins, I hope the next generation of hunters respect and cherish what I've loved for 50 years.

I am so fortunate that both my sons were able to get a few trophy bull elk with me and that my daughter, Dawn, took a summer trip there just to see my camp. I don't think it took her very long to realize why I loved this place so much.

I wish my Marie could've seen it up there. Then she'd understand why I was so addicted to it. I didn't venture up those mountains just to kill elk – this was my home for a couple weeks every year.

I'll close with a couple of words of advice for you hunters:

1. Stop on your way home and pick up something for your better half. It helps.
2. If you're going to purchase a horse and trailer, make sure you put a damn good lock on the doors.
3. Install good fencing for the horses.
4. Most importantly of all, make sure you buy a horse that doesn't hate Pontiacs.

Great Hunting to You All!!
The Chaz

Next Year??? ⟶

Charlie and Tom

Bob and Charlie

Epilogue:
A Few Things I've Learned
Over the Years

- When in the mountains, take small steps and, if the trail is slippery, take side steps. Better to take it slow on purpose than have a fall force you to take it slow.
- When climbing, try to stop on a level area; this will help you get your balance back. Also take deep short breaths and exhale slowly.
- Keep the grips on your boots clean by kicking heel to toe.
- If you're heading to high elevation, dress light; but have a jacket in your backpack. It gets chilly when you stop moving.
- When you're in the thick woods, look far ahead and you'll probably see the trail the elk use.
- With crunchy snow, walk toe to heel. This really helps.
- While stalking or posting, move your eyes first.
- Absorb everything around you. There's lots of entertainment out there – chipmunks, birds, etc.
- This one may cause some controversy but… When walking up or down the mountainside with a group, never sling your gun on your shoulder. If you fall, odds are you just pointed your weapon at your partner.
- Be Safe and Enjoy God's Creations!

GLOSSARY

Enjoy learning and using some of the wacky words we used while hunting:

Badadas = potatoes

Mamatas = tomatoes

Chickie = chicken

Sitcheation = situation

Oreknized = organizing

Tank you = Thank you

Shiiittt = shit

Learnin' = learning

Meischt = Shit in German

Yep, uh-huh = Yeah, right

Speckmouse = fat mouse

RECIPES

Use your favorite beef recipes when cooking elk meat. I think you'll find it to be delicious and healthy. You can't beat elk burgers on the grill.

Try any of the following:

- Swedish meatballs
- Pan-fried steak with mushrooms and onions
- Slow cook or oven roast with butter and jalapenos

The main consideration with all elk recipes is to <u>never</u> overcook it!

Ironically, the first ten years or so, I was hunting with a butcher (Noris) and a federal meat inspector (Bob). So, our field dressing involved gutting and thoroughly washing the entire cavity.

After skinning, we would crosscut the carcass behind the last rib bone then cut straight down the spine as is done in a butcher shop. We would then quarter the meat (including the ribs) and pack this heavy load to camp in our backpacks.

Since we were outdoors in the elements (wind, rain, snow, cold, etc.) and using a take-down meat saw, this process was rather challenging.

Then, for several more years, we decided to quarter the front and hind quarters and just debone the rib area. This certainly helped with the bulkiness for packing down.

Over the last 20 years, we skinned the animal, quartered it, and deboned it. What a difference! I highly recommend the process.

Always get as much blood off the meat as you can. We would then hang the meat in mesh game bags. If the weather is on the warmer side, stick something in the bag to separate the meat from bag such as branches or pine bows to help keep insects off the meat. Obviously, keep the bags in the shade.

What a difference it makes leaving the bones for the coyotes instead of carrying the extra weight on your back. Also, if you plan to carry the entire hide out, dry it as best you can to lighten the load.

Anyone who has eaten elk meat knows that it is healthy and delicious. Whether or not you process the elk meat or a butcher shop does it, I recommend adding 30% of beef suet (fat) to the elk meat because it is so lean.

Chicken-fried Elk steak

Cut backstraps into one-inch steaks. Run these through a tenderizer or hammer out to a quarter inch thick.

Dredge in seasoned flour (seasonings are your choice), then place in an egg and milk mixture. Remove from egg and milk and place in Panko breadcrumbs.

Heat oil. Add a quarter stick of butter in a frying pan. Drop a small pinch of Panko in the oil. If it bubbles up, it's ready. Cook each side until brown. (around two minutes or so per side).

Remove from oil and sprinkle coarse sea salt to taste. Pour your favorite gravy over the steaks. Enjoy!

About the Author

Charlie "Chaz" Butz, Jr. started his hunting journey at the age of twelve, when he headed out into the fields with family chasing pheasants and ducks – albeit strictly as an excited retriever.

By the age of 14, Charlie's passion for the outdoor tradition grew as he headed out with his own shotgun — this time, a single shot 16 gauge. His ability to use his "16" with slugs for deer and 6-shot for birds made him a force to be reckoned with. It wasn't long before he added a 243 Remington to his arsenal, which many a whitetail and mule deer would succumb to over the years.

Over the next 60 years, Charlie stayed loyal to his Browning semi-auto shotguns, bringing down hundreds of upland birds and waterfowl.

It wasn't until 1967 that Charlie experienced elk hunting for the first time. Born and raised in the Bismarck, North Dakota area, Charlie didn't have much opportunity to hunt elk. In fact, the only opportunities at that time were hundreds of miles away, so elk hunting wasn't taken seriously.

Using his whitetail hunting experience, he thought elk hunting would be a walk in the park. Like any hunter on that first elk hunt, he was left humbled by the majestic and mighty Wapiti. In 1974, Charlie's chance meeting with Bob McManus and invitation to Colorado for an archery elk hunt changed his life.

This began the 50-year tradition that would consume Charlie's passion for and admiration of the outdoors, pursuing the mighty elk. Like any tradition, it was more than just an obsession. The thrill of time spent with friends and family while sharing the majestic Rocky Mountains with this tremendous animal was much more valuable than the hunt and kill.

YOUR REVIEW MATTERS

Reviews are like candy to authors – or like a jaw full of anise!. It's the best way to help booksellers know which books their customers love and, consequently, which they should show to more prospective buyers. So, take two minutes and twelve seconds (yes, we timed it!) to log onto Amazon.com and write a short review. **Thanks for your support.**